GUITAR WORLD CLASSIC ROCK

ROCKERS' DELIGHT!
Portraits of the hot and heavy guitarists behind Led Zeppelin, Pink Floyd, the Grateful Dead, the Eagles, the Doors and all your favorite classic rock bands.

From the pages of
GUITAR WORLD
magazine

Edited by
Jeff Kitts, Brad Tolinski
and Harold Steinblatt

Published by Hal Leonard Corporation
In cooperation with Harris Publications, Inc., and Guitar World Magazine
Guitar World is a registered trademark of Harris Publications, Inc.

7777 W. BLUEMOUND RD. P.O. BOX 13819 MILWAUKEE, WI 53213

ISBN 0-7935-9008-6
Copyright © 1999 by HAL LEONARD CORPORATION
International Copyright Secured   All Rights Reserved

No part of this publication may be reproduced in any form or
by any means without the prior permission of the Publisher.

Executive Producer: Brad Tolinski
Producer: Carol Flannery
Editors: Jeff Kitts & Harold Steinblatt
Art Director: John Flannery
Cover Photo: Angus Young of AC/DC by Neil Zlozower

Visit Hal Leonard Online at
www.halleonard.com

Guitar World Presents CLASSIC ROCK

Table of Contents

Classic Rock Rules!
1   The Stories Behind Rock's Most Famous Songs
    Guitar World, October 1993

The Interviews
15 **Hard as a Rock: AC/DC's Angus Young Explains Why He Loves to Take His Show on the Road** *Guitar World, January 1993*

27 **The Road Goes on Forever: The Story of the Allman Brothers Band** *Guitar World, January 1993*

45 **David's Harp: David Gilmour Reflects on His Role in Making Pink Floyd One of Rock's Most Innovative Bands** *Guitar World, February 1993*

57 **Strange Days: Robby Krieger Sheds Light on the Doors, One of Rock's Greatest and Most Mysterious Bands** *Guitar World, March 1994*

75 **Perfectly Frank: The Life and Times of Frank Zappa–Composer, Satirist and Towering Giant of the Electric Guitar** *Guitar World, April 1994*

89 **Not F-F-F-Fade Away: A look at 30 Years of the Who, and Their Brilliant Guitarist Pete Townshend** *Guitar World, June 1994*

107 **The Long Run: Eagles Guitarist Don Felder Offers a Candid Appraisal of The Band's Great Past** *Guitar World, August 1994*

120 **Smash Hits: Pete Townshend Offers the Final Word on the Who's Tumultuous Three-Decade Career** *Guitar World, October 1994*

141 **Peace of Mind: Musical Trends May Come and Go, but Tom Scholz, Boston's Reclusive Rock Man, Couldn't Care Less** *Guitar World, February*

161 **Journey Through the Past: The History of Neil Young's Long and Distinguished Career** *Guitar World, September 1995*

175 **American Beauty: A Tribute to Jerry Garcia, One of the Most Influential Musicians of Our Era** *Guitar World, November 1995*

187 **Trick or Treat: The Feast-or-Famine Story of Rick Nielsen and Cheap Trick** *Guitar World, October 1996*

203 **Classic Rocks: Aerosmith Takes a Disc-by-Disc Journey Through the Albums That Made It America's Greatest Hard Rock Band** *Guitar World, April 1997*

221 **Rastaman Vibration: The Story of Bob Marley and the Music He Introduced to a Grateful World** *Guitar World, December 1996*

237 **Gimme Three Chords: Gary Rossington Explains the Origins of Some of Lynyrd Skynyrd's Finest Moments** *Guitar School, July 1993*

245 **Songs for America: An Overview of Kansas' 20-Year Career with Guitarist Richard Williams** *Guitar School, October 1995*

253 **Time and Motion: Alex Lifeson Dissects Several Key Songs from Rush's Past** *Guitar World, November 1996*

259 **El Loco: ZZ Top's Billy Gibbons Recalls Three Decades of Texas Excess** *Guitar World, November 1996*

265 **Good Times, Bad Times: The Greatest Guitar Stories Ever Told** *Guitar World, April 1995*

Jimmy Page of Led Zeppelin

one day he said, 'Hey, we don't have enough songs. You guys try writing some.' I thought, well, okay.

"What really amazed me was you'd think that a guy of Jim's caliber would have only wanted to do his own stuff. Can you imagine going up to Bob Dylan and saying, 'Hey, Bob, I wrote this tune for you?' That shows you something about Jim. He wanted it to be 'The Doors,' not 'Jim Morrison and the Doors' He was adamant about that."

"The End" *The Doors* (Elektra, 1967)
"That started out as just a cute little love song: 'This is the end, my friend, my beautiful friend.' And I got the idea to do an Indian tuning, because I was into Ravi Shankar in a big way. I ended up using a dropped-D, and from there it started getting longer and more weird. And every time we'd play it, Jim would add more weird stuff to it."

GENE SIMMONS AND PAUL STANLEY (Kiss)
"Deuce" *Kiss* (Casablanca/Polygram 1974)
GENE SIMMONS: "That was the first song I ever wrote for Kiss; it was thrown together in about half an hour. I ripped off the lick from 'Bitch' by the Rolling Stones and changed it so it starts in A and goes to a C. I purposely set out to create a repetitive lick—like in 'Satisfaction' or 'Bitch.' Lyrically, I had a slight thread of a story line, but I was more concerned with conveying attitude than making sense of the word 'deuce.' I'm not quite sure what the line, 'You know your man is working hard, he's worth a deuce!' means, but it sounds right."

"Detroit Rock City" *Destroyer* (Casablanca/Polygram 1976)
PAUL STANLEY: "From the very beginning, the people of Detroit took us in as one of their own. While we were still an opening act in most parts of the country, we were headlining there, and I wanted to write a song about that. Then someone was hit by a car and killed outside one of our concerts in Charlotte, North Carolina. I found it very strange that somebody on his way to see something that would have been so much fun, something that was such a testament to being alive, would get killed—which is where the song's car crash intro

comes from. The whole song is really about somebody getting ready to go to a concert to have a great time, and ending up dying."

GEORGE THOROGOOD
(George Thorogood & the Destroyers)
"Bad to the Bone" *Bad to the Bone* (Capitol, 1982)

"I came up with the phrase 'bad to the bone,' then it took me several months to write all the lyrics. I wanted them to be like an old Muddy Waters or Bo Diddley song—exotic, tough, mythic lyrics like 'Who Do You Love,' 'I'm Ready,' or even 'Jumping Jack Flash.' Muddy Waters could sing songs with mythic proportions—and mean it. Not many people can do that and I actually wrote 'Bad to the Bone' for him to sing, because I just couldn't hear myself doing it. We tried to peddle it to Muddy, but he declined. Then I wanted Bo Diddley to record it, and he liked it, but he was without a record deal at the time. So I was my own third option; I literally could not peddle it to anyone, so I recorded it myself. And it became the song I'm best known for."

JOE WALSH (The Eagles)
"Hotel California" *Hotel California* (Asylum, 1976)

"That tune was written by Don Felder, regardless of what [Glenn] Frey and [Don] Henley say. He brought that tune in with no lyrics—Henley, Frey and J.D. Souther got together late at night for a month to put those together—but the song's signature descending chord progression was all Felder's. I thought up the lead parts, and was 75-80 percent responsible for their arrangement. But if Felder hadn't been there kicking me in the butt, I would not have played like that. He is a serious guitar player, and he's completely underestimated and undervalued."

GARY ROSSINGTON (Lynyrd Skynyrd)
"Free Bird" *pronounced leh-nerd skin-nerd* (MCA, 1973)

"Ronnie [*Van Zant, Skynyrd vocalist*] didn't like it in the beginning. He complained that the opening chord progression was too complicated, and he couldn't find a melody for it. Every once in a while we'd bring it up again, and he'd just tell us to forget about it.

"Then one day we were at rehearsal and Allen [*Collins, guitar*] started playing the chord progression again, and Ronnie said, 'That's pretty.' Allen played it again, and Ronnie said, 'Okay, I got it.' And he wrote the lyrics in three or four minutes—the whole damned thing! He came up with a lot of stuff that way.

"So we started playing 'Free Bird' in clubs. Initially it was just a slow ballad. Then Ronnie said, 'Why don't you do something at the end of that so I can take a break for a few minutes?' So I came up with the ending chord progression and Allen played over them, then I soloed and then he soloed... It all evolved out of a jam one night. We started playing it that way, but Ronnie kept saying, 'It's not long enough. Make it longer.' We were playing three or four sets a night, and he was looking to fill them up."

"Gimme Three Steps" *pronounced leh-nerd skin-nerd* (MCA, 1973)
"The lyrics to 'Gimme Three Steps' are based on a true story. Ronnie went into a bar one night to look for someone. Allen and I were too young to get in so we waited outside. Suddenly, he came running out with a big ol' guy chasing him. It turned out that Ronnie had started dancing with this chick. Unfortunately, she had a redneck boyfriend who was drunk and had a gun—a nasty combination. Ronnie said, 'Just give me three steps and I'm gone. If you're going to shoot me, it's going to be in the ass or the in the elbow.' And he took off like a bat out of hell.

"We got in the car and split. He told us what happened and we laughed, and we kind of wrote the song right there."

"Sweet Home Alabama" *Second Helping* (MCA, 1974)
"It's basically a joke song. We used to travel through Alabama a lot and just marvel at how pretty it was and how nice the people were. Then Neil Young came out with 'Southern Man' and 'Alabama,' which criticized the South. So we said, 'Well, what does he know? He's from Canada.' So we threw that line about him in there. The funny thing is, Neil Young was and is one of our favorite artists."

DAVID GILMOUR (Pink Floyd)
"Comfortably Numb" *The Wall* (Columbia, 1979)

"I'd written 'Comfortably Numb' when I was doing my first solo album [*David Gilmour, 1978*]. It was very, very simple to write, but we had arguments on how it should be recorded and mixed. We'd done one track with Nick Mason on drums that I thought was too rough and sloppy. We had another go at it, and I thought that the second take was better. Roger [*Waters*] disagreed. It was more an ego thing than anything else. In retrospect, it was probably stupid to go head-to-head with each other over such a minor thing. I probably couldn't tell the difference if you put both versions on a record today. But anyway, it wound up with us taking a drum fill out of one version and putting it into another.

"I just went out into the studio and bunged down five or six solos. From there I just followed my usual procedure, which is to listen back to each solo and make a chart, putting ticks and crosses on different bars as I count through: two ticks if it's really good, one tick if it's good, and a cross if it's no go. Then I just follow the chart, jumping from phrase to phrase and trying to make a really nice solo all the way through. That's the way we did it on 'Comfortably Numb.' It wasn't that difficult."

"Money" *Dark Side of the Moon* (Columbia, 1973)

"It's Roger's riff. He came in with the verses and lyrics for 'Money' more or less completed. And we just made up middle sections, guitar solos and all that stuff. We also invented some new riffs—we created a 4/4 progression for the guitar solo and made the poor saxophone player play in 7/4. It was my idea to break down and become dry and empty for the second chorus of the solo.

"I really wanted to make a dramatic statement with each of the three solos. The first one is artificially double-tracked. And the third one is actually double-tracked. I think the first two solos were performed on a Fender Stratocaster, but the last one was done on a different guitar—a Lewis, which was made by some guy in Vancouver. It had a two-octave neck, which meant I could get up to notes that I couldn't play on a Strat. I imagine I used a Hiwatt, but I'm not too certain. I used Fender Twin Reverbs in the studio a lot, too. But I'm certain the effects consisted of a Fuzzface fuzz box and a Binson echo/delay."

NEAL SCHON (Journey)
"Wheel in the Sky" *Infinity* (Columbia, 1978)
"We were driving through the middle of a desert one night—nine of us in a station wagon. We pulled over to get some gas and to stretch, I grabbed my acoustic, sat on the hood of the car and started to play. That's how I wrote it!"

TED NUGENT
"Cat Scratch Fever" *Cat Scratch Fever* (Epic, 1977)
"That song came from a lick at soundcheck. My wife had come up with this antique medical journal that listed a disease called 'cat scratch fever.' My brain is like a computer; it catalogs everything. And when this guitar pattern came up, the words 'cat scratch fever' just fit perfectly."

"Stranglehold" *Ted Nugent* (Epic, 1976)
"This was a road product. I was on the road constantly between 1967 and '75, playing 250 to 300 nights a year. You discover connections between the audience and your guitar. That guitar lick may be the most identifiable lick on the face of the earth. It came from unrestricted jams, but developed into what I consider to be the quintessential Nugent musical maneuver. That song has kept America moist for years!"

LESLIE WEST (MOUNTAIN)
"Mississippi Queen" *Mountain Climbing* (Legacy, 1970)
" 'Mississippi Queen' took over where Clapton left off when he quit Cream. To make up for my lack of speed I added in a lot of vibrato from the blues guys—like a chef adding ingredients to a stew—and worked on my squeals and pig grunts. [*laughs*] And the tone was fat, just like me. I used my Les Paul Junior and two Sunn stacks with the Coliseum PA heads. They were Hendrix's old amps, re-tolexed and

re-coned. I turned both the mic volume and the master volume all the way up and overdrove the thing like crazy."

MIKE CAMPBELL
(Tom Petty and the Heartbreakers)
"American Girl" *Tom Petty and the Heartbreakers* (Shelter, 1976)

"A lot of people think we're using electric 12-strings, but it's actually two six-strings playing different inversions of D major in unison.

"The song wasn't a conscious attempt to emulate Roger McGuinn, like some people think, but we were heavily influenced by the Byrds. We initially wrote several songs with that flavor, and when I started working with Tom we were both listening to the Byrds. But if anything, we tried to avoid that sound because we knew that we leaned in that direction naturally. It came as a complete surprise when Roger called us up and said he wanted to cut the song. We went over to his place and showed him how to play it. It was funny, because he said that when he heard 'American Girl' on the radio he thought he had written it and forgotten about it. We showed him the parts, and he ended up using a 12-string."

JIMMY PAGE (Led Zeppelin)
"Stairway to Heaven" untitled (Atlantic, 1971)

"I'd been fooling around with an acoustic guitar and came up with several different sections, which I married together. I knew I wanted something that would have the drums come in at the middle and then build to a huge crescendo. Also, I knew I wanted the piece to speed up, which is against all musical...I mean, that's what a musician *doesn't* do.

"So I had all the structure, and I ran it by [*bassist*] John Paul Jones so he could get the idea of it—[*drummer*] John Bonham and Robert [*Plant, singer*] had gone out for the night—and then on the following day we got into it with John Bonham. You have to remember that at first there was a hell of a lot for everyone to remember on this one. But as we were sort of routining it, Robert started writing down these lyrics, and a huge percentage of them were written there and then.

"When it came time to record the solo I warmed up and did three of them. They were all quite different from each other, but the one we used was the best, I can tell you that!"

"Whole Lotta Love" *Led Zeppelin II* (Atlantic, 1969)
"I used distant miking to get this rhythm guitar tone. Miking used to be a science, and I had heard that distance makes depth, which in turn gives you a fatter guitar sound. In my studio session days, the mikes were right up close to the amps and I would have to turn down the amp volume. In Zeppelin, I learned to always use a distant mic.

"The amp was turned up very high. It was distorting, just controlled to the point where it had some halls to it. I also used a depressed wah-wah pedal on the solo, as I did on 'Communication Breakdown.' It gets you a really raucous sound."

ROBIN TROWER
"Bridge of Sighs" *Bridge of Sighs* (Chrysalis, 1974)
"I had the opening guitar riff for about six months before I could come up with the turnaround section. I loved that opening lick so much that I was determined to make the second half just as perfect. So I waited and waited… Then it came to me. The band played it for the first time at the Winterland in San Francisco, and we received, like, a 10-minute standing ovation. It obviously had magic."

PAT SIMMONS (The Doobie Brothers)
"Jesus Is Just Alright" *Toulouse Street* (Warner Bros., 1972)
"That song was always well-received—even in the roughest of biker bars. The heaviest of heavy-duty people would come up to us and say, 'Man that's great. You really said it, brother.' Redneck bikers everywhere loved it. It was like someone was telling them they were worth the trouble, you know?"

JOAN JETT
"I Love Rock 'N' Roll" *I Love Rock 'n' Roll* (Blackheart, 1981)
"I cut the demo for 'I Love Rock 'n' Roll' in England with Steve Jones and Paul Cook of the Sex Pistols. Twenty-three record com-

panies turned it down; I have the letters. They all say, 'This is interesting, but we don't hear a hit.' "

JIMI HENDRIX
"Foxey Lady" Are You Experienced? (Reprise, 1976)
"I can't write happy songs. 'Foxey Lady' is about the only happy song I've written. And I didn't feel very happy when I started writing."

ERIC CLAPTON
"I Shot the Sheriff" 461 Ocean Boulevard (Polydor, 1974)
"I didn't think we had got it as good as Bob's [*Marley*] version. I thought we'd prettied it up a lot, and just not done it justice. And that disturbed me to the point where I wasn't keen on even having it on the album. I was overruled, and thank God I was because Bob, in fact, was one of the first people to say, 'Thank you.' "

"Strange Brew" Disraeli Gears (Polydor, 1967)
"I'd bumped into Jimi [Hendrix] by then, and he was instrumental in turning me on to Albert King. We used to listen to things like 'Crosscut Saw' together; they were actually being played in London discos. And Albert's soloing became a major influence on me. On 'Strange Brew,' I really just played Albert as well as I could."

"White Room" Wheels of Fire (Polydor, 1968)
"We were all very much into experimentation. The intro to 'White Room' was made up of me feeding back on every string, so it was like six tracks of single strings feeding back. I thought that was a landmark in recording history. We were all going places we didn't think anyone had been before."

"Layla" Layla (& Other Assorted Love Songs) (Polydor, 1970)
"The album was the culmination of about a year of hippie living. We lived in my house in England, playing non-stop, 24 hours a day. We were on a lot of dope and taking a lot of different things, but we were just playing all the time, just writing and riffing. When we went

into the studio we didn't actually have too many concrete songs, but there was so much stored up that it just came together.

"Duane [Allman] hadn't even been talked about at that point; that was very coincidental. We were in the studio in Miami and heard that the Allmans were playing nearby. We went to see them and they came back to the studio, and we played them some stuff and jammed together. Duane and me hit it off right away—instant soul mates—and I asked him if he'd like to come back to the studio and play and help me out with the record. Of course, he agreed."

BRIAN MAY (Queen)
"Bohemian Rhapsody" *A Night at the Opera* (Hollywood, 1975)

"Freddie [*Mercury, singer*] used to come into the studio armed with sheets and sheets of paper, with notes scribbled all over them in his own particular fashion. It wasn't standard musical notation—it looked like buses zooming all over his bits of paper. He had the song all worked out when he came in. We played a backing track, which left the gaps. And he would go, 'Bum bum bum bmm, that's what happens here…' He knew exactly what he was doing all along. It was Freddie's baby. He had it in his head. We just helped him bring it to life.

"We were stretching the limits of technology in those days. Since 'Bohemian Rhapsody' was entirely done on 16-track, we had to do a lot of bouncing as we went along; the tape got very thin. This 'legendary' story, which people think we made up, is true: we held the tape up to the light one day—we'd been wondering where all the top end was going—and what we discovered was virtually a transparent piece of tape. All the oxide had been rubbed off. It was time to hurriedly make a copy and get on with it."

"We Will Rock You" *News of the World* (Hollywood, 1978)

"That was a response to a particular phase in our career—when the audience was becoming a bigger part of the show than we were. They would sing all the songs. Sometimes, they'd be so vociferous that we'd have to stop the show and let them sing to us. So both Freddie and I thought it would be an interesting experiment to write songs with audience participation specifically in mind—everyone can stamp and clap and sing a simple motif. We recorded that in an old converted church with a good, natural sound. There are no drums on there. It's just us, stamping on boards, with many primitive delay machines, and clapping. A bit of singing, a bit of guitar playing and that's it.

"It's amazing to go to sports events and hear people do it. It's very gratifying to find that it has become part of folklore. I'll die happy because of that."

MICK JONES (Foreigner)
"Feels Like the First Time" *Foreigner* (Atlantic, 1977)
"This was the first song I wrote for Foreigner. I'd just come out of a band with [*Mountain guitarist*] Leslie West that had fizzled out, and I wasn't feeling too optimistic about music. I thought about going back to England to become a dentist or something. [*laughs*] But then I started to write, and three or four songs came out. I thought, 'What do I do with these?' "

"Hot Blooded" *Foreigner* (Atlantic, 1977)
"My playing was so hot, my amp actually caught fire while we were recording this!"

RITCHIE BLACKMORE (Deep Purple)
"Smoke on the Water" *Machine Head* (Warner Bros., 1972)
"Simplicity is the key to this song's endurance. And it is simple—you can still hear people playing it at music stores. I never had the courage to write until I heard 'I Can't Explain' and 'My Generation.' Those riffs were so straightforward that I thought, 'All right, if Pete Townshend can get away with that, then I can, too!' "

PETER BUCK (R.E.M.)
"Driver 8" *Fables of the Reconstruction* (I.R.S., 1985)
" 'Driver 8' is probably the quintessential R.E.M. song of that period; the chord changes, melodies and harmonies are very representative of what we were doing then.

"Since 'Driver 8' is kind of a folk song, I originally thought I should play banjo on it. But since I can't really play banjo, I hit upon the idea of doing a real Ventures-sounding surf-guitar riff instead."

"It's the End of the World as We Know It (And I Feel Fine)" *Document* (I.R.S., 1987)
"That's Bob Dylan's 'Subterranean Homesick Blues' filtered through Chuck Berry's 'Too Much Monkey Business,' filtered through some old medicine-show singer in the South somewhere. Of course, ours has a chorus, which Dylan's didn't. I like the song because it's so apocalyptic. I wish it had been a hit, because it would have been fun hearing it on the radio right after Sheena Easton's 'My Baby Takes the Morning Train.' "

MICK RALPH (Bad Company)
"Can't Get Enough (Of Your Love)" *Bad Company* (Atlantic, 1974)
"I wrote this in open A, but the key was wrong for Paul [*Rodgers, singer*], so we changed it to C. Being in open C [low to high, G, C, G, C, E, G] gives it a really distinct sound. The guitar was a '57 Les Paul Jr. that I found in a pawn shop for $75. I had to put lighter strings on it because of the tension the tuning put on the neck."

JIM CREGAN (Rod Stewart)
"Hot Legs" *Footloose and Fancy Free* (Warner Bros., 1977)
"It came together in one day. But we didn't get the actual take for a few days, because we were having trouble getting the groove to sit down. Carmine Appice, who's a very talented drummer, was probably overqualified to play that kind of music. He finds it very hard to sit on a groove and do almost nothing—which is what was required. So we struggled for a while, until he got comfortable."

BILLY GIBBONS (ZZ Top)
"La Grange" *Tres Hombres* (Warner Bros., 1973)
"Harmonic City. The solo on 'La Grange' is one of my best. I like savage sounds, but my obscenity comes in harmonics rather than a grind for tone."

Guitar World Presents CLASSIC ROCK

Angus Young of AC/DC

Guitar World, January 1993

Hard as a Rock

The world's favorite overgrown adolescent is back to rock the school. In an in-depth interview, AC/DC's Angus Young explains why he loves to take his show on the road.

By Alan di Perna

GREAT ROCK AND roll needs no explanation. It hits you so squarely in the chest that you start feeling good long before your brain has had time to figure out what happened. AC/DC knows this. For 16 years they've been making powerful, masterful rock and roll—without pretense, self-analysis or the slightest regard for the never-ending parade of fashion.

Those 16 years are summed up beautifully on AC/DC's new live album—a collection of classic after classic from the quintessential live hard-rock band. Through it all, Angus Young's lead guitar rages like a house afire. He stands no taller than five feet, but he throws every ounce of his compact frame into each power chord and stinging lead, playing with unmistakable conviction. As singer Brian Johnson says, "You cannot bullshit the kids." AC/DC wouldn't know how to try.

In New York to promote their new record, *Live*, Johnson and Young come on like a duo from a Charles Dickens novel: a roisterous highwayman from the chilly north of England and a diminutive, wise-cracking Artful Dodger. Though Angus has lived in London for years, his speech is still peppered with the sharp cadences of

Australia, where he and his brother, Malcolm, started AC/DC all those years ago. With each wry observation, Angus squints one eye behind a perpetual cloud of cigarette smoke that trails up and gets lost in his fine, auburn hair. He and Brian throw themselves wholeheartedly into the business of talking barre chords, bared bottoms, busty lasses and other rock essentials along the Highway to Hell.

GUITAR WORLD: Your performance style is so strenuous, Angus. Have you ever hurt yourself on stage?
ANGUS YOUNG: Sure. I've lost teeth. I mean I don't go out there to do myself a deliberate injury. But when you're on the road for that length of time, you're bound to twist an ankle or something. I once had splints on my fingers. I soon learned how to play slide with them on! I've jumped off amps and fallen ass over tit—made a complete fool of myself.
GW: What was your most embarrassing moment on stage?
YOUNG: Well, I've had my pants fall off. All of a sudden I'm out there in my wedding tackle for all to see. You know, I've even had my shorts stolen a couple of times.
GW: What's the origin of that time-honored part of your show where you strip off and moon the audience?
YOUNG: A lot of that came from the days when we'd be playing clubs and it'd be hot inside. So I'd take off my jacket, and half the audience would go "whooooooo." Especially with my physique—I'm not exactly Mr. Arnold Schwarzenegger. So it's all built off that. I'd take off my shirt and the drummer would go *ta-dump*. A bit of cheap cabaret, really.

And the mooning thing…well, it's a great way to shut up a heckler. Or to get attention back up on the stage. One time we were playing this big festival in England and there was this woman photographer with a real Dolly Parton physique, you know? She gets up and walks across the front of the stage. And of course more than half the audience are hotblooded males; so they're all following her like this. [*rolls his eyeballs to the right*] And my brother says, "You better do something quick to get their attention back." So I mooned 'em. That

certainly jolted them back quick. Very popular with the law, too.
GW: I'll bet!
YOUNG: Oh, yes. On one of the early tours of Britain we had the vice squad on tour with us the whole time. 'Cause Bon [*the late Bon Scott, AC/DC's first singer*], he took the French language, you know. Well, he had a colorful language anyway. I remember there was many a time in Australia, playing in these outback places, where we'd have to put up bail money. And if we did anything wrong—like me pulling my pants off or Bon swearing or anything—we'd lose the bail money. The mayor and the councilmen would come along to the show to monitor us. They thought it was a great thing. They invented it. Not us. It was their way of trying to stamp us out. So I remember once Bon getting up there and saying, "I've been told we can't say fuck. Okay, we won't say fuck. I've been told we can't say shit. Okay, we won't say shit. They left out suck. But we won't say that either...." You know? Our bankbook didn't grow, but our popularity did.
GW: You've said somewhere that you can't play guitar well unless you're jumping around like a lunatic.
YOUNG: Yeah, well I go with the guitar, because I'm pretty small. On most people, a Gibson SG looks small—like a violin. On me, it looks like a big guitar. I've got small fingers, too. Now, when most people bend a string up, their finger bends the note. With me, my whole body's got to go. [*He falls into Angus stage move number 1, miming how he uses his entire forearm to bend a string.*] I hug the guitar, if you want to get technical about it. Now for vibrato [*he convulses with laughter as he illustrates*] I've got to shake me leg a little. When you're a little guy, there's not much pull on the strings—especially with the heavier gauges.

The most important thing for me on stage is playing the guitar. The whole epileptic routine—whatever I do up there—comes out of that. I do become a little...possessed, as Malcolm says. But there's nothing Satanic in it. I do become another person. But that other person comes from me concentrating really hard on playing the guitar.
GW: Do you feel that AC/DC is essentially a live band?
YOUNG: I think that all good bands are essentially live bands. The

great ones—the ones that last—are the ones that had that approach. Your Stones, Who, whatever. Your only real gauge for AC/DC is if we play someplace and people come to see us the next time we play there. That's the only way we know if we were good the last time. You can't trust the hype side of it.

GW: Do you see a lot of fans from the beginnings of your career—1976?

YOUNG: Sure we do. There's a lot. You can tell. The older ones are in the back.

BRIAN JOHNSON: We're just about on first-name terms with some of them. Some guys have got a standard pass to get in. They know the crews and all.

YOUNG: Europe accepted us before America did. So when we went through Europe last time it was like an army following us. Kids with tents coming out and stuff. You walk in and they give you the set list they want you to play.

JOHNSON: We feed 'em, too. There's always a lot of food backstage—more than we can eat. So as we're leaving the venue, we say, "Okay guys!" And the kids come in with haversacks and fill them up—so they can get to the next gig.

YOUNG: They've got great networks, the fans. They can tell you what happened the night before. Like if you played a few different songs or did a song a bit faster the previous night, they know all about it.

GW: Is it kind of like the Grateful Dead phenomenon?

YOUNG: Naaooowww. I mean, the last four letters of the Grateful Dead say it all, don't they?

GW: Brian, you joined AC/DC in 1980, after the band had enjoyed a bit of success. Did the band live up to your preconceptions of what they were like?

JOHNSON: Well, I hadn't known about AC/DC long enough to have a preconception of them. I was up in Northern England. And it was just six months before I auditioned for them that I first *heard* them. A couple of me buddies...Malcolm Waley, I'll never forget...he brought back an album, 'cause he'd seen them at the Newcastle Mayfair. And he said [*his voice drops even lower than usual*], "You gotta fookin' hear these! Fook!" [*To Angus:*] You know Mal.

At the audition, we started doin' "Whole Lotta Rosie"; I knew it 'cause there was a big buzz in England on that song. Europe and England was the first place where the boys were really gettin' red hot. It was great 'cause it was right in the middle of the big punk thing. Now, I heard punk and I said, "I fuckin' don't get it. I know everybody's raving about it...." But I didn't like it at all. So with the boys, at least there was something out there that was decent. Ya could tap ya foot to it—know what I mean?

YOUNG: At that time he's talking about—the middle Seventies—we were giving punk music a good name. Because that was the word they used to describe us—punk band. They'd get a wrong idea. We weren't a punk band, but they'd put us on the same bill as punk bands. And they sure got a shock when they started spitting at us and we spat back. We were never ones for getting slumped under a tag or filed under A, B, or C. We started as a rock and roll band. That's what we play—what we do best. We never claimed to be anything else. And then in the Eighties, they'd slump us in as a heavy metal band. Even before that they had other things: power pop. Crap.

JOHNSON: You put all the names together and it spells bullshit.

YOUNG: It's true. I mean, okay, the word "blues" conjures up something definite. You know where you're going. It says it right. But the heavy metal thing? I immediately think of men in armor. And then that split leg routine. You know what I mean? There's more to playing the guitar than being able to do a leg split and wearin' a pair of tights. The heavy metal tag offended me more than the punk thing. 'Cause I thought, "Jesus, what have they conjured up now?" Then just because you call an album *Highway to Hell* you get all kinds of grief. And all we'd done is describe what it's like to be on the road for four years, like we'd been. A lot of it was bus and car touring, with no real break. You crawl off the bus at four o'clock in the morning, and some journalist's doing a story and he says, "What would you call an AC/DC tour?" Well, it *was* a highway to hell. It really was. When you're sleeping with the singer's socks two inches from your nose, that's pretty close to hell.

GW: Presumably it's gotten a little better now.
YOUNG: It has. He can do his laundry now.
JOHNSON: I've got two pair of socks now.
GW: So Angus, did you listen to a lot of blues early on?
YOUNG: Sure. That was my diet. Other kids would come to school with the latest Top 40 thing. I was always buying a lot of imports: Muddy Waters. That music. When I was young, one of the earliest records I heard was Little Richard's "You Keep a Knockin'." I think I nearly invented rap with that record: I'd take the needle and keep putting it back to the same spot, to the blues bit, over and over again; 'cause that was the best part of the song. My mother said, "You touch that needle one more time and you're going to have a very sore fist." But I couldn't help it. I just loved that one bit. And I was never a lover of the harmony-type stuff. For some reason that seemed to...eeuuuewww...it brought in that sweetness. When I heard the Beach Boys, I just thought it was an older version of the Chipmunks.
JOHNSON: Hah—at the real speed!
YOUNG: You know what I mean. 'Cause it was like [*sings in a hilariously nasal California accent*], "We're suurrfun Yew Ess Ayy." Then when my family immigrated to Australia [from Scotland, in the mid Sixties], you'd see these kids that had nothing to do with the real thing, but they all looked like they came out of *Hawaii Five-O*. Standing there with these great wooden lumps of board. I'd never seen a surfboard in my life. But they've all got these bits of wood, and they're all going, "Surrrfun Yew Ess Ayy." I went home to my mother and said, "Mum, I think they put us on another planet."
JOHNSON: In Newcastle [England] we didn't know what water was.
YOUNG: It was oil.
JOHNSON: The only water we had was what you put in your whiskey.
YOUNG: That's right, Newcastle invented the word pollution.
GW: So you weren't impressed by the "American-ness" of it all?
YOUNG: Oh, no, no, no, don't get me wrong. I love what's come from America, musically. But I don't think the people here see it for what it is a lot of times. For me, the culture is blues music. That's what I grew up on, and I have great respect for Muddy Waters, B.B. King,

Chuck Berry, Willie Dixon... If those people weren't there, you wouldn't have your Stones, your Zeppelins, the Who...all the big blues-based bands. The Beatles—same thing. I mean if Paul McCartney played in Boston tomorrow, he would finish off the night with seven or eight Little Richard songs. That, to me, is rock music. The other things are really the housewife, "cry in the tea towel" shit. That ain't rock music.

GW: When did you start up with that SG, Angus?

YOUNG: Just as I came out of school. I saved up my pesos and went to the guitar shop. I always wanted an SG. I had a friend, an American guy, who had a Gibson catalog. As soon as I saw the SG, I knew that was the one I wanted; I think it was because the horn things [*i.e., the sharp cutaways*] reminded me a bit of myself. And the other thing, when I saw the Beach Boys with a Stratocaster, I think that also swayed me the other way. It didn't look right. And that surfin' thing was popular at the time.

GW: That Fender sound.

YOUNG: I'm not condemning it. You've got your Hendrixes and all that. But even he said he didn't like playin' surf music.

GW: The Who did.

YOUNG: Well, yeah. They were a strange case.

GW: So you discovered the guitar of your life pretty early on.

YOUNG: Well, not *right* off the bat. I mean I played other guitars. I had an acoustic guitar first. My mum got it for 10 bucks when I was nine or so. She got both me and Malcolm one each, so there'd be no fighting over it. There was always a guitar around the house, always some brother that had some guitar lying about somewhere.

GW: Were you influenced by your brother George being in the Easybeats? [*The Easybeats were a mid Sixties beat group that had a worldwide hit with "Friday on My Mind."*]

YOUNG: Not that much, 'cause he formed that band as soon as we arrived from Scotland—formed it from the immigrant camp. So from the moment we arrived, he was out playing a lot. I never really saw him much. And then I had another brother, a saxophone player, who had also taken off. He went to London and then ended up in Hamburg, Germany, during the Beatles' times. My father wanted to get us all off the music kick—he thought we should be working. That was his thing. That's why he moved to Australia. So at school, I wasn't allowed to tell anyone that my brother was a member of a band. I remember one headmaster found out and gave me a hard time over it.

GW: Did you and Malcolm start your thing together?

YOUNG: Not really. We just used to play away. George would say to Malcolm sometimes, "Here Mal, pick up the guitar." Like if he was working out an idea or something. 'Cause Mal was very competent. He's a great all-around guitarist. I know it says "rhythm guitar" on the albums. But for me, if he sits and plays a solo, he can do it better than me.

GW: Does he ever play solos on records?

YOUNG: In fact, there's a couple of solos from him on our first album. But even then it's the *way* he plays rhythm—it's got that distinct sound, especially with that Gretsch [Firebird]. I've tried to emulate his rhythm style myself, at home, with one of his guitars, and it's no easy task. He's got those big thick strings on it, like tram tracks, you know? It's all in his little wrist.

GW: You guys have an amazingly tight thing together.

YOUNG: I think that's part of the brother thing, too. It used to be a game, sort of. It becomes instinct with you. And my other brother George was so quick that you learned a lot when you were with him. Especially when you were 14 or something. He'd pick up a bass and hand you the guitar. And you'd think you were incompetent, but before you knew it you were playing with him. He'd go "G...A..." And you were away. He also taught me...like say you play a song five nights in one key, but on the sixth night the singer's throat ain't makin' it. You might have to go down a tone or so. George was really used to that, and he got me used to that.

GW: Instant transposition!

YOUNG: Right. And he was into some crazy things too, you know. Like he'd tell me the D string annoyed him. The G string too. "Too sweet for rock and roll," he'd say—so off went the G string! When

I last saw him in the Easybeats, he had like four strings on that guitar. He was never a fan of light strings either—especially when those slinky strings came out. He'd say, "You can't tune 'em."

GW: So now Malcolm uses real heavy gauge strings and you use lighter ones.

YOUNG: Well, Malcolm just seems to get heavier and heavier with his strings. Now he's at the point where they're not making that gauge any more, since the youth want them lighter and lighter. These days, you see, they all want to run from one end of the fretboard to the other. They want to practice their scales. I mean, that's all very good, so long as they do it at home.

GW: Why should we have to hear it?

YOUNG: Right.

GW: A lot of your greatest hooks are single-string riffs where you alternate between fretted notes and playing the string open—like "Thunderstruck," for example.

YOUNG: Yeah, I was just fiddling with my left hand when I came up with that riff; I played it more by accident than anything. I thought, "not bad" and put it on a tape. That's how me and Malcolm generally work. We put our ideas on a tape and play them for one another. Malcolm came in to me once when we were on the "Highway to Hell" tour and said, "I've got this riff and it's driving me nuts." It's three o'clock in the morning and I'm trying to sleep, and he's saying, "Well, what do you think of this?" I said, "It sounds fine to me." And that was "Back in Black." Bang.

GW: So you like being in a band with your brother, then?

YOUNG: Well, it's good and bad. When I play something in the studio and the producer says, "Oh, that's great," I always look around and say, "Yeah, but what does Malcolm think?" 'Cause Malcolm knows me, and if he says yay or nay, it's the difference between getting to go home or sitting in the studio all night. So sometimes it's like having two producers. But that's good, because it keeps you on your toes. And if I really get disheartened, I can just hand Mal the guitar and say, "Here, you try it." Then he'll show me up and I'll say, "Right, I'll beat him."

GW: What can you recall about your first tour of the States?

YOUNG: When we first came here, we toured around with a station wagon. We got put on with Kiss. This was when they had all the makeup and everything—the whole hype. They had everything behind them: the media, a huge show and stuff. And here we were—five migrants, little micro people.

JOHNSON: Migrant workers—that just about describes it! "Where's your green cards?"

YOUNG: It was tough to even get into the show with that station wagon. Many a time they wouldn't let us in the venue 'cause they didn't see a limo. [*Another nasal Yank accent*] "Wheeahs duh limo? If yaw duh rock band, wheeahs yaw limo?"

GW: When was this?

YOUNG: 1977 was the first time we got to America. So this would have been '78. It was pretty strange. I hadn't even heard of a lot of the music here at the time—I thought there would be more rock. But when we got here it was a disco-type thing.

GW: It was a dismal place in 1977.

YOUNG: What was real strange was that although the media was pushing this really soft music, you'd get amazing numbers of people turning out to hear the harder stuff. We were playing big stadiums and getting a great reaction. We'd be on the bill with a whole heap of acts—like in Oakland, playing a Bill Graham "Day on the Green" event. We were on at 10:30 in the morning—the first act. But at 10:30 in the morning there was 65,000 people. And they knew what we were about when we came on. We were only on for 35 minutes. But in 35 minutes you had to do a lot. It was fun. It was exciting. I'd do it again.

JOHNSON: Yeah, yeah, that was excitin' times, that. Pick yer best and go out. Pow.

YOUNG: Sometimes we could be real mercenary. Like if another band was givin' us a bit of stick—the headlining band or something. We get on and just sort of say, "Okay, we'll just turn up to 11 here, and let's go." Blow 'em away. We were good at that too.

JOHNSON: Fuck 'em. Hah!

GW: Were you overwhelmed by the groupie scene here?
YOUNG: No, no, no, no, no. In those days, girls were only interested in…well, not us. You met more of that when you started in clubs and pubs. Because in that time, you got rich people coming to slum it, and other people coming to see what the fuss was about. So those were your times when you could meet more of the weird and wonderful women. The crazy people. But during those first tours in the States…no. No more than what would be now. Same thing. And we were never that sort of band, anyway. I never ever saw a girl out there that would faint over me. Maybe she'd look and go, "Mmmm, I've never seen something as ugly as this!" Maybe I'd get some of *that*. But not a—what would you call it?—a fan sort of thing.
JOHNSON: The *Top of the Pops* syndrome.
YOUNG: But in a way that's always worked for us. You don't see an audience of young little girls screaming for us. So other people say, "Now *that's* a real band. That I like. It's real." 'Cause we aren't the prettiest things in the world. With AC/DC, it's not like we're here to steal your wife and your girlfriend and your daughter. We may *borrow* them, but…
JOHNSON: Only for a while.
GW: But don't girls like the schoolboy suit?
YOUNG: Well, they used to come out in England. But then, the English have been known for their craziness in the, um, sexual department.
JOHNSON: The public toilet department. "Vicar, please, take yer hands off me. It's not yer turn!"
YOUNG: I guess there's something a bit sexy in the blues element of what we do. That's probably more what's associated with the old strip club routine. I think that's somewhere in the back of people's heads when they hear that sort of music: the strip club image, you know? The smoke-filled room and the girl on stage. Well, I would *like* to believe that.
JOHNSON: I was startin' to feel good.
GW: One last thing: what's the origin of the schoolboy?
YOUNG: My sister. As a kid, I'd come right home from school and

pick up my guitar, without changing out of my school suit. At dinner time, I'd still be in the school suit, playing away. My sister always remembered that. She thought it was cute. And she was the one who said to Malcolm and me, "You know, it would be great if he'd get on stage with that school suit. It'll give people something to look at." I suppose she was right. At least it's worked for us.

Guitar World, January 1993

The Road Goes on Forever

Their career has been marked by wild triumphs, unspeakable tragedies and an unshakable devotion to their music. Now, insider Kirk West tells the story of the Allman Brothers Band—rock and roll's great survivors.

By Kirk West, as told to Alan Paul

DICKEY BETTS AND Warren Haynes stand at mid-stage, their guitars locked in a burst of delirious harmonies as they drive "Whipping Post" to a frenzied peak. Gregg Allman, his voice quivering with emotion, howls the song's final verse. The entire Allman Brothers Band sustains the final notes and brings the song—and the four-hour concert—to a shuddering climax. The drained crowd files out as the band retreats slowly backstage.

That the Allman Brothers have reclaimed their rightful place as one of rock's most hellacious live bands is but one aspect of what is a truly remarkable resurrection story. Few bands have experienced, let alone survived, the extreme ups and downs which have characterized the Allmans' career.

Once hailed as "America's best rock and roll band," the Allman Brothers Band, featuring the legendary twin guitars of Duane Allman

Guitar World Presents CLASSIC ROCK

Duane Allman

and Richard "Dickey" Betts, formed in 1969. The sextet blended elements of blues, r&b, jazz, country and rock into a dramatic, improvisational style that has influenced several generations of rockers, from Lynyrd Skynyrd to the Black Crowes. The band's incendiary *At Fillmore East* (Polydor, 1971) is simply rock's greatest live document, capturing the Allmans on a magical night at the height of their formidable jamming powers—and demonstrating repeatedly why Duane is considered the greatest rock slide guitarist ever.

The seminal Southern rock band was formed when Duane Allman, a well-regarded session guitarist who had worked with such r&b giants as Aretha Franklin and Wilson Pickett, decided to strike out on his own. Allman immediately enlisted an eclectic collection of players with a wide range of playing experiences: drummer "Jaimoe" Johanny Johanson was a veteran of numerous r&b sessions; bassist Berry Oakley and guitarist Dickey Betts were members of a popular Jacksonville, Florida, psychedelic band; Butch Trucks played drums with an acoustic-based Jacksonville band; and, of course, organist/vocalist Gregg Allman, Duane's brother, was quickly developing into the world's greatest white blues singer.

The band was quickly signed to Phil Walden's fledgling Capricorn Records, releasing their self-titled debut in November 1969. In 1971, just as the Allman Brothers' popularity began catching up to their critical reputation, Duane was killed in a motorcycle accident. The guitarist's death was just the first in a series of bizarre tragedies and mishaps to afflict the band, including the death of bassist Berry Oakley, a scandalous drug trial, numerous personnel changes and ever-shifting tastes in popular music. But for all their difficulties, the Allmans have proven to be remarkably resilient, countering each apparent knockdown blow with such brilliant albums as *Eat a Peach*, *Brothers and Sisters* and *Shades of Two Worlds*.

With the recent release of *The Fillmore Concerts* (Polydor), an expanded and remastered version of *At Fillmore East*, the time seemed ripe to take a long, deep look at this turbulent and towering musical force. Kirk West, currently the Allman Brothers' "tour mystic," has known the band since 1970. The associate producer of *The Fillmore*

Concerts, as well as *Dreams*, a four-CD boxed set released in 1989, and several other Allman Brothers collections, he is the band's archivist and unofficial historian. What follows is based on his personal recollections and on his interviews with each surviving band member.
—*Alan Paul*

Duane was the band's visionary. He inspired the other guys. He gave them courage and he challenged them to play what was in their hearts, even when times were tough. Butch came from acoustic folk music; Dickey and Berry from electric psychedelia; Gregg and Duane from a pretty formatted blues background; and Jaimoe from straight jazz and r&b. The amazing thing is, Duane got all of them pulling in the same direction.

Duane obviously practiced his ass off and worked incredibly hard at getting better, as any great musician must. But there was something else there, something that can't be learned—a spark that was, I suppose, genius, and that made everyone else around him better and more confident. I think Duane always had a sense of his gift, and towards the end he began to realize what that could do. His session work was a great source of confidence, because it was the first time that he realized that he had ideas which people would listen to.

When he talked about the Herbie Mann sessions [Push Push, *Atlantic*], which he did two months before he died, he said, "I can't get better than this. I played this stuff perfectly." He said similar things about recording *Layla* with Clapton. And [*producer*] Tom Dowd will tell you that that album session had been dead in the water. Everyone was so stoned and uninspired that it almost collapsed—until Duane came in and lit a fire under it. That was part of his gift, and it had a lot to do with his own band's success.

There hasn't been much said about Duane and Dickey's relationship, because Dickey doesn't talk about it much, but there was, obviously, a tremendous mutual respect and a healthy competition between them. It wasn't the one-upmanship type of competition where you try to make the other guy look bad. Rather, they used what each other did to inspire themselves to play better; it was a competition where nobody lost. Dickey has always said that he's never played with anyone who inspired him more, and Duane used to say similar things about Dickey. In fact, Duane talked about Dickey being a *better* guitar player than him, period. Yet Duane got all the spotlight—and still does to a certain extent. But Dickey brought a lot to Duane's playing. They always left room for each other and fed each other ideas. And they both had an amazing sense of restraint. They understood the philosophy that someone like Albert King lives by: that it's the holes you leave, the gaps, the notes you don't play, that makes the notes you *do* play more important.

It's unusual enough for someone to have that innate sense of restraint, but for two guitarists, particularly that young, to have it and share it perfectly, almost as one sense, is phenomenal. It's like two people running down the beach tossing a football to each other and, without ever breaking stride, never once underthrowing or overthrowing one another. And they didn't look at each other's fingers; they always looked into the other's eyes when they played harmony together or were getting ready to swap leads, which tells you a lot about how they communicated.

That dynamic extended beyond Duane and Dickey, and ran throughout the whole band. You can really hear it on all those really long, out-there jams which became their trademark. If somebody got lost during something very unstructured—"Mountain Jam" or "In Memory of Elizabeth Reed"—and was out there floating, then someone else, usually Oakley or Trucks, would go grab him and bring him back. The two people on stage with the most presence were Duane and Berry, and Dickey, Duane and Berry were constantly playing in a little circle. Jaimoe says all the time that the reason that unit was so good is they all listened to each other. There was a jazz sense to Duane's approach that freed him to take major risks, and this ability to take chances, to not be a perfectionist, was, on a musical level, the band's catalyst.

Up until 1970 the band lived together, first in Jacksonville, later in Macon. They'd eat together, they'd get high together, they'd sleep in the same house. They traveled in a van together, and would get one or two hotel rooms on the road, when they'd get them at all. They shared everything. It was constant, in-your-face companionship, like being in an army unit together. If you go through strife or turmoil together, you learn how the others are going to think and respond. And that's indicative of the way they played together. It wasn't a job; it was their life, and they were doing something they really believed in.

After a year of living together, barnstorming the South, but making only occasional, haphazard forays up North, the Allman Brothers were booked by Bill Graham to open for Blood, Sweat and Tears at New York's Fillmore East auditorium in December 1969. Though the band was not well received, Graham was impressed, and it marked the beginning of the end of the Allmans' tenure as a regional band. It also was the beginning of a long and fruitful relationship between the band and the promoter, which lasted until Graham's death in 1991.

They were actually booed at the Blood, Sweat and Tears show. Afterwards, Bill Graham, who had been knocked out by them, said, "I'm sorry guys, it was bad booking on my part. Who do you like?" And they said, "Any of the Kings [*B.B., Albert or Freddie*], the Grateful Dead and [*jazz saxophonist*] Roland Kirk." Two weeks later, they were at the Fillmore West playing with B.B. King and Buddy Guy. Two weeks after that they were back at the Fillmore East, playing with the Grateful Dead and Love. And shortly after that, they played with Kirk back in San Francisco. So Graham gave them a big break, but he was zigzagging them across the country in the middle of winter, when their only transportation was a Ford Econoline van with no heating. Snow would form on the inside, and they would lie head to foot, covered by blankets and equipment, trying to stay warm. It was a rough couple of months.

Two months before the first Fillmore show they had their first major gig outside the South: opening for the Velvet Underground at the Boston Tea Party. The club liked them and booked them again for a performance two weeks later. They had nowhere to stay, so they found an abandoned building and squatted there. They played a couple of free shows at the Boston Commons during that time, then met the J. Geils Band and had a few jam sessions with them. Then they played the Tea Party again and headed back to Macon.

This wasn't atypical of the way they did things; they'd get a gig and go do it, regardless of where it was. They'd play in Atlanta, pile in a van and go play a show in Virginia, then drive back to Macon. And they weren't making any money or getting any tour support, though Phil Walden was buying them lots of equipment. So while they had no money, they had great gear. But they drove that Ford van into the ground. In the spring of '70, they parked in front of Walden's office and said they weren't leaving until they got something better. And he bought them a Winnebago and a Ryder truck, which was a huge step up.

Times were tough in 1969-70, but the Allmans were doing exactly what they wanted: playing great music and staying buzzed. Though they weren't selling any records—the first album came out in November and sold 30,000 copies, and *Idlewild South*, which came out 11 months later, sold maybe twice as many—I don't think they ever started doubting themselves, because they were seeing progress: every time they returned somewhere, the crowd would be four times as big.

When they were living in Jacksonville, they'd set up anywhere. They played high schools and Sunday "Be-Ins" in the park—and that continued for the first year or so in Macon. They just wanted to play in front of people. And all these experiences brought them together, as did having Jaimoe in the band, which was not a small thing at the time; they experienced a lot of shit for being a bi-racial band in the South. Actually, at the time, hippies weren't much better than blacks in a redneck's eyes, so they had six strikes against them. It was like being in a war or a carnival act together. Six band guys and three road guys all alone in the South, which was a dangerous place.

The roadies were as important to the operation as the band. That's why they were pictured on the back of *Fillmore East*. In fact, Duane had a policy that the crew got paid before the band did. There was absolutely no division between the band and the crew for the first few years, in large part because for a long time they lived off of the government checks of Twiggs [*Lyndon, tour manager*], who'd been in the Army, and Reddog [*the Allmans' first roadie, still with the band*], who was a disabled Marine. They both got $100 or $150 a month, and that's what the whole band lived on.

In March 1971, the Allman Brothers played two nights at the Fillmore East. Recordings of the shows were released in July as At the Fillmore East. *The double album contained only seven songs, of which three clocked in at over 12 minutes, including the 22-minute opus, "Whipping Post." The band was captured in all its sonic fury, exploring the jazzy, psychedelic improvisations of "In Memory of Elizabeth Reed" and storming through the bone-cutting blues of "Done Somebody Wrong" and "Statesboro Blues." The album firmly established Duane as a guitar hero of the first magnitude and him and Dickey as rock's finest guitar team. It also proved to be the band's commercial breakthrough, garnering rave reviews and earning the Allmans their first Gold record.*

The band just stayed on the road after *Fillmore* came out and started to really see progress. They were playing much bigger places, and were generally accepted by critics as the greatest live rock and roll band. They rented a ski lodge in Tennessee to work on songs for their next album—what became *Eat a Peach*—and there are incredible tapes of those sessions: Betts playing the chorus of "Ramblin' Man" (then called "Ramblin' Country Man"); the whole band playing a jazzy, free-form version of Rodgers and Hammerstein's "My Favorite Things"; and three different versions of "Blue Sky," with Dickey showing it to the band and everyone working out their parts. That's how they worked songs out—individually bringing ideas in and jamming them into songs. A few months later, they went to Miami and began recording.

At the end of October, the Allman Brothers took a well-deserved break from the sessions and returned to Macon. After showing up at the band's "Big House" to offer birthday greetings to Berry Oakley's wife, Linda, on October 29, Duane took off on his motorcycle. He swerved to avoid a truck and was killed in the resulting fall. He was one month shy of his twenty-fifth birthday.

Duane's funeral was a somber, devastating affair. The Brothers played, as did Dr. John, and [*Atlantic Records' executive*] Jerry Wexler gave the eulogy. It wasn't a private ceremony; there were huge crowds surrounding the church and the whole town was in shock. Strangely enough, they didn't bury Duane, because there were some disputes over what kind of monument to put up, where to bury him and who would pay for it. He sat in cold storage for more than a year. It was some pretty funky stuff, but typical of the way Phil Walden does things. There wasn't going to be anything done until there was a financial arrangement. He wasn't buried until Berry died and [Duane's widow] Donna got together with Berry's widow, Linda, and they buried them side by side, with matching tombstones, in the Civil War section of a Macon cemetery. It was very near where the band used to go write and hang out and get high—where Elizabeth Reed is buried.

There was also a big controversy when Duane died over who his widow was. He and Donna had never married, but they had a daughter, Galadrielle, and if you have a child in Georgia, you're married and have to get a divorce. He was separated from Donna and living with another lady—and in Georgia, if you lived together, you were also considered married. There was a big legal battle over who would be the recipient of his estate, but Donna won because they were never legally divorced.

Gregg wrote "Ain't Wasting Time No More" within three weeks of Duane's death, and it was the last thing put on *Eat a Peach*. It's a perfect summation of the band's view of how they were going to handle things. The band played Carnegie Hall on Thanksgiving (three weeks after Duane's death), so they clearly never thought about not continuing; it was just a matter of figuring out how. Berry took on a much more prominent musical role. He had always played bass like a lead instrument, but he started really playing lead bass and there was an awful lot of interplay between him and Dickey. But Berry was really devastated by Duane's death, and he stayed loaded and in a sort of a haze all the time. It was a real problem; he couldn't even always finish shows.

The tone of the band started to gradually change, with more of Dickey's country stuff seeping in. In a way, it had already been a major influence, because a lot of his and Duane's approach to arranging lead guitar structures was based on Dickey's experiences with the twin fiddles of Western Swing music. And it probably would have happened whether Duane had died or not—"Ramblin' Man" was written in 1971, and they had played "Blue Sky" live several times with Duane—but the process was accelerated out of necessity; there were holes that had to be filled.

After Duane died, a lot of people suddenly started realizing that Betts is a hell of a guitar player. Reviewers were almost unanimously astounded that Dickey was so good, and that had a huge impact on him, as did the weight of being the sole guitar player in what was known as a two-guitar band. But it was a combination compliment/slam, because he had always been that good, and he wondered why no one had ever realized it.

And he had to start playing slide on certain songs—and play it like Duane—which he never really liked to do. So he was in a very, very complicated position: he had to be his own guitar player and play his own way, yet he had to occasionally replicate Duane's parts. And right up to this day, he's had to deal with being a central figure in a band called "The Allman Brothers," which was never really an issue until Duane was gone.

After several performances as a five-piece, the band added keyboardist Chuck Leavell and, returning to Macon, began recording Brothers and Sisters, the title of which reflects the communal lifestyle they led at the time.

Chuck brought a lot to the band, and he was added for a couple of reasons. They were looking to expand from a five-piece and add another lead instrument, but they knew that they couldn't try to replace Duane, so Chuck seemed like a perfect answer. He fit right in, and everything was going extremely well. Everyone was happy with the songs and Oakley started really pulling out of his black hole, which was a huge relief. He got very wrapped up in recording the album, and was staying much cleaner. Then it happened to him.

Mid-way through recording the album, almost exactly one year from the day Duane died, Oakley was killed in an eerily similar motorcycle accident. He was quickly replaced by Lamar Williams and the album was completed, with the band actually reaching something of a creative peak. With Betts taking on a larger role and the band's musical interplay re-invigorated by Leavell's jazzy/honky tonk piano playing, the album included the band's only Top 40 hit, "Ramblin' Man," as well as two instant classics, the instrumental "Jessica" and "Southbound"; all three songs were penned by Betts. The Allmans returned to the road, playing to larger crowds than ever. But Oakley's death weighed heavily on them. Williams never quite adapted to the group's unique sound, and the seeds which would lead to the band's demise were already being sown. By the time they recorded Win, Lose or Draw *in 1975, communication within the band had broken down and their creative spark was nearly extinguished.*

Success had a lot to do with the diminished interplay and communication among the band. They made a lot of money in 1973-74 and they started living like it. They all had nice homes, big cars and lots of expendable income. They started traveling in jets and limos and a lot of the forced interaction diminished—they stopped hanging. Gregg wasn't even present for the recording of *Win, Lose or Draw*. They sent him the tapes in L.A., where he was living with Cher, which the other guys thought was totally ridiculous. But they thought Gregg had done a lot ridiculous things, so it was shocking but not surprising.

Of course, all this wasn't unique to the Allman Brothers. Often when a band experiences success, the event overwhelms the performance. The Brothers would perform a show which they knew was half-assed, and everyone would tell them it was great. And it gets to where you don't believe anybody. You quit having faith in anyone. They were making lots of money, selling lots of records and hundreds of thousands of tickets, but they had quit having any belief in it. It was just happening, and they were a band who had *lived* their music.

What happened when Berry died is that two people who weren't leaders were thrust into leadership roles. Duane and Berry were the two who really had the vision, and Gregg and Dickey weren't very well-versed in how to inspire and motivate people. There was a big loss in inspiration and vision. Dickey has always said that while losing Duane was a tremendous shock, there was never any question about what they were going to do. Staying together and making music was the way they all dealt with the loss; they leaned on each other. Berry's death was the one that really cut the legs out from under them and left them grasping. Things started becoming more individualized; there was a lot less of everyone bringing in a song and jamming it out.

It was a band that communicated so well on stage—and stopped communicating at all off stage. It was indicative of the times, but they weren't the Eagles or Fleetwood Mac; they couldn't just rehearse their songs and play them while they hated each other. The whole point of their being was to be a jazz band at maximum volume; the interplay and improvisational stuff were what made them special—and that's what suffered. They would just break down during any of the stuff where the whole point was to just get out there and explore musical boundaries.

And Lamar was a totally different kind of bass player. Since he had always played bass, he tried to lock in with the drummers, which was impossible to do, because Jaimoe and Butch play so completely differently. Berry had been a guitarist and he played bass like a lead instrument—around the drums.

In '75 they did 52 shows as the best-paid band in the country—making anywhere from 250 to 500 grand a night, guaranteed. They came home from that 52-date tour and had $150,000 profit to split between the partners. They had pissed it all away. They had roadies hiring roadies to do their jobs. The roadies, who had a band, met a chick who was a great keyboard player, and they hired her to play in the band that did soundchecks and opened a few shows. It was pretty indulgent.

The Allman Brothers' 1976 breakup has often been attributed to outrage by the other band members at Gregg, who testified for the prosecu-

tion at the drug trial of the band's assistant road manager, Scooter Herring. According to West, this is an overly simplistic explanation.

Phil Walden had gotten them involved in fundraising for [presidential candidate] Jimmy Carter, who, as governor [of Georgia], would occasionally come hang out at the studio. Meanwhile, the Ford White House was looking for ways to slander and diminish the Carter campaign. Since there had been a lot of money raised by Capricorn and its acts—and as far as Republicans are concerned, rock stars are all drug addicts, anyway—they sent Federal attorneys down to see what they could find.

Scooter had come into the picture in 1973, when he painted a motorcycle for Gregg, and they hit off. He was a well-connected, nice guy, so they put him on the payroll as a valet/assistant tour manager. And he hooked up with this pharmacist who had a drugstore in a little strip mall right by Gregg's house. When his little drugstore suddenly started going through a ridiculous amount of pharmaceutical cocaine, a red flag went up with the Food and Drug Administration. Meanwhile, a directive came down from the White House: Walden and Capricorn are funding the Carter campaign, so let's see just how dirty they are. All this stuff came together, and they busted Scooter and forced Gregg back from L.A. to testify before the grand jury.

Scooter, Phil, Gregg and all of their lawyers met, and Scooter said, "The buck stops here: They're not going to take Gregg down, they're not going to take Phil down and they're definitely not going to take Jimmy Carter down. It obviously isn't what they think it is, so let's just stop it with me." So Scooter's lawyers were paid for, Gregg bought him a house, and Scooter took the heat—voluntarily.

Gregg testified at the trial and Scooter was sentenced to the maximum—75 years. An appeal was set up immediately and he spent about eight months in prison while it went through the process. Then the sentence was overturned and he went into a drug rehab program for 12 months. He was home free in two years, and there was a big party for him—paid for by Gregg. But the headlines read, "Gregg Allman testifies. Road manager gets 75 years." The reality is that it was a no-win situation, and that Scooter willingly took the heat. He remained on friendly terms with Gregg and it all calmed down, but it was the final nail in the band's coffin, because no one ever asked Gregg his side of the story. None of the band were at the trial, so all they knew was what they read in the papers or what a reporter who called them for comment told them.

But from the way things were going and everyone was living, the band wouldn't have made it through 1976, anyhow. The whole thing had just sort of run its course; the music wasn't happening any more. What with their profit margin after the '75 tour, their inability to record an album in one place, and the lack of communication, no one was to blame, and everyone was to blame. Everyone pointed their finger, but they had four or five pointing back at them. Then the Scooter thing happened and all of a sudden Gregg was a bad guy.

Following the band's 1976 dissolution, the members went their separate ways: Allman returned to Los Angeles and Cher, with whom he recorded an album, Allman and Woman, *as well as the solo* Playing Up a Storm; *Betts formed the country-rock outfit Great Southern; while Leavell, Williams and Jaimoe remained together as Sea Level. After Great Southern released two albums to critical acclaim but lukewarm public interest, Allman expressed tentative interest in a reconciliation. In December 1978, the Allman Brothers Band was reunited, filled out by Great Southern's guitarist, Dan Toler, and bassist, David Goldflies. The band went back to Step One: resigned with Capricorn Records, enlisted producer Tom Dowd, who had been behind the boards for* Idlewild South, At the Fillmore East *and* Eat a Peach, *and returned to Miami's Criteria Studios, home of many of their early triumphs. The result was* Enlightened Rogues, *an album which captured much of the Allmans' original spirit. But trouble was lurking just around the corner.*

By 1978, the rest of the band realized that all their condemnation of Gregory was misplaced. They also realized things weren't happening for them financially on their own, and that they weren't making nearly as inspired music as they were capable of. Contrary to some opinions, getting back together was not a totally monetary decision.

Everyone felt good about *Enlightened Rogues,* and they hit the road. The album sold well, the crowds were there and the band played great. Then Capricorn went down the toilet and the band signed with Arista, which had also just signed the Dead. Clive Davis [*Arista president*] had this warped vision of what he could do with these bands—he took two totally unique, self-sustaining entities and tried to change them. The Brothers were given a pop-oriented production team, and they recorded *Reach For the Sky*, an album which no one in the band can bear to listen to today. When they went back on the road, things started to fall apart a bit. The record wasn't selling, the crowds were getting smaller, and the band's attitudes started to sour; they weren't playing with the same fire. Although there were some great shows and great playing in any given show, the spirit started to diminish. They changed lighting companies and sound men. This sounds minor, but they had always worked on a family basis with their crew, and now they had a crew of rock and roll mercenaries. The unified, family-style feeling had just disappeared completely.

In 1981, they recorded *Brothers of the Road*, which sold even less than *Reach For the Sky*, and they didn't know where to turn. Arista was leaning on them to be more songwriting-oriented, to get radio airplay and get on *Solid Gold*, so they were making music they weren't particularly good at. They stayed on the road and kept playing smaller places to littler crowds in further out-of-the-way places. They returned to Florida and recorded demos of a dozen songs, and Gregg went to New York to play them for Davis, who rejected every one of them. Gregg said, "Fuck you. I'll take my name and go." And Davis said, "You can't take your name. I own it." So they had their hands tied; they couldn't record and they couldn't go anywhere else because they were under contract.

The final performance by this version of the Allman Brothers Band was on *Saturday Night Live* on January 23, 1982. The last song they played was "Leaving" [*Brothers of the Road*], a song with strangely appropriate lyrics: "Gonna take my guitar/I don't care if I'm a big star/I'm leaving."

The Allmans' 1982 breakup appeared to mark the end of the band's remarkable history. Gregg quickly formed the Gregg Allman Band, while Betts went through several phases, often playing with Leavell and Trucks, and making consistently good music which failed to impress the public. In 1986 Allman and Betts toured together, concluding each performance with an hour-long set of Allman Brothers material. The joint tour led to two Allman Brothers Band reunions that year, both at benefit concerts. Following these shows, the band went their separate ways, with Gregg recording two albums for Epic Records: 1987's I'm No Angel *and 1988's* Just Before the Bullets Fly. *The title track of* I'm No Angel *was a moderate hit, reflecting the fact that, thanks to Stevie Ray Vaughan, the Fabulous Thunderbirds and Robert Cray, the music world had begun to grow more favorable to blues-based rock.*

Meanwhile Betts, now hooked up with guitarist Warren Haynes and pianist Johnny Neel, had also signed with Epic, for whom he recorded Pattern Disruptive *in 1988. Though the album didn't sell much, it demonstrated that, in Haynes, Betts had at last found a guitar foil good enough to stand up to the inevitable comparisons to Duane. Epic soon asked the Allmans to record yet another comeback album but the band refused, insisting on touring first. They had their way, and a 20th anniversary tour in support of the four-CD retrospective,* Dreams, *was planned. The newest incarnation of the Allman Brothers included original members Betts, Allman, Trucks and Jaimoe, Betts Band alumni Haynes and Neel, and bassist Allen Woody, who was selected from among dozens of applicants. The band hit the road, with no plans beyond seeing if they were still a viable unit.*

Dreams gave the band a big boost. It shined a light on all of their accomplishments and verified their status as one of rock's greatest bands; and it gave them a record to go out and promote, without having to record anything new. Epic wanted them to record an album and then tour, but the band flatly refused; they had to make sure that there was still something there. So without writing any new material, they rehearsed for two weeks and jumped off—and it clicked right away.

One of the keys to the original unit was that if someone had a bad night, the band would pull them out of their funk. While that stopped happening during the first reunion, when they didn't play as a unit in the same way, it became the case again in 1989. The unit was stronger than any one person, and was thereby able to overcome individual shortcomings or bad nights. The level at which they played during the reunion tour astounded everyone, and they were able to record *Seven Turns* with a great deal of confidence.

1990's Seven Turns *was indeed a strong comeback album, immediately re-establishing the Allmans as a vibrant musical force. The following year's* Shades of Two Worlds, *recorded after months of intensive touring, was even stronger, proving that the band had managed to revive its original spirit while developing its own distinct personality. All this was thanks in large part to Woody and Haynes, a magnificent improviser who lit a fire under Betts' playing.* An Evening with the Allman Brothers Band, *a live album released last fall, serves as an exclamation point to the band's comeback, as it is recorded evidence of what anyone who has seen the band in the past three years already knows: There is no more adventurous, skilled and hard-rocking live band around today.*

Seven Turns was a strong album, but as they toured, they just got better and better. The interplay between Warren and Dickey grew more confident. The band became tighter and Gregg was singing incredibly well. Before recording *Shades*, Johnny Neel left the band, leaving Gregg as the sole keyboardist, which has resulted in him playing more and better than he has in years. They've all just been astounded at their musical strength.

Warren has made an amazing contribution, as has Allen, who plays more like Oakley than any other bass player they've ever had. And Warren plays more like Duane, not in the sense of copying him but in that he plays with tremendous confidence and originality—copying Duane would be the exact *wrong* way to capture his spirit.

And he adds an incredible dynamic to Dickey's playing, because they play very differently—as did Duane and Dickey. That musical tension and contrast is the real key to why the band was so good and is today. They are by far the closest that they've been to the original unit since Berry died.

Guitar World Presents CLASSIC ROCK

Roger Waters and Syd Barrett of Pink Floyd

Guitar World, February 1993

David's Harp

David Gilmour reflects on his creative partnership with Roger Waters and his own role in making Pink Floyd one of rock's most innovative and experimental bands.

By Alan di Perna

SWINGING LONDON, 1967: Amid the psychedelic explosion of new groups making their debut in that charmed era was a quartet called The Pink Floyd. In small, smoky clubs like UFO and the Roundhouse, the Floyd galvanized the London scene with their extended, free-form instrumental jams. Fledgling flower children grooved to the heady new sounds in rooms that seemed to bob and levitate as blobs of multi-colored liquid light melted the walls around them. Perhaps even more than Cream and the Jimi Hendrix Experience (two other groups that debuted in '67), The Pink Floyd were psychedelia personified.

But by the following year, it was no longer possible to ignore the rapidly deteriorating mental condition of Syd Barrett, the band's brilliant but unstable guitarist and leader. In 1968 The Pink Floyd dropped the "The" from their name—and they dropped Syd Barrett. Guitarist David Gilmour, an old school friend of Syd's, was drafted to replace him. Barrett invented The Pink Floyd, and his troubled genius would later furnish the subject matter for some of the band's best songs. But it was David Gilmour and his lyrical guitar work that provided Pink Floyd with the sonic signature that helped carry them to international stardom in the Seventies. The smoky clubs of Swinging London gave way to vast arenas and stadiums. The Floyd's ever-evolving trippy instrumental textures evolved to new levels of complexity, along with their otherworldly concert visuals.

Pink Floyd's next big crack-up didn't occur until 1985, when David Gilmour and bassist Roger Waters came to a bitter parting of the ways. Gilmour assumed sole leadership of the band in 1987. With Waters' brooding lyrics out of the mix, Gilmour's searing, expansive guitar style became the keystone of Pink Floyd's identity more than ever—the consistent factor runing all the way back to the days of Flower Power.

These days, David Gilmour is a portly gray-haired English gentleman who becomes instantly youthful once he gets a guitar in his hands. To celebrate *Shine On* (Columbia), the new Pink Floyd box set, Gilmour consented to share some of his memories with *Guitar World*.

GUITAR WORLD: Long before Pink Floyd, you and Syd Barrett hung out together in college, in Cambridge, playing guitars. Can you recall what you played or how you influenced each other?
DAVID GILMOUR: We were friends first, then we picked up guitars later on. I was playing professionally in groups before Syd. So technically speaking, I was a little better than Syd when we were at college. We sat around learning Beatles songs, Rolling Stones songs, r&b, blues songs... I can recall spending some time working on "Come On," the first Stones B-side or whatever it was, working all that out, playing harmonicas and stuff. He'd know something, I'd know something and we'd just swap, as people do in back rooms everywhere. He then left that college and moved up to an art college in London, which is when Pink Floyd got formed.
GW: There's a famous story about Syd being phased out of the band in 1968. You were all in a van, on your way to a gig in Southampton...
GILMOUR: Not in a van, no. In a Bentley.
GW: Right. And someone said, "Oh, let's just not pick up Syd tonight." Can you recall who said that?

GILMOUR: Probably Roger. Certainly not me—I was the new boy. I was in the back. Someone probably said, "Shall we go and pick up Syd?" And Roger probably said [*in conspiratorial tones*] "Oh no, let's not!" And off we went down to Southampton. We were playing with the Incredible String Band and Tyrannosaurus Rex that night.
GW: In the early days of Pink Floyd, did you feel like you were just a Syd surrogate?
GILMOUR: Oh, I was; no question about it. They wanted me to play his parts and sing his songs. Nobody else wanted to sing them, and I got elected. That was my job as far as live shows were concerned, anyway. Me and Syd played only five gigs together in Pink Floyd. Or maybe four. Maybe Southampton was supposed to be the fifth one; I don't remember. While all this was happening, we were also trying to make the new album, *A Saucerful of Secrets*. But live, we didn't play the tracks from that. We were playing virtually all Syd's stuff. Because there wasn't anything else to do. It was either that or back to Bo Diddley covers.

"A Saucerful of Secrets" *A Saucerful of Secrets* **(Capitol, 1968)**
GW: What made the band decide to take on a lengthy, abstract instrumental like "Saucerful"?
GILMOUR: That's hard to say. I had just joined the group shortly before that. I don't think the band really knew quite where they wanted to go after Syd had left. "A Saucerful of Secrets" was the first hint at a direction. I just remember watching Roger and Nick [*Mason, Pink Floyd's drummer*] drawing weird shapes on a piece of paper.
GW: You mean diagramming the dynamics?
GILMOUR: Yeah. It all came out of that diagram, basically, and got made up as we went along. It started off with the edge tones of two cymbals, beaten very softly. My natural bent within the whole thing, I suppose, was to try and make it a bit more musical, and to help create a balance between formlessness and structure, disharmony and harmony.
GW: The producer, Norman Smith, wasn't too keen on "A Saucerful of Secrets," was he?

GILMOUR: No. Norman worked as an engineer on the Beatles and had seen another one of his contemporaries, George Martin, move up to the pinnacle of success by producing the Beatles. That was the route he wanted to take. He tried that out with us and the Pretty Things. One of us was supposed to become the next Beatles. But you know, people have their own ideas of how they want to be. Norman was a great teacher in terms of studio techniques, however. We got along very well. But once or twice he just had to accept the fact that we weren't going to do it the way he thought.

GW: There are varying opinions as to whether or not Syd is on the "Saucerful of Secrets" track.

GILMOUR: No, he's not. That's totally false. He's on three or four other tracks on the album, including "Remember a Day" and "Jug Band Music" [*Syd's sole composition on the* Saucerful *album*]. He's also on a tiny bit of "Set the Controls for the Heart of the Sun." I think I'm on "Set the Controls" as well.

GW: Can you recall any of the techniques you used to get unusual guitar tones back then?

GILMOUR: Well, on the middle section of "A Saucerful of Secrets," most of the time the guitar was lying on the studio floor. You know how mic stands have three steel legs about a foot long? I unscrewed one of the legs and just whizzed one of those up and down the neck—not very subtly. Another technique, which came a bit later, involved taking a small piece of steel and rubbing it from side to side across the strings. You just move it and stop it in places that sound good. It's something like an E-bow.

"One of These Days" *Meddle* (Capitol, 1971)

GW: Another technical point: the instrumental "One of These Days" was born when someone plugged a bass into a "Binson Echorec." What is this device?

GILMOUR: The Binson was an Italian-made delay unit. It was strange because it didn't utilize tape loops, but used a metal recording wheel instead. [*Binson's Echorec was basically a wire recorder—a precursor to magnetic tape. It had six knobs, an input volume, one to control the length,* *volume and tone of a swell, a three-position selector knob and a 12-position switching knob. The selector accessed either echo (one repeat), repeat (more than one repeat) or swell (reverbs cleverly devised by feeding the outputs of the heads back to themselves), while the switching knob accessed 12 variations of these.—GW Ed.*] You could get some wonderful delay effects that aren't attainable on anything that's been made since. "One of These Days" evolved from some of my experiments with the Binson, as did "Echoes" [*also from* Meddle]. One day, Roger decided to take some of the techniques that I was developing and try them out for himself on bass. And he came up with that basic riff that we all worked on and turned into "One of These Days." For the middle section, another piece of technology came into play: an H&H amp with vibrato. I set the vibrato to more or less the same tempo as the delay. But the delay was in 3/4 increments of the beat and while the vibrato went with the beat. I just played the bass through it and made up that little section, which we then stuck on to a bit of tape and edited in. The tape splices were then camouflaged with cymbal crashes.

GW: So you played the bass on that track?

GILMOUR: Yes. The opening section is me and Roger. On "One of These Days," for some reason, we decided to do a double track of the bass. You can actually hear it if you listen in stereo. The first bass is me. A bar later, Roger joins in on the other side of the stereo picture. We didn't have a spare set of strings for the spare bass guitar, so the second bass is very dull-sounding. [*laughs*] We sent a roadie out to buy some strings, but he wandered off to see his girlfriend instead.

GW: How did you hit on the idea of playing slide guitar on the track?

GILMOUR: I guess I was never particularly confident in my ability as a pure guitar player, so I would try any trick in the book. I'd always liked lap steels, pedal steels and things like that. I can't remember exactly what I used on "One of These Days"; I may have bought a lap steel by that point, but maybe I used a regular guitar. Certainly for touring, I got hold of two cheap Jensen lap steels and put Fender pickups on them. And then I just tuned them up differently. The lap steel on "One of These Days" is tuned to an open E minor chord—E, B, E, G, B, E, low to high. The other lap steel is basically tuned to a modified open G chord [D, G, D, G, B, E, low to high]. I use that for "The Great Gig in the Sky." Instead of tuning the top string down to a D, which would be a full, open G chord, I kept it an E so that I could do major and minor chords on the first three strings.

So that's basically how I deal with lap steel. I have a lot of different tunings. The one thing I don't do is regular slide guitar with the thingie on your finger. I've never had any interest in that.

"Money" *Dark Side of the Moon* **(Capitol, 1973)**
GW: Where did the famous 7/4 time signature for "Money" come from?
GILMOUR: It's Roger's riff. Roger came in with the verses and lyrics to "Money" more or less completed. And we just made up middle sections, guitar solos and all that stuff. We also invented some new riffs—we created a 4/4 progression for the guitar solo and made the poor saxophone player play in 7/4. I got to do mine in 4/4. It was my idea to break down and become dry and empty for the second chorus of the solo.
GW: Were you purposely trying to get away from just playing a 12-bar blues on guitar?
GILMOUR: No, I just wanted to make a dramatic effect with the three solos. The first solo is ADT'd—Artificially Double-Tracked. And the third one is actually double-tracked. I think I did the first two solos on a Fender Stratocaster, but the last one was done on a different guitar—a Lewis, which was made by some guy in Vancouver. It had a whole two octaves on the neck, which meant I could get up to notes that I couldn't play on a Stratocaster.
GW: What amp did you use on that?
GILMOUR: I imagine it was a Hiwatt, but I'm not too certain. I used Fender Twin Reverbs in the studio a lot, too. But I'm certain the effects consisted of a Fuzzface fuzz box and the Binson echo/delay.
GW: What was [*producer/engineer*] Chris Thomas' role on *Dark Side of the Moon*?
GILMOUR: Chris Thomas came in for the mixes, and his role was essentially to stop the arguments between me and Roger about how

it should be mixed. I wanted *Dark Side* to be big and swampy and wet, with reverbs and things like that. And Roger was very keen on it being a very dry album. I think he was influenced a lot by John Lennon's first solo album [*Plastic Ono Band*], which was very dry. We argued so much that it was suggested we get a third opinion. We were going to leave Chris to mix it on his own, with Alan Parsons engineering. And of course on the first day I found out that Roger sneaked in there. So the second day I sneaked in there. And from then on, we both sat right at Chris' shoulder, interfering. Luckily, Chris was more sympathetic to my point of view than he was to Roger's.

GW: Was that the first album where tension emerged between you and Roger?

GILMOUR: Ah, there's always been tension. But it was all quite controllable until after *The Wall* album.

GW: There's creative tension and then there's outright hostility…

GILMOUR: There's creative tension and there's total egocentric megalomaniacal tension, if you like.

GW: Did the prospect of having to follow the huge success of *Dark Side of the Moon* create a lot of pressure during the sessions for *Wish You Were Here*?

GILMOUR: Yeah, that's what the album's about, I think, as far as Roger's concerned anyway. It's about that feeling we were left with at the end of *Dark Side*—that feeling of "What do you do when you've done everything?" But I think we got over that. And for me, *Wish You Were Here* is the most satisfying album. I really love it. I mean, I'd rather listen to that than *Dark Side of the Moon*. Because I think we achieved a better balance of music and lyrics on *Wish You Were Here*. *Dark Side* went a bit too far the other way—too much into the importance of the lyrics. And sometimes the tunes—the vehicles for the lyrics—got neglected. To me, one of Roger's failings is that sometimes, in his effort to get the words across, he uses a less-than-perfect vehicle.

"Dogs" *Animals* **(Columbia, 1977)**

GW: On the next Pink Floyd album, *Animals*, "Dogs" is the only song not written solely by Roger. What was your part in co-writing "Dogs" with him?

GILMOUR: I basically wrote all the chords—the main music part of it. And we wrote some other bits together at the end.

GW: There are those fantastic sections with the two-part harmony leads.

GILMOUR: Three-part, in some cases. It's two-part in the melody sections. But the last line of the first solo, I believe, is a three-part descending augmented chord. Which is quite nice, and I was very proud of. I thought it was very clever. Then Roger went and wiped it and I had to recreate it.

GW: On purpose?

GILMOUR: By mistake, by mistake.

GW: What were you playing on that?

GILMOUR: A custom Telecaster. I was coming through some Hiwatt amps and a couple of Yamaha rotating speaker cabinets—Leslie-style cabinets that they used to make. I used to use two of those on stage along with the regular amps. That slight Leslie effect made a big difference in the sound.

GW: Throughout the Seventies and Eighties, each successive Pink Floyd album grew slightly more elaborate. Was it difficult bringing that to the stage?

GILMOUR: Actually, very difficult. We spent years gathering experts around us—just gaining the necessary expertise in all the areas we wanted to be good in. It was always a lot of work, but we looked forward to playing.

GW: Would you say you felt more at ease in the very early days of the band's free-form psychedelic experimentation on stage, or in the later days of carefully orchestrated stage extravaganzas?

GILMOUR: Somewhere in the middle, really. For me, *The Wall* show was terrific fun, and a great achievement. But I had to take on the role of music director, if you like, and deal with a lot of purely mechanical things on stage so that Roger didn't have to think about them. I had a huge cue sheet up on my amps, because we had all these cues coming up on monitors or on screen, and different delay settings which I had to transmit with very primitive equipment to all the delay lines on stage. Very tricky. Once you got over being satisfied with how clever it was and how wonderfully it all worked, there were virtually no moments except for the solo in "Comfortably Numb" when you could say, "Forget it, just blow. Just play." Having said all that, though, I should add that I like structure. I'm very keen on melody, I'm a big Beatles fan, and just about everything else I love—like the blues—is highly structured. Totally free-forming is not my thing. But totally rigid structure isn't either.

"Comfortably Numb" *The Wall* (Columbia, 1979)

GW: "Comfortably Numb" is one of your few co-writing credits on *The Wall*. By all reports, it wasn't born easily.

GILMOUR: Well, there were two recordings of that which me and Roger argued about. I'd written it when I was doing my first solo album [David Gilmour, *1978*]. We changed the key of the song's opening from E to B, I think. The verse stayed exactly the same. Then we had to add a little bit because Roger wanted to do the line, "I have become comfortably numb." Other than that, it was very, very simple to write. But the arguments were over how it should be mixed and which track we should use. We'd done one track with Nick Mason on drums that I thought was too rough and sloppy. We had another go at it, and I thought that the second take was better. Roger disagreed. It was more an ego thing than anything else. We really went head to head with each other over such a minor thing.

GW: Have disagreements between you and Roger ever reached the point of physical violence?

GILMOUR: They've threatened to. But it's never actually come to that. Once Roger and I had a real shouting match at this Italian restaurant in North Hollywood. We'd gone there with [*producer*] Bob Ezrin to have it out over something on *The Wall*—probably "Comfortably Numb," because the only thing I'd really argue with Roger over was my own music. With his music, I wouldn't bother to argue.

GW: While the earlier Pink Floyd records were concept albums, *The Wall* is the first one with an outright plot. What were your feelings about that?

GILMOUR: I *liked* Roger's story line. Although I didn't totally agree with it, you've got to let a chap have his vision. I just had a different view of our relationship with our audience than Roger did. Roger didn't like touring. And he felt there was no connection between him and the audience in front of him. I had a different view of it; I still do. And my view of what *The Wall* itself is about is more jaundiced today than it was then. It appears now to be a catalogue of people Roger blames for his own failings in life, a list of "you fucked me up this way; you fucked me up that way."

GW: What about your solo on "Comfortably Numb"? Did that take a long time to develop?

GILMOUR: No. I just went out into the studio and banged out five or six solos. From there I just followed my usual procedure, which is to listen back to each solo and mark out bar lines, noting which bits are good. In other words, I make a chart, putting ticks and crosses on different bars as I count through—two ticks if it's really good, one if it's good, and a cross if it's no go. Then I just follow the chart, whipping one fader up, then another fader, jumping from phrase to phrase and trying to make a really nice solo all the way through. That's the way we did it on "Comfortably Numb." It wasn't that difficult. But sometimes you find yourself jumping from one note to another in an impossible way. Then you have to go to another place and find a transition that sounds more natural.

GW: When you do a comp like that, are you concerned that you'll wind up with a result that's physically impossible to play?

GILMOUR: Not if it sounds all right. I'm perfectly happy to puzzle the hell out of people who try to work out how it was done.

GW: You've got an extensive guitar collection—a world-famous collection. When you go to record, how much of it goes into the studio with you?

GILMOUR: Well…not much, really. Generally, I just use a Stratocaster and that's the end of it. The ones I tend to use these days are modern '57 reissue Strats with EMG pick-ups. Apart from that, I've got a few different acoustics and slide guitars. For some of the rhythm things, I have a black Gretsch Duo-Sonic that sounds really nice.

GW: Who are your favorite guitar players?

GILMOUR: I'm not a fan of many rock guitar players. Jeff Beck's my favorite; a damned fine player.

GW: You're not keen on the modern school of technique?

GILMOUR: No. It's probably just sour grapes, because I'll never be able to do it. Eddie Van Halen has done a few things that I like a lot. But for the most part, no, that kind of thing doesn't interest me. Guitar just happens to be the instrument I can best express my feelings on. I'm not very fast on it, but you don't have to be. You hear something like John Lee Hooker doing "Dimples." Between the vocal lines he just hits the bottom string on the guitar—*boom!*—that one note says it all. My guitar influences are people like Pete Seeger, Leadbelly, Hank Marvin and Jeff Beck. But there hasn't been anyone recently that I've been turned on by.

GW: It's great to hear you acknowledge a guy like Pete Seeger.

GILMOUR: Oh, Pete Seeger's a wonderful, fantastic human being. "America's Tuning Fork," they called him at one time. I learned guitar off his *Pete Seeger Teaches Guitar* record. That was the first instruction I had. The first track taught you how to tune the guitar. That was pretty important.

"One Slip" *A Momentary Lapse of Reason* (Columbia, 1987)

GW: Let's move on to Pink Floyd's most recent studio album, *A Momentary Lapse of Reason*. How did you hook up with Phil Manzanera [*Roxy Music*] to write "One Slip"?

GILMOUR: Phil is an old friend of mine. We've known each other for years and years, and we always talked about doing something together. So I went and visited him over at his studio, and we started playing around. During that whole period of time, I was trying things out with a number of people, to see if there was anyone I felt comfortable working with who could help to make the load a little lighter in doing the new Pink Floyd record without Roger. Phil basically wrote the music to "One Slip."

GW: On *A Momentary Lapse*, how did you deal with the whole issue of maintaining continuity with the old Pink Floyd?

GILMOUR: By totally ignoring it. I didn't bother with any of that stuff. I know it's something that came up in Bob Ezrin's mind; he felt a certain responsibility to make it sound like Pink Floyd. But that's something I had no interest in whatsoever. If it's done by me, it's going to sound like Pink Floyd to a certain extent. Because it's my voice, my guitar playing and my musical taste that are plastered all over everything Pink Floyd ever did, going back to *A Saucerful of Secrets*.

GW: *A Momentary Lapse* is certainly a return to the lushness of pre-*Animals* Pink Floyd.

GILMOUR: Yes. That's what I like. "Signs of Life," for example, is actually an old demo. I had to re-record a lot of things, but the rhythm guitar chords in the background are from a demo from way back in '78.

GW: So on *A Momentary Lapse* you got to follow through on ideas that, perhaps because of Roger's dominance, you didn't get to pursue earlier?

GILMOUR: Yeah. I went back to this balance of more music and not quite the same preponderance of words. You do what you're good at, you see. Roger's very good at lyrics. I'm certainly not as practiced as him, so I wouldn't put myself up there.

GW: Was *A Momentary Lapse* a good experience for you, Nick and Rick [*Wright, Pink Floyd keyboardist*] in the sense that you assured yourselves that you could do it without Roger?

GILMOUR: Yes. The album and the tour were a rehabilitative process for all of us.

GW: It was good to hear you and Rick playing together again. [*Wright, ejected from the band in 1979, rejoined for* A Momentary Lapse.] The guitar and keyboards worked together so sympathetically on a lot of these old tracks we've been talking about.

GILMOUR: Well, it's like Bob Dylan says [*in "My Back Pages"*]: "I was so much older then, I'm younger than that now." You learn things about yourself and other people as time goes by. When the three of us sit down and play, it sounds like Pink Floyd. There's a very distinct value in that which was important for me to discover. There's something there that's bigger than any one person's ego.

actually Krieger who penned many of the Doors' greatest songs and biggest hits, including "Light My Fire," "Love Me Two Times" and "Touch Me."

Remarkably, when Krieger joined the Doors in 1965, he was only 18 years old and had been playing guitar for just two years—electric guitar a mere six months.

"I really learned to play as a member of the Doors," he asserts. "I just tried to sound like myself—I consciously avoided copying Chuck Berry or B.B. King because that's what everyone was doing. I tried to come up with the right part for the song and play something that would complement Jim's singing.

"It must have worked," he adds coyly. "I think we came up with a pretty good body of work."

Pretty good, yes. Good enough to have gotten the Doors inducted into the Rock and Roll Hall of Fame last January and to have inspired Oliver Stone's reverential 1991 biopic. And, most of all, good enough to enthrall three decades of rock fans with music that remains as powerful and profound in the Nineties as it was in the Sixties.

Robby Krieger cannot escape his past with the Doors, even though the band essentially died with Morrison in 1971. Although he has remained active, touring regularly and recording seven solo albums dominated by instrumental music, Krieger says, "I realized pretty quickly that I would never again have another band like the Doors. Music has become more of a fun thing for me, much like painting is—something that's personally rewarding. It's what I do and how I identify myself: I'm Robby Krieger, guitarist."

Most people would say: Robby Krieger, *Doors* guitarist. What follows are Krieger's recollections of the Doors' career, from their 1967 self-titled debut to 1971's brilliant swan song, *L.A. Woman*.

THE DOORS (Elektra, 1967)

GUITAR WORLD: What was your first impression of Jim Morrison?

ROBBY KRIEGER: I first met him when he came to my house with John Densmore and he seemed pretty normal. I didn't really get a sense that there was anything unusual about him until the end of our first rehearsal. Initially, everything was cool. Then this guy came looking for Jim. Something had gone wrong with a dope deal, and Jim just went nuts. Absolutely bananas. I thought, "Jesus Christ, this guy's *not* normal."

GW: What were your impressions of Ray Manzarek?

KRIEGER: When I first met him, he was the "big man on campus" at the UCLA film school. In fact, our first gig as a band was to provide music for one of his student films. Afterwards Ray got up in front of an auditorium full of people and gave a speech. I remember it well, because he had them in the palm of his hand. He was downright mesmerizing. He was a major character, but Jim kind of kept him in his place. Jim was so out there that Ray's personality was overwhelmed, which, oddly enough, created a good balance.

GW: And you were pretty much what you appeared to be: a nice, quiet guy who fit in between these two powerful personalities?

KRIEGER: Well, dealing with Jim kind of changed me, too, because I was pretty crazy myself. I was the first one at my school to try acid and I was always the one pushing things. Then I got into the Doors and I couldn't hold a candle to Jim and Ray. [*laughs*] But I had already gone through acid and I was onto meditation by the time I joined the Doors—I actually met John at meditation class—so I had already mellowed out.

GW: When were the Doors thrown out of the Whisky-A-Go-Go for performing "The End"?

KRIEGER: Well, that's overstating it a little bit. That whole incident has been blown out of proportion. There was a fight with the owner and we were thrown out, but I don't think we were actually fired. We kept playing at the Whisky after that.

GW: Jim's antics are held in such reverence now. Were they funny at the time?

KRIEGER: It was always a bummer. We had this group which we all knew had the potential to be something really big, and Jim was trying to sabotage it by fucking up at every turn. We would call a rehearsal, Jim wouldn't show, and we'd get a call from Blythe, Arizona, telling us that he was in jail.

GW: Yet you guys were amazingly productive. You produced six studio albums in three or four years. Were his work habits really that bad?

KRIEGER: No. The music was all he lived for. A lot of times he was at the office when we weren't. He'd even live there sometimes, because that was his whole life. We all had lives other than the Doors, but he didn't, and he kind of resented that. He felt like he was living it 24 hours a day, and we weren't. And he was right.

But the recording sessions really bored him. We had to hang around interminably until they got the drum sound down and all that shit, so I can't blame him for going crazy. Paul Rothchild, our producer, was a real perfectionist.

GW: How important was Paul to your music?

KRIEGER: It really differed from album to album. On the first one, he just turned on the mic and stepped out of the way. The second album, when we actually had a budget, Paul really got involved in the sound.

We were all kind of freaked out recording the first album because we didn't know what it would be like. For example, it really bothered us that we couldn't turn up as loud as we wanted.

GW: Yet it really sounds like you were all playing with total abandon.

KRIEGER: That's because we had been playing those songs for so long that we really had the material down cold. Everything was cut in one or two takes.

GW: Your version of "Back Door Man" is really effective. Were there ever any debates about how faithful you should be to the original version?

KRIEGER: No. For one thing, we probably weren't good enough musicians to do exact copies and we knew that Jim would never sing it anywhere near the original anyhow. So we just went on our own.

GW: For years it was a little-known fact that you wrote "Light My Fire." That changed when Oliver Stone made it a point to show how the song evolved in his movie, *The Doors*. Was it as simple as pulling a crumpled piece of paper out of your pocket and offering it to the band like the movie suggests?

KRIEGER: [*laughs*] It's pretty close. Jim had been writing all the songs and then one day we realized we didn't have enough tunes, so he said, "Hey, why don't you try and write songs?" I wrote "Light My Fire" that night and brought it to the next rehearsal. It was my idea to have that scene in the movie, by the way. I wanted it there because it's always kind of bugged me that so many people don't know that I was the composer.

GW: Your solo on "Light My Fire" is truly one of your shining moments as a guitarist. Did it bother you when the solo was edited out of the single version?

KRIEGER: A little. We never wanted to cut it. But our first single, "Break on Through," flopped, and radio stations around the country told us that "Light My Fire" would be a hit if we edited it. We didn't have much choice. FM wasn't very big and to get on AM you had to have a short song.

GW: Was the "Light My Fire" solo improvised in the studio?

KRIEGER: It was the kind of solo that I usually did, but it was different every night. To be honest, the one on the record is not one of my better versions. I only had two tries at it. But it's not bad; I'm glad it was good as it was.

GW: Do you have any particularly vivid memories from those recording sessions?

KRIEGER: Well, there's the famous story about recording "The End." Our engineer, Bruce Botnick, had brought in a TV to watch the World Series, and Jim, who was on a lot of acid, got kind of pissed at that; baseball wasn't exactly conducive to setting the right mood for "The End." So he threw the damn television through the control room window. That got everyone's attention. [*laughs*]

I also remember Jim sitting at the table out in the snack-bar area, ranting on and on, "Fuck the mother, kill the father. That's where it's at, man. Fuck the mother, kill the father." So we're going, "Yeah, right Jim, but we've got to record. How about singing?" We finally got him into the studio for two takes, and we nailed it. We thanked God because we knew we weren't going to have many shots because of Jim's state of mind.

Guitar World, March 1994

Strange Days

The Doors' Jim Morrison lit the world on fire, but it was guitarist Robby Krieger who supplied the matches. In an exclusive interview, the legendary axeman sheds light on one of rock's greatest and most mysterious bands.

By Alan Paul

"IT WAS HARD living with Jim."

Robby Krieger is talking about his days as guitarist with the Doors, reflecting on his role as creative sidekick to one of rock's all-time great lyricists, singers, sex symbols and extreme personalities, Jim Morrison. "It would have been so great if we'd just had a guy like Sting," says Krieger wistfully. "You know, a normal guy who's extremely talented, too. Someone who didn't have to be on the verge of life and death every second of his life."

The guitarist laughs at his own fantasy. He knows better than anyone that it was Morrison's inner demons, which surfaced all too frequently, that gave the Doors' music its resonance and power. But while Morrison was undoubtedly one of rock's great visionaries, the contributions of the other Doors to the band's unique sound and success cannot be overlooked. The blues-based, often hypnotic music created by Krieger, organist Ray Manzarek and drummer John Densmore perfectly complemented Morrison's commanding, sensual vocals and mesmerizing lyrics. And it was

Guitar World Presents CLASSIC ROCK

The Doors: Standing, Jim Morrison and Ray Manzarek. Seated, Robby Krieger and John Densmore.

GW: Was the whole album recorded live?

KRIEGER: No. Jim always sang with us, but they rarely used the scratch vocal. "The End" was an exception.

GW: What do you think of the song now?

KRIEGER: I think that particular version of "The End" was nowhere near as good as the way we played it many other times. All the songs on the first album were like skeletons of how we really played them. It was just a combination of not having any studio experience and having to do everything so fast. I also think that studios are, by nature, limiting. You cannot get the sound of five big amplifiers on a little piece of tape.

GW: Did you ever think about how strange it was not to have a bass player?

KRIEGER: Definitely. We *always* thought about that. We wanted a bass player, and we auditioned a few—but we never could find one who was right. Looking back, I'm glad we didn't, because the Doors' sound was largely a result of the fact that Ray had to play really simple bass lines, which gave the music a hypnotic feel.

And not having a bass player affected my guitar playing a lot. It made me play more bass notes to fill out the bottom. Not having a rhythm player also made me play differently to fill out the sound. And then, of course, I played lead, so I always felt like three players simultaneously.

GW: "Light My Fire," the first song you ever wrote, was a Number One hit. That sudden success must have been mind-boggling.

KRIEGER: It wasn't that sudden. It actually felt like forever to us. We started the band in 1965, and nothing happened for two years. We were going crazy. Finally, after being turned down by everyone in town, Elektra signed us. Our first single bombed, and it was another six months before "Light My Fire" hit. So it seemed like a long time. We felt like veterans.

GW: Did you use your standard gear in the studio? Were you playing an SG?

KRIEGER: Yeah, though the first red one I had was actually a Melody Maker. I had a few red SGs in the Doors, but they're all gone now, most-

ly stolen or lost. Amp-wise, I usually used a Twin Reverb in the studio.
GW: You almost allowed "Light My Fire" to be used in a car commercial before Jim put an end to it. Did Jim do the right thing?
KRIEGER: Oh yeah, absolutely. In fact, it's been our policy to reject any subsequent offers—and we've had quite a few. I really hate it when I see other bands selling their music to commercials. And by the time a big corporation is interested in using your music, you don't need the money. So there's really no excuse.

STRANGE DAYS (Elektra, 1967)

GW: When the second album came out it was attacked by many critics as being a retread of the first. Do you think that was valid criticism?
KRIEGER: Only on one count. I'll admit that "When the Music's Over" was similar to "The End" in length and structure, but so what? Something works, so you do it again. It's one of my favorite songs.
GW: I don't think that Morrison's poetry rap is quite as interesting on "When the Music's Over" as "The End."
KRIEGER: No, it's not. How could you possibly top "The End"? What's left once you've fucked your mother and killed your father? [*laughs*] The reason it's my favorite song is my solo—I think it's my best.
GW: That solo is composed of two solos played simultaneously. Did you improvise both of them on the spot?
KRIEGER: Pretty much. In fact, I've never been able to reproduce them. That solo was really a challenge because the harmony is static. I had to play 56 bars over the same riff, which isn't easy. It's a lot easier to play something over an interesting chord progression. But we did that a lot because we were really into [*saxophonist*] John Coltrane, who pioneered "modal" jazz and soloed brilliantly over static harmonies and minimal chord progressions. I was always trying to play something that sounded like him—just totally out there in terms of tonality. I think "When the Music's Over" is the closest I ever came.
GW: You recorded *Strange Days* less than a year after your debut. Did Elektra put a lot of pressure on you?
KRIEGER: No, we were ready. We had tons of material for the first two albums; the pressure came on the third album. We ran out of

stuff and Jim was pretty fucked up on liquor by then, so it was hard to write with him, and that's when I started writing more of my own songs. It was also difficult to write while we were touring, so we started writing a lot more in the studio.

GW: What was life on the road with the Doors like?

KRIEGER: Not as crazy as you would think. At first, it was mostly teenyboppers and groupies and a few local nuts hanging around. But a couple of years down the road, when people realized how weird we were, we really started drawing some creeps. We still do, I might add—Morrison wannabes show up on my doorstep all the time. And they always want to sing. [*laughs*]

GW: Speaking of weirdos, "People Are Strange" has a great chord progression. Did you write that?

KRIEGER: Yeah. Jim came up to my house in Laurel Canyon one night, and he was in one of his suicidal, downer moods. So John said, "Come on Jim, we'll go see the sunset. That'll get you out of this." We went up to the top of Laurel Canyon and it was incredibly beautiful—we were looking down on the sun reflecting off the top of the clouds. Jim had a total mood flip-flop, and said, "Wow! Now I know why I felt like that. It's because if you're strange, people are strange." And he wrote the lyrics right there. Then I came up with the music and we went back down the hill.

GW: Why wasn't "Moonlight Drive," the first song you wrote and rehearsed together, on the first album?

KRIEGER: It wasn't really the first song; "Indian Summer" was, and "Moonlight Drive" was the second. But we didn't think the version that we cut was good enough, so we decided to drop it off the first album and try again next time. Unfortunately, we've never been able to find the damn master for the first version. I think we may have found it now, and I hope I'm right because I, personally, always thought it was good. It was totally different than the one on *Strange Days*. It was real dark and laid back, very spooky.

GW: Any strange memories from the *Strange Days* sessions?

KRIEGER: One time, we were getting ready to leave for the night and Jim didn't want to stop because he was feeling good. He kept saying, "Man, I want to play all night." But we were all tired and wanted to go home. Jim finally left, but he came back half an hour later, climbed over the fence, broke into the studio, took out the fire extinguisher and sprayed it into the piano and all over everything. It was quite a surprise in the morning. [*laughs*]

GW: Were you guys around when Jim recorded "Horse Latitudes"?

KRIEGER: Yeah. He said he had a poem he wanted to read and he wanted something real weird to back it. There were all these instruments in the studio from an orchestra session—harpsichords and pianos and timpani. We all started banging on them and fumbling around inside the pianos, and there were 10 or 12 people just screaming at the top of their lungs. After we laid that down, Jim overdubbed the poem.

The funny thing was, as we were listening back at full volume and Jim was reading, the guys from the Jefferson Airplane came straggling in—high as kites, of course. They stared at us like we were out of our minds, but we just acted casual and said, "Oh yeah, this is one of our songs." [*laughs*]

GW: Were you friends with them?

KRIEGER: Sort of. We always played on the same bill, but we didn't really hang out much. There was always a bit of a competitive vibe—to see who could blow who off the stage. We didn't hang out with other musicians that much—just Van Morrison when he came to town, and occasionally the guys in Buffalo Springfield. We didn't get too close with the San Francisco groups—especially the Grateful Dead, who wouldn't let us use their amps one night.

We had a gig at Beverly Hills High School in the afternoon and then one about an hour up the coast in Santa Barbara, so we left our gear, figuring the Dead would let us use their stuff. You'd always let people use your amps in those days, but they just refused. I ended up playing through a Pignose or something equally ridiculous.

Ray was aghast at the fact that Pigpen wouldn't let him use his organ. He kept saying, "Pigpen? Someone named Pigpen won't let me use his instrument? I could catch cooties from his organ." He couldn't believe it.

WAITING FOR THE SUN (Elektra, 1968)

GW: It seems like the band was in a creative lull and feeling a lot of pressure by the third album. Do you see a band like Pearl Jam going through a similar thing?

KRIEGER: Their situation is a lot different, but, yes, I see the similarities. I know Eddie [Vedder]—he sang with us at our induction to the Rock and Roll Hall of Fame last year—and he wants to be like Jim. He was drilling me about Jim—asking me a million questions about how Jim would have reacted to various situations. And he is kind of a troubled person and a very serious guy, like Jim was. But I don't think he, or anyone else in that band, is too fucked up to write good material. They may not be the straightest people in the world, but it's not like our situation, where you have a guy who's really out of control. Eddie's not like that; he knows what he's doing.

GW: Does it trouble you to see someone emulate a person whose self-destruction you witnessed?

KRIEGER: Yeah, it really does. I always tell people, "Don't drink because Jim drank. That was a mistake. That's what fucked him up." If it weren't for the booze he might still be writing songs today.

GW: Had his drinking gotten considerably worse when you were recording *Waiting for the Sun*?

KRIEGER: Definitely. That's when the liquor really started being a problem. Before that, everything was more or less fine. LSD was no problem because it was a creative thing. There's nothing good about liquor—it just fucks you up—though at first it relaxes you, which is what you probably need after taking eight-zillion acid trips. [*laughs*]

GW: "Hello, I Love You" was a Number One hit and *Waiting for the Sun* topped the album charts. Can that kind of success get you through a creative lull?

KRIEGER: It helped a lot. In fact, we were just going out on tour when "Hello, I Love You" hit Number One, and it really buoyed our spirits. People always think that we stole that track from the Kinks' "All Day and All of the Night," but we weren't thinking of them at all. What I did steal was the drumbeat; I told John to play something like "Sunshine of Your Love." So we ripped off the Cream, not the Kinks.

GW: What specific recollections do you have of these sessions?
KRIEGER: A lot of very horrible ones. By that time, Jim was being taken advantage of by various hangers-on. He would bring them to the studio and Rothchild would go crazy—all these drunken assholes would be hanging around, fucking in the echo chamber and pissing in the closets. It was a mess.

Jim would drink with anybody because we wouldn't drink with him. He would take on all these assholes who used him: "Hey, we're hanging with Jimbo." And they wouldn't care how fucked up he got—they'd leave him on somebody's doorstep in his own puke.
GW: At what point did you guys refuse to drink with him?
KRIEGER: I never drank with him because I didn't like to drink to excess and he loved to go until he couldn't see. I knew what was coming and hated to see it, so I would usually be gone by that point. John and Ray felt the same way.
GW: Were you three using a lot of drugs at that point?
KRIEGER: No. Not at all. And the fact that Jim was using so much made us use even less. The romance was definitely gone. Once in a while he would talk me into taking acid—like you saw in the movie—but not often.

THE SOFT PARADE (Elektra, 1969)
GW: *The Soft Parade* features several heavily orchestrated, intricately arranged songs. Were you compelled to go in this direction because of the Beatles?
KRIEGER: Yeah, totally. In those days you had to try to keep up with the Beatles! But, to be honest, I didn't really like orchestrating the songs. It definitely wasn't my idea—it was Paul Rothchild's. I never would have done it.
GW: Does it sound better to you now?
KRIEGER: Actually, it does sound better with time. But I never thought it sounded bad—I just thought it didn't sound like us. The Doors were lost. It was Jim and the orchestra.
GW: This was the first album where you had individual songwriting credits.

KRIEGER: Right. Jim originally wanted everything to say "written by the Doors" to keep things mysterious. But everybody just took it for granted that he wrote everything. I think he realized that wasn't fair and wanted to give others credit.

GW: Did he actually write the music on those songs where he alone is credited?

KRIEGER: No. He would hear the song in his head. But he didn't play anything, so he would sing a vocal melody, and we would have to figure out what to do. But a lot of times he just had a poem on paper and I would come up with something. Other times I would come up with a melody, and he'd put words to it.

GW: What about the *Soft Parade* sessions sticks out in your mind?

KRIEGER: The endless mixing sessions. That was a very long, drawn-out album. We spent more money on it than we did on any other album. And Jim was hard to find. All the mixing bored the hell out of him. But I think his drinking problem wasn't as bad as it was on *Waiting for the Sun*, because he had started making a film, which kept him busy.

There was one funny thing that happened. This crazy guy appeared and apparently he thought that "The Celebration of the Lizard" [*a Morrison poem which appeared on* Waiting For the Sun] was written about him. He was yelling, "How did you know that *I'm* the Lizard King, goddamn it! That's me. You wrote a song about me!" And he smacked Ray right in the eye because he thought Ray was Jim. Ray had his glasses on and they just crumpled. It was a mess.

GW: Before the poem appeared had you ever heard Jim refer to himself as the Lizard King?

KRIEGER: He was always obsessed with lizards—he loved that kind of stuff because he'd seen it on acid a lot. But I don't know when he came up with, "I am the Lizard King." I think he wished he had never said that. It was just another thing he had to live up to.

GW: During the *Soft Parade* tour, your Miami concert erupted in pandemonium and was canceled. Later Jim was charged with indecent exposure. What do you remember of the concert?

KRIEGER: Well, first of all, Jim did *not* pull it out. But it was bedlam, just total craziness. The place was oversold, thousands of people swarmed the stage, and it collapsed. I remember Jim just rolling around in the midst of all those people and I was wondering if we would ever get out of there. It was very much like in the movie—they did a real good job on that one.

GW: But you had no sense that the incident was going to turn into such a big thing?

KRIEGER: No, hell no! Okay, the concert was fucked up, and we didn't finish, but nobody was angry, nobody asked for their money back. And the cops were friendly—they sat around drinking beers with us after the show. Nothing happened until a week later, when somebody decided to make a stink about it. Some politician decided to make their career at our expense. Then it fucked everything up. We couldn't play anywhere for a year. The Hall Managers' Association basically banned us.

GW: Did Jim feel very persecuted?

KRIEGER: I'm sure he did. But he wasn't surprised. He knew he was pushing authority as far as it could go. We really did have the sense that we had pushed the system to the edge and finally it was pushing back.

MORRISON HOTEL (Elektra, 1970)

GW: "Roadhouse Blues" and a couple of other songs on *Morrison Hotel* hinted at the changes to come on *L.A. Woman*—heading in a bluesier, more bare-bones direction.

KRIEGER: I think it was a reaction to the overproduction of *The Soft Parade*. We wanted to get back to basics. "Roadhouse Blues" is one of my personal favorites. I was always proud of that song because as simple as it is, it's not just another blues. That one little lick makes it a song, and I think that sums up the genius of the Doors. I think that song stands up really well as an example of what made us a great band. And the session was really cool—one of my fondest memories of the band. We cut the tune live, with John Sebastian playing harp and Lonnie Mack playing bass—he came up with that fantastic bass line.

GW: How did Mack end up on there?

KRIEGER: He just happened to be hanging around. I think he had a contract with Elektra and wasn't recording so they gave him a job at the studio. We just said, "Hey, why don't you play bass?"

GW: You cowrote "Peace Frog" with Jim...

KRIEGER: Yes. I had written the music, we rehearsed it up, and it was really happening, but we didn't have any lyrics and Jim wasn't around. We just said, "Fuck it, let's record it. He'll come up with something." And he did. He took out his poetry book and found a poem that fit. But it always seemed kind of forced to me, to tell you the truth.

GW: The legend has Ray and Jim being very tight, but you're the one who wrote with him a lot.

KRIEGER: In the very early days Ray was very close with Jim; Jim actually lived with Ray and his wife. He was almost like their son, and he was great for a while—he wasn't drinking or anything. The problem was that Ray became a father figure, so Jim rebelled. He fucked their house up—trashed it on more than one occasion—and took advantage of them in many ways. Then I joined the band and sort of latched on to Jim, and we hung out a lot.

Ray worked up all the early songs with Jim—everything on the first album. Then I wrote a lot with Jim—before I started really writing on my own—and those songs went mostly on the second and third albums.

GW: Did you ever talk about lyrics with Jim?

KRIEGER: Not much. He didn't like to explain lyrics because he wanted people to interpret them themselves. But he thought about that stuff a lot. He was also somewhat into pure impressionism—which I think is what he liked about my songs. I always tried to write something that just fit the music, even if it didn't especially mean anything.

L.A. WOMAN (Elektra, 1971)

GW: Legend has it that *L.A. Woman* was cut entirely live.

KRIEGER: Not entirely, but a lot of it was live, and the song "L.A. Woman" was completely live. I think that could be the quintessential Doors song, and the way we came up with it was amazing. We just started playing and it came together as if by magic. Jim made a lot of it up as he went along, which is amazing because I think it's one of his most poetic songs. I can remember Jim sitting in the bathroom with the mic, singing, and all of us just having a great time.

GW: That album was the first time you had a rhythm guitarist—Marc Benno.

KRIEGER: That was basically just so we could do it live. It freed me up. And we thought it might add a different flavor. I actually enjoyed it, and I didn't have to do as much overdubbing.

GW: You still did some overdubbing; it sounds like there are at least four guitar tracks on "I've Been Down So Long."

KRIEGER: Yeah, there probably are. Ray played a guitar and Benno played, and I probably overdubbed one too. I think I also overdubbed two or three slide parts.

GW: That slide solo is one of your craziest.

KRIEGER: Definitely. I was just trying to capture a mood without worrying about technique.

GW: The beauty of your slide playing—and your blues playing in general—is you don't mimic the originators. And you never really cleaned your blues up—you left it a little messy. Some white guys tend to be very anal.

KRIEGER: [*laughs*] That's right. That's what I didn't like about Mike Bloomfield—too perfect. I always just tried to do my thing. I could play traditional blues slide, but all the other guys reacted more enthusiastically to my untraditional slide playing. In fact, that's what got me into the band. Jim always loved my slide playing—he wanted me to play it almost exclusively.

GW: Did Jim ever critique your playing?

KRIEGER: He would always tell me that I was the most underrated guitar player around. What's funny is that the four of us hardly ever criticized the others' playing—or even suggested anything. We worked so well together that we hardly ever had to talk about it. Everybody just played the right part in the right place at the right time.

GW: "Cars Hiss by My Window" is a rather unusual blues.

KRIEGER: Yeah. That was our Jimmy Reed piece. Jim was really getting into the blues at that time and he loved it when I would just play straight blues. He'd sit there and make up songs on the spot. He just wanted to play all night. It's too bad because I really think that had we done another album it would have been a lot more straight blues stuff, which I always loved.

GW: How did "Riders on the Storm" develop?

KRIEGER: We were fooling around with "Ghost Riders in the Sky" one day and somehow it turned into "Riders on the Storm." It just happened. Ray was playing a Fender Rhodes instead of his organ.

GW: Another change on *L.A. Woman* is the absence of reverb, particularly on Jim's voice, which was so heavily reverbed on your first few albums.

KRIEGER: Well, Sunset Sound, where we recorded the first two albums, had one of the best echo chambers in the world. It was a live chamber, which they don't make anymore. And it sounded so great that we used it a lot more than we might otherwise have. We piped everything through there.

But *L.A. Woman* was recorded on an eight-track in our rehearsal space and Paul Rothchild was gone, which is one reason we had so much fun. The warden was gone.

GW: So, even after all your success, you still had that sort of relationship with the producer, where he was cracking the whip?

KRIEGER: Yeah, we just kind of took it for granted that he would produce and we would do things his way—you stick with success. And, finally, he was like a rat deserting a sinking ship. I think he figured it was time to bail.

GW: So there really was a sense that the Doors were a sinking ship?

KRIEGER: Yeah, definitely. We couldn't play anywhere; we were fucked because of the Miami incident. *Morrison Hotel* didn't do that well, Jim looked bad and was getting fat… All things considered, I thought it was pretty cool that *L.A. Woman* did well.

I think we came up with something so loose because there was no pressure. We figured we were already screwed, so we were having fun again. We were so far gone that it was like our first album.

GW: Just weeks after the album entered the Top Ten, Jim was dead. Do you remember finding out?

KRIEGER: Yeah, I got a phone call and I didn't believe it because we used to hear shit like that all the time—that Jim jumped off a cliff or something. So we sent our manager over to Paris, and he called and said it was true.

GW: People often talk about the inevitability of him dying young. Do you buy that?

KRIEGER: No! I thought he would never die. I thought he'd outlive everybody, like one of those Irish drunks who drink a fifth of whisky a day and live until they're 80. He seemed invulnerable, the way he would do things like jump out of windows without getting hurt. I never saw those things, but I would hear about them the next day. For some reason, he was fairly well behaved around me. Somehow our relationship developed where he stayed fairly calm around me, thank God. [*laughs*]

GW: After Jimi and Janis died, Jim supposedly told people that he would be the third to die at age 27. Did you remember him saying such things?

KRIEGER: Yeah. He was definitely obsessed with death. He talked about it all the time.

GW: There's always been talk that he's not dead, and Ray has occasionally fueled that idea. Have you ever thought that?

KRIEGER: Yes and no. I've allowed myself to fantasize at times, but I'm sure that if he wasn't dead he would have gotten hold of us by now. But then again, if there's anybody who could pull something like that off, it was him. I still think about him quite a bit. I always have dreams that he's alive, and we're playing together again. Wishful thinking.

Guitar World, April 1994

Perfectly Frank

The life and times of Frank Zappa—composer, satirist and towering giant of the electric guitar.

By Alan di Perna

"THERE'S NO SINGLE ideal listener out there who likes my orchestral music, my guitar albums and songs like 'Dyna-Moe-Hum,' " Frank Zappa told me in 1988. "That's why sometimes I'll do an orchestral album, and the people who like guitar stuff can't stand it. And then a guitar album comes out, and the people who liked the orchestral album can't stand *that*. But you know, they're all my friends in their own way. So why not accommodate them all?"

Now that Frank is gone, it's somehow comforting to reread those words. Frank Vincent Zappa was notoriously intolerant of the imperfections in human nature. With a few curt remarks, he could decimate an audience member foolish enough to shout out a song request, or a journalist presumptuous enough to concoct a half-assed theory about him. Yet he was willing to consider all of us who love his music as "friends."

There are rabid Zappa fanatics out there who would insist that it *is* possible for one person to admire Zappa's knotty, inventive orchestral compositions, his honking, brilliant guitar work *and* the prickly combination of sociology, satire and schoolboy scatological that went into his song lyrics. But it's no small undertaking. Frank

Guitar World Presents CLASSIC ROCK

Frank Zappa

Zappa's 60-album oeuvre is an imposing body of work. Some of the records are better than others, but the overall quality level is astonishingly high. Unlike many of his contemporaries, Zappa was still in top creative form at age 52, when he succumbed to prostate cancer—on December 4, 1993—after battling the disease for several years.

We'll never know what he would have achieved had he lived another 20 or 30 years. But we can console ourselves with the fact that, in the brief time allotted to him, he accomplished far more than most humans. Beyond his having been a superb composer and musician, Frank Zappa was also a committed and capable political activist, an innovative filmmaker, able businessman and one of our century's all-around *bona fide* smart guys. He raised rock's IQ more than a few notches.

FRANK'S FIRST STEPS

"Scientists believe that the universe is made of hydrogen, because they claim it's the most plentiful ingredient. I claim that the most plentiful ingredient is stupidity." That's what Zappa said in an interview, just a few months before his death, with *Pulse!* magazine's Dan Ouellette. The "hydrogen" quote was one of Frank's favorites; it cropped up a lot in interviews down through the years. And in many ways, Zappa's whole life was a battle against stupidity—the stupidity of mass media conformity, the stupidity of greedy, inept, ignoble government, the stupidity of thinking it's *cool* to be stupid.

Frank liked facts, so here are a few now. He was born on December 21, 1940, in Baltimore, Maryland. (His childhood is hilariously chronicled in his 1989 autobiography, *The Real Frank Zappa Book* [Poseidon Press].) When he was around 10 his family moved to the dismal suburban environs of Lancaster, California. There, he became interested in two strangely dissimilar forms of music: the black r&b and blues sounds of the day, and the early 20th century avant garde compositions of Edgard Varese, Anton Webern and Igor Stravinsky. Both influences can be heard throughout his music. But his blues inspiration is most strongly felt in his guitar work. In 1988, he told me about one of the key experiences of his youth:

"It was when I first heard the guitar solo in 'Three Hours Past Midnight,' by Johnny 'Guitar' Watson. That's probably one of the most important musical statements I ever heard in my life. And also the guitar solos on 'I Got Something For You' and 'The Story of My Blues,' by Guitar Slim. And 'Lover Man' by Wes Montgomery."

Another blues artist influenced Zappa in a way that is often overlooked. In a 1980 interview for *Trouser Press*, Frank told Michael Bloom that he first grew his trademark goatee and mustache because he "thought it looked good on bluesman Johnny Otis."

As a teenager, Zappa played drums and guitar in a variety of local r&b hands. By the time he reached his early twenties, he'd owned and operated his own recording studio (Studio Z), composed B-movie scores, tried his own hand at filmmaking and co-authored a doo wop tune called "Memories of El Monte," which was recorded by the Penguins. Around 1964, Zappa took control of the r&b bar band he was then playing with—the Soul Giants—persuading them to try some songs he'd written. He also changed the name of the band to the Mothers, an event of incalculable sociological importance.

The Mothers came into their own on the mid Sixties Los Angeles freak scene. It is generally accepted that hippiedom began in San Francisco. "But the scene in Los Angeles was far more bizarre," Frank wrote in his autobiography. It was the L.A. underground that gave birth to the Doors, the Byrds, the Seeds and several other fine bands whose names have not become part of Official Rock History. Needless to say, the Mothers were far weirder than any of these acts.

In an era when even the "dangerous" rock bands were still pretty clean and cute, the Mothers were unkempt and ugly, and some of them would very obviously never see 25 again. The wild melange of sounds they generated included some decidedly unfashionable musical styles like doo wop and lounge jazz. But at this particular juncture in cultural history, the weirder something was, the better it was generally esteemed to be. This was one of those times when record companies couldn't figure out what the hell was going on with "those crazy kids" and their music, so they were signing all kinds of interesting acts with "no commercial potential." This included the Mothers, who were offered a contract with MGM's Verve label.

FREAKING OUT THE WORLD

Nineteen sixty-six saw the release of *Freak Out!*, the debut album by the Mothers of Invention. (The record company suggested adding "of Invention" to the band's name, since the word "Mothers" by itself sounded too close to the popular shortened form of "motherfucker," which—for reasons too complex to detail here—was a very potent word in the hippie counterculture of the mid to late Sixties.) By any reckoning, *Freak Out!* is one of the most influential rock albums of all time. It is generally considered the first "concept album" and also the first double album in rock. It contains the seeds of all Zappa's later work. The first two sides are devoted to songs—satirical, humorous, angry, topical, carefully and resourcefully arranged songs, played with exacting precision. On the second disc, the presentation grows increasingly free-form, culminating in "The Return of the Son of Monster Magnet." This piece takes up all of side four (pretty revolutionary in '66) and offers an aural glimpse of "what freaks sound like when you turn them loose in a recording studio at one o'clock in the morning on $500 worth of rented percussion equipment," to quote Zappa's liner notes.

Freak Out! and the Mothers' subsequent Verve albums did much to establish the Zappa mythology. Frank's log cabin home at 2401 Laurel Canyon Blvd., in an L.A. neighborhood heavily populated by rock stars, assumed Olympian proportions in the minds of his fans. John Mayall even wrote a song about his stay there. Frank's friends and associates—who bore names like Suzy Creamcheese, Dakota and Motorhead—acquired the larger-than-life stature of Zeus, Hera, Pan and Aphrodite to a generation of suburban teenage misfits. These youths felt tremendously empowered by *Freak Out!*, and its implication that not only was it okay to be a bit strange, frizzy-haired, unpopular and a little too intelligent, it was positively *cool*. But not everything about the Zappa myth was pleasing to the man at its center. *Freak Out!* almost instantly acquired a reputation as the

Number One Album to Take Drugs To, much to the chagrin of its composer, who was resolutely straight all his life.

By 1967, Zappa and the Mothers had migrated to New York, where they began their now-legendary six-month residence at the Garrick Theatre in Greenwich Village. The Mothers basically moved into this decaying old 300-seater, doing two shows a night. Nobody could be certain in advance what was going to occur on any given evening. Jimi Hendrix was one of the notable musicians who came down to jam. But in many ways, it was the audience who often provided the real entertainment. Here, during the height of the Vietnam War, Zappa one night convinced three drunken Marines to attack a baby doll with a bayonet on stage.

According to eyewitnesses, the ensuing spectacle made a more powerful anti-war statement than any protest song or political speech ever could.

These "audience participation" segments were to become a popular element of Zappa concerts throughout his career. There's something completely emblematic of his work in the contrast between the perfectionist discipline of his music and his willingness to entrust a portion of his concerts to some inebriated schmoes randomly selected from the crowd. It's as though he wanted, not to *impose* order on chaos, but to *incorporate* chaos into the ordered perfection of his art. If the universe was gonna insist on being inherently stupid, Zappa was determined to find some positive, creative use for all that stupidity.

His entrepreneurial energies were boundless. 1967 also saw the release of his first solo album, *Lumpy Gravy*. The following year, after his relationship with Verve ended, he started two record labels of his own: Bizarre and Straight, both distributed by Warner/Reprise. Straight was Zappa's label for presenting new talents he had discovered. It was Frank Zappa who brought the world the first recordings by Captain Beefheart and Alice Cooper, as well as less-well-remembered artists like folksinger Tim Buckley, the aptly named Wild Man Fischer and the GTOs. The last was a vocal ensemble comprised of Hollywood scenemakers—including kiss-and-tell rock diarist Pamela Des Barres—who apparently had enough "pull" to entice talents like Jeff Beck and Rod Stewart to perform on their disc.

Bizarre was the label for the Mothers' own records. The first to appear on the new imprint was 1968's *Uncle Meat*. This double-album set is another landmark Zappa work, exhibiting a compositional flair and a gift for woodwind arrangement that far exceeded anything that had come before. The liner notes describe this record as "an album of music from a movie you will probably never get to see." Which was almost true. It took the invention of the VCR and the formation of Zappa's own Honker Video company in the Eighties for the world to see this bizarre cinematic document of the Mothers' first incarnation.

MY GUITAR WANTS TO KILL YOUR MAMMA: ZAPPA IN THE SEVENTIES

Zappa had never abandoned the interest in moviemaking that he developed back in his pre-Mothers Studio Z days. But it wasn't until 1971 that he was able to get a film into commercial release. This was *200 Motels*, a surrealistic inquest into the proposition that "touring can make you crazy." *200 Motels* deserves a place in film history because of the video editing and effects techniques that Zappa pioneered in making it. Also, it has become a perennial favorite among zonked-out midnite movie patrons everywhere.

The accompanying soundtrack album is an essential Zappa work for several reasons. For one, it fully exploited the considerable capabilities of the new Mothers of Invention line-up that Zappa had debuted on the previous year's album, *Chunga's Revenge*. Zappa disbanded the original Mothers in 1969, largely for economic reasons. (By this point, by the way, he was firmly ensconced back in Los Angeles.) The newly formed Mothers were fronted by humorists/vocalists Howard Kaylan and Mark Volman, formerly of the mid Sixties teen pop group, the Turtles. The line-up also included jazz piano ace George Duke and British drummer Aynsley Dunbar, fresh from a stint with John Mayall's Bluesbreakers. True to form, Zappa had surrounded himself with a fantastically diverse assortment of musical personalities.

200 Motels was also the first recording on which Zappa fans got the opportunity to hear his music played by a real symphony orchestra, Britain's Royal Philharmonic, under the baton of Elgar Howarth. In stark Zappa-esque contrast, *200 Motels* was also one of the first albums where Frank played really heavy guitar. Even today, tracks like "Magic Fingers" and "Mystery Roach" stand up as sterling examples of mastodon unison riffology and extended fretboard exploration. When I spoke to him in '88, Zappa ascribed much of this to the influence of Aynsley Dunbar:

"Remember that, earlier in the Mothers of Invention, we had an assortment of drummers who were okay for keeping a beat. But when it came to playing a solo along with them, there really wasn't much interaction. Aynsley was the reason why I was able to go in more of an extended guitar solo direction at that time. He just loved playing that way. We'd sit in my basement for hours and jam. It's been a long time since I've known any drummers who like to do that."

Zappa regarded his guitar solos as a form of "instant composition. It's basically the same intellectual process that I would go through writing music on a piece of paper, except that I don't have to write it down; it gets done right away. But it's really no different. You have a certain amount of time that you're going to fill up by making a piece of music. And you hope that the people who are working with you on stage are also interested in inventing music on the spot. When it works, which is not very often, I'm glad I have a recording truck. I can snag it. Because it's gone after that. That's the only time it exists."

Zappa was incontestably one of the most interesting guitar soloists of all time. His blues grounding gave him an insistent earthiness, while his sense of avant garde, dadaist absurdity pushed him in directions that confounded all expectation. But more than anything else, it was his tone that made him a fiercely distinctive player. His guitar sounded like a gander with a bad sinus condition. He made brilliant use of a wah wah pedal, and was one of the few guitarists of the Seventies and Eighties to exploit the lower strings and fret positions to their full potential. He laughed when I complimented him on this.

"Well, I think most guitarists have a tendency to play in some way like they talk," he said. "And since I'm not much of a squealer—I happen to be a baritone kind of guy—to play on the low strings is a little more in phase with my reality."

Zappa really came into his own as a gonzo guitarist in the Seventies. The decade's inaugural year saw the release of his exquisite, heavily guitar-driven solo album, *Hot Rats*. The same year also brought the Mothers' aforementioned *Chunga's Revenge* and *Weasels Ripped My Flesh*. Both feature some flaming beauties of guitar solos. The latter album includes the original recording of Zappa's axe anthem, "My Guitar Wants to Kill Your Mamma."

The line-up in Zappa's bands changed regularly throughout the Seventies and early Eighties. His groups became increasingly polished from a technical standpoint as he found himself more and more able to draw on top session talent and noted players from every field of music. Zappa was a formidable, notoriously demanding band-leader. His band was generally recognized as a hothouse for extremely proficient players; it's alumni include the guitarists Lowell George, Adrian Belew and Steve Vai.

Some fans of the original Mothers felt that Zappa's work had become a little slick at this point. The truth is, however, that he'd always used session players. Examine the liner notes to *Freak Out!* and you'll find studio aces like Carol Kaye—and even Lawrence Welk's guitarist, Neil Le Vang—clearly credited. Frank never paid much attention to his musicians' underground credibility. Original Mothers fans also tended to find Kaylan and Volman's brand of humor a little too broad, obvious and infantile. A new legion of fans, however, liked it just fine.

What *did* happen during the Seventies is that Zappa's albums began growing more "unidirectional." He began sorting out the different strands in his work. His early albums combined satire, serious composition, gross-out jokes and jazzy improvisation, all in one gloriously multifaceted package. Later on, he would focus on just one of these elements for any given album.

A record like 1973's *Overnite Sensation* is heavy on humor, whereas *The Grand Wazoo* (1972) is mostly about composition and jazz-based soloing.

THE HIGHLY SPECIALIZED EIGHTIES

In the Eighties, Zappa took this trend toward specialization to a new level with the release of the *Shut Up 'N Play Yer Guitar* series, an orgy of guitar solos and nothing else, directed straight at the coterie of Zappa axe junkies. By this point, he had started a new label, *Barking Pumpkin*, and his own marketing/mail order operation, Barfko-Swill, after his deal with Warner/Reprise and a subsequent arrangement with Mercury Records had gone sour. Zappa maintained close ties with his fans. Unlike many rock stars he was highly accessible.

"When we're on the road there are kids who follow us from town to town," he explained in 1988. "If we see the same faces when we arrive at the venue for an afternoon soundcheck, we let them in and they sit through the soundcheck. And you know, I talk to these people. They tell me interesting things. For example, a fan in Germany was the first to point out that there were incorrect dates and locations in the liner notes for *You Can't Do That on Stage Anymore*.

Frank deemed this kind of networking essential in the face of what he regarded as an increasingly incompetent, crooked and imbecilic music industry. Marketing his own music was "the only way I can exist," he told me. "There's no way that what I do can fit within a corporate format. In the United States, radio is a cultural embarrassment. Most of the music that's broadcast is harmful to your mental health."

The early Eighties brought many opportunities for Frank's orchestral and chamber compositions to be recorded and performed. 1983 saw the release of the first *London Symphony Orchestra* disc, which was followed a year later by *The Perfect Stranger: Boulez Conducts Zappa*. During this period, there were also performances of Zappa's music by ensembles such as the Kronos String Quartet and Aspen Wind Quintet. These developments were very gratifying to the composer, who had long sought an outlet for his more serious work. But he entertained no illusions about the classical music power structure. He found it every bit as frustrating and foolish as the pop music industry. Zappa was no snob.

"I have no following or any pretensions to a following in the normal classical consumer environment," he told me in a 1984 interview. "The normal audience for an orchestral piece wouldn't be caught anywhere in the vicinity of what I write. It's just not relevant to their lifestyle, nor is it written for their tastes. Basically, the material is written to amuse me and anybody else who has a similar musical outlook."

Zappa may have found his ideal musical collaborator in the Synclavier computer music system (a high-end music workstation), which also entered his life in the mid Eighties. "What I've been waiting for since I started writing music was a chance to hear what I write played without mistakes and without a bad attitude," he said in 1984. "The Synclavier solves that problem for me."

The Synclavier-based *Jazz From Hell* album won Zappa a Grammy in 1988. He was somewhat obsessed with the device. When I spoke to him in 1988 he estimated that he had some 500 new compositions stored on computer disc: "I work every night on that. My Synclavier hours are usually from about 11:00 at night until 7:00 in the morning." Nocturnal in his work habits, Zappa preferred to be asleep while the rest of the world went about its dubious business.

Frank embraced the digital revolution wholeheartedly. As soon as the Compact Disc format established itself, he threw himself into the monumental task of remastering his entire back catalog for CD release through Rykodisk. Later he embarked on the equally ambitious "Beat the Boots" series for Rhino Records, offering quality masterings of his live concerts as an alternative to the unauthorized bootleg Zappa product that has been flooding the market ever since the Sixties.

The pristine digital perfection of the Synclavier took Zappa entirely away from guitar playing from 1984-'88; he said he didn't touch the instrument once during that period. But in 1988, he assembled a band, its members culled from the cream of the players he'd worked with during the Eighties—including guitarists Ike Willis and "stunt" axeman Mike Keneally—for a world tour. The results, which are among Zappa's last public performances on guitar, can be heard on two discs: *Broadway the Hard Way* and *The Greatest Band You Never Heard in Your Life.*

Amid all these projects, Zappa also found time to become a vigorous political activist. In 1985, he testified at the U.S. Senate's "porn rock" hearings. He became one of the most outspoken and eloquent campaigners against the censorship of rock music, a tireless free speech activist and protector of constitutional rights. In 1989, after the collapse of communism in Eastern Europe, Zappa was invited to Czechoslovakia by the country's new president, Vaclav Havel, as an economic advisor. For several months, he acted as the country's economic representative to the West. Zappa was increasingly drawn to politics. It's reported that he was planning a serious presidential campaign.

This was one of many plans that were canceled when he was diagnosed as having prostate cancer in 1990. According to an article in *Pulse!*, the condition had been developing for some eight to 10 years before it was detected. Rumors of Frank's illness began to spread in the music industry shortly after the diagnosis. At first, they were widely disbelieved; it just seemed like another stupid, obviously untrue Frank Zappa story. But when the family confirmed the rumors, there was no more denying the grim fact.

Zappa continued working right up until the end. As a result he was able to see the release of one last recording of his music, *The Yellow Shark*, performed by Frankfurt's Ensemble Modern. This lavish and beautifully realized album reaches all the way back to compositions from *Uncle Meat*—a fitting end to a wondrously rich career.

But we've hardly heard the last of Zappa's music. Frank's unflagging creative energy left behind a legacy of unreleased compositions and recordings that will sustain us for many years to come. Plans are already underway for the release of a new orchestral work, *Civilization Phase III*, slated to come out in April on Rhino.

"I am a realistic kind of guy," Frank told *Guitar World's* John

Swenson in 1982. "I just try and look at things the way they are, take them for what they are, deal with them, and go on to the next case. But Americans thrive on hype and bloated images and bloated everything. They turn away from anything that's realistic. They want the candy gloss version of whatever it is."

And that's the one version that Frank never played.

Pete Townshend of the Who

Guitar World, June 1994

Not F-F-F-Fade Away

They smashed their instruments, broke musical barriers and composed some of rock's most powerful anthems. *Guitar World* looks at 30 years of the Who, and their brilliant guitarist Pete Townshend.

By Alan di Perna

THOSE WHO THINK of the Who as a bunch of guys with beards playing stadium rock must try to realize that they were *very different* in 1967. They were on the cusp of psychedelia then—four ultra-foppish Swinging London dandies looking slightly stunned to find themselves staring out into America's armpit. That's how I first saw them, from the lip of a plywood stage at the grubby Commack Arena in Long Island, New York. The Who had never played anywhere in the United States before 1967. So it seemed nothing short of miraculous that they'd actually come to perform in the depressing, shithole suburban town where I was then undergoing puberty.

The speedy, bruising rock and roll they played that night offered a stark contrast to their ruffled shirts and Pete Townshend's sequined coat. By '67, the Who had already evolved into an incredibly intense live band—a powerful, yet graceful, juggernaut fueled by the psychotic combustion of four conflicting personalities. Keith Moon wasn't a fat drunk back then, but an unbelievably flashy young drummer, just barely out of his teens and enthroned behind his fabled "Pictures of Lily" drum kit—all Union Jacks and Victorian nudes and psychedelic colors.

Roger Daltrey was genuinely frightening. When he wasn't spitting angry lyrics or twirling the microphone cord high out over the audience, he'd be brandishing a cymbal stand to ward off the town greasers, who'd come to the hall to beat the hell out of one another and hurl cherry bombs at the band. (Most of the crowd was there for the opening set by local spaghetti rock faves the Vanilla Fudge, anyway.) If anyone wanted trouble, Daltrey looked ready to show them that a street kid from Shepherd's Bush—even one in a frilly ruff—was a damn sight rougher than any little suburban toughies.

Between songs, Townshend played the nice guy: "Oh no, Mr. Officer, it's your job to tell them not to climb on the stage. I couldn't possibly. You see, they wouldn't like our group then. And they might not buy our records…" But after each frail witticism, the guitarist would kick off another tune with a violent windmill, convulsively propelling his body back into his Marshall stack like some self-abusive lunatic. In direct opposition, the only movement from John Entwistle's side of the stage came from the bassist's plectrum and fleet fingers. The Ox stood stolidly, even as some teenage girls right behind me threw bits of paper at him all night.

Then, at the climax of the set, came the moment my friends and I had read about in teen mags but dared not think we would actually witness. Pete Townshend slipped the strap of his beautiful Lake Placid Blue Fender Stratocaster off his shoulder and proceeded to slam it onto the stage, repeatedly, violently, strap peg downward, gripping the dual cutaway horns with his long, slender hands. My face was just inches from the stage, so I could feel each resounding impact. The instrument squealed each time it was struck. *Feedback.* Yeah! The Strat started to splinter. Pete grabbed the neck and began destroying the guitar in earnest, slamming it against every available surface: speaker cabinets, drums, mic stands, stage…

After that evening, I joined the small coterie of New York Who crazies who followed the band from gig to gig around the

Metropolitan area. The Fillmore East, Central Park, Westbury Music Fair, the Singer Bowl—we were there. In those days you could pay $3.50 at the door and get right up front to see the Who. Nobody knew who the fuck they were—except us New York Who crazies. It's hard to fathom this now, but from 1965 to 1969 the Who was an obscure cult band in America. Much as people would later do with indie punk rock singles, we avidly sought out then-little-known Who 45s like "I Can't Explain," "Substitute," "I'm a Boy" and "Pictures of Lily." These jolting three-minute doses of pure rock euphoria perfectly encapsulated the experience of having been born in some Lower Middle Class Nowhere: awkward, angry, clueless and young, with your hormones erupting and your shirt not fitting properly.

These concerts (along with punk's first flowering) are the reason why I'm now hacking out a Who tribute for a guitar magazine instead of pursuing some more lucrative and dignified profession. (Thanks, Pete.) So I'm here to tell you first hand:

The Who was *not* just another rock band. And Pete Townshend was never your run-of-the-mill guitar hero. Without Townshend, the terms "power chord," "Marshall stack" and "feedback" might never have entered the modern guitarist's vocabulary. Instrumentally speaking, the Who was the first power trio, and Townshend defined what the electric guitar could do within that context. But he was never one to riff on mere notes. The guy riffs on *ideas*—ideas which have profoundly affected the way rock music is performed and presented. He increased rock's vocabulary a hundredfold, dramatically expanding what can be said with a song, a show or an album.

This year is the Who's 30th anniversary. If you're a brand new rock fan wondering what the excitement was all about, MCA's box set, *The Who: Maximum R&B*, is a good place to start. It must be said that, in the end, any recording is just a substitute for the completely cathartic experience of seeing the Who live.
Wish you could've been there.

BACK NUMBERS

The story starts out much like any rock band's history. Peter Dennis

Blandford Townshend and John Alec Entwistle met at Acton County Grammar School in west London. In 1959, when both were around 14, they formed a trad jazz band called the Confederates. ("Trad," or traditional American Dixieland jazz, was popular in Britain during the late Fifties and early Sixties.) Pete played banjo and John was on trumpet. Pete came from a musical family. His father was a well-known sax player in Britain and his mother a big band vocalist. But it was John who was the more accomplished musician, a fact that was to have an important bearing on the way the Who's sound ultimately developed. By the time he started rehearsing with Pete, John had won all sorts of school prizes and community honors for his brass playing.

"When [the Confederates] asked me to join them, I had to run out and get a chord book," Pete told his friend and biographer Richard Barnes for the latter's essential Who bio, *Maximum R&B*. "As I'd been buggering about playing guitar for nearly two years, I wasn't getting anywhere. They expected me to play and were fairly impressed, which I couldn't work out. Perhaps they thought that if you could play three chords you could play the rest."

Pete started out on a very cheap acoustic he'd received from his grandmother. In his last year at Acton Grammar he got something a little better: a £3 special from Czechoslovakia. By this point, Entwistle had added bass guitar to his instrumental repertoire. He and Townshend started a Shadows-influenced rock band that they first called the Aristocrats and then the Scorpions (thus pre-figuring both German rock history and John's "spider thing").

Shortly thereafter, Roger Daltrey moved to Pete and John's neighborhood from nearby Shepherd's Bush and lured Entwistle into his own band, the Detours. By all accounts, Daltrey was quite a go-getter in those days—energetic, ambitious, ready to win a point with his fists when verbal persuasion failed. Townshend soon joined the Detours, too—enticed, it is said, by the group's possession of a real Vox amp. Roger Daltrey was the Detours' lead guitarist at first, but eventually decided to concentrate solely on vocals. Drummers came and went, until a fateful Thursday evening in March of 1964 when a lunatic from a local surf band, dressed in ginger from head to toe, sat in on "Roadrunner" during a gig at the Oldfield Hotel. He managed to break the hi-hat and bass drum pedal, thus establishing himself as the man who'd been put on earth to play drums for Townshend, Entwistle and Daltrey. Keith Moon had arrived.

By this point, Townshend had already begun attending Ealing Art School, where he eagerly absorbed bohemianism, marijuana, pop art, avant garde music, and obscure American blues, r&b and jazz records. It was one of Pete's art school friends, the aforementioned Richard Barnes, who came up with the Detours' new name—the Who—during a hemp-fueled brainstorming session at the flat he and Pete shared. As the Who, the group started to become the musical choice of London's Mod movement. They played the current r&b and Tamla/Motown songs which, along with Jamaican ska, were the mainstays of the Mods' musical diet. For a brief period they were managed by Mod pacesetter Pete Meaden, who changed the group's name to the High Numbers ("number" being slang for a regular street kid kind of Mod, a humble foot soldier in the great Mod army). Under Meaden's aegis, they made their first single: "I'm the Face"/"Zoot Suit." The sides—reworkings of familiar blues riffs with Mod buzzword lyrics penned by Meaden—didn't sell too well. Meaden was dropped and the band name reverted to the Who.

During this period, circa 1964, many key elements of the Who's approach to the guitar fell into place. It was John Entwistle who first bought one of the new 4 x 12, closed-back speaker cabinets that London music store owner Jim Marshall had begun to manufacture. The Marshall cabinet gave John such a boost in volume that Pete was compelled to get one as well. And from there, it was just a short step to Townshend's pioneering use of feedback. It was at the Oldfield Hotel, where the band had first discovered Keith Moon, that Townshend made an equally momentous discovery.

"Where I stood on the stage was a piano, and I stuck my cabinet on it and it was dead level with the guitar," he explained to Barnes. "And I started to get these feedback effects that I really liked. When I went to other gigs and put the speakers on the floor, it wouldn't happen. So I started to put it up on a chair and then I decided to stack the things so that I could *induce* feedback."

Thus was born the Marshall stack. Equally essential to Townshend's developing style were the Rickenbacker guitars he had started playing. He'd admired them ever since he saw the Beatles using them. But he soon began adapting the Rick's eccentricities to his own musical needs. "The strings are closely spaced on a narrow neck," Pete explained to Rickenbacker historian Richard R. Smith. "The fingerboard is lightweight but superbly balanced. This suited my chordal style, and I invented several new chord shapes using that neck which have since become standard rock shapes. What falls under the fingers on a Rick might dislocate your hand on an old acoustic Martin. The lightweight neck allowed me to produce vibrato techniques by moving the neck backwards and forwards. This became another characteristic of my style. The weak points of the [Rickenbacker] guitars were that the necks would literally break off in my hand if I went too far."

That fateful weak spot, however, was to change rock history forever. Townshend's menacing, strident feedback squeals must have seemed shocking enough to compulsively polite Britons out for a few nice pints after a hard day at the gasworks. They'd certainly never heard anything like *that* before. Nobody on earth had, for that matter. But imagine how badly it must have startled them to see a young lad wantonly smashing a perfectly good electric guitar—one that for many audience members was clearly worth at least several week's wages.

Townshend was just as surprised as his spectators as he performed the first guitar smashing in history, at the Railway Hotel in London. It was a venue with a particularly high stage and correspondingly low ceiling.

"I started to knock the guitar about a lot, hitting it on the amps to get banging noises and things like that, and it started to crack," Pete told Barnes. "It banged against the ceiling and smashed a hole in the plaster, and the guitar head actually poked through the ceiling. When I brought it out, the top of the neck was left behind. I couldn't believe what had happened. There were a couple of people from art school I knew at the front of the stage and they were laughing their heads off. One of them was literally rolling about on the floor, laughing, and his girlfriend was kind of looking at me, smirking. So I just got really angry and got what was left of the guitar and smashed it to smithereens. About a month earlier I'd managed to scrape together enough money for a 12-string Rickenbacker, which I only used on two or three numbers. It was lying at the side of the stage, so I just picked it up, plugged it in and carried on playing as if I'd meant to [smash the other guitar]."

The guitar smashing thing was completely emblematic of Mod culture, with its celebration of fast-paced consumerism and glib disposability. The serious Mod had to discard and replace costly items of clothing on a weekly basis in order to keep up with small-but-crucial changes in the vogue for lapel widths, pocket stitching, fabric patterns, etc. Tiny sartorial details like these made or broke the aspiring Mod. And the ones who did make it often found themselves extremely broke as a result. But here was this bloke in a pop group who not only spent £60 a week on clothes (so the legend went), but who also went through expensive electric guitars like they were pocket squares. With his art school training and his gift for eminently quotable interviews, Townshend was quick to align his Rickenbacker wreckings with the Auto-Deconstructionist movement in contemporary art. Along with Pete's windmill guitar strum and the Bird Man—a stage pose which saw the guitarist stand stock still with his limbs extended while feedback from his instrument swelled cataclysmically—the Who's equipment destruction became part of a compelling stage act that netted them the title "World's Most Exciting Teenage Group" in the mid Sixties.

Of course, the Who couldn't afford the guitar smashing ritual that quickly became expected of them. It actually kept them constantly on the verge of total bankruptcy, up until the massive success of *Tommy* in 1969. And that is the essence of the Who's entire career: They acted out our wildest fantasies, living dangerously, irresponsibly and beyond all known laws. And then they had to foot the bill.

ON THE RECORD

But in early 1965, things were looking up. The Who had new management, Kit Lambert and Chris Stamp, who had secured them a record deal and hooked them up with expatriate American record producer Shel Talmy, who'd just taken the Kinks to the top of the charts. "I Can't Explain," the Who's first single, came out in January of '65 and climbed to Number Eight in Britain. The tune was penned by Pete, who'd set up a recording studio at his loft in Ealing Common and had begun to experiment with songwriting. With its slashing, chordal guitar riff, "I Can't Explain" owes an obvious debt to the Kinks' "You Really Got Me," but the glassy roundness of Townshend's Rickenbacker tone makes the riff distinctly and unmistakably Who. (Talmy's number one session jobsworth, Jimmy Page, was also present, but the story is that Townshend refused to lend Page his Rick 12-string. So all the 12-string parts on "I Can't Explain"—i.e., the song's principal guitar parts—are generally attributed to Townshend.)

It's often been noted, however, that the *real* lead instrumentalist on "I Can't Explain" is Keith Moon, whose terse, belligerent drum fills set up the song's choruses and insistently push the rhythm. Moon was integral to the Who's musical chemistry. With another drummer, John Entwistle's virtuoso bass tendencies might easily have gotten out of hand and overpowered Townshend's chordal guitar playing. But with Moon's defiant refusal to be a conventional rock and roll timekeeper, the bass had to assume a fair share of the "anchoring" duties. This give-and-take between Moon and Entwistle made for one of the most propulsive rhythm sections ever heard in rock.

The Who were able to assert their unique identity even more strongly on their next two singles, UK hits both: "Anyway Anyhow Anywhere" and "My Generation." Two of the finest teen rebellion anthems ever written, both are Townshend compositions. "Anyway" features an extended feedback middle section, with Townshend madly flicking the pickup selector toggle switch on his Rickenbacker for extra effect. He was the first guitarist to make musical use of the instrument's mechanical appendages—its switches and knobs—and of the "accidental noises" generated by electric guitars and amps. He thus pointed the way not only for psychedelic guitarists like Syd Barrett and Jimi Hendrix, but also for modern alternative noise guitar bands like Sonic Youth and My Bloody Valentine.

John Entwistle comes to the fore with a thwacking fine bass solo on "My Generation," but the real fireworks come at the end: another extended feedback raveup that became the basis for the destructive orgy with which the Who now regularly closed their shows. Daltrey's enraged, stuttering vocal delivery and the venomous line, "I hope I die before I get old" represented an extraordinarily powerful evocation of teenage frustration and anger. By 1965 standards, the song was like a middle finger defiantly raised during Sunday services. Even the Rolling Stones had never made quite so rebellious a statement. "My Generation" became the title track of the Who's first album, released late in 1965 in Britain and in early 1966 in the U.S., under the somewhat unfortunate title, *The Who Sings My Generation*. (Their first American label, Decca, was to prove sadly adept at such clownish touches.) The album contains some early Pete Townshend songwriting gems, including the sublime "The Kids Are Alright," together with vestiges of the Who's r&b club repertoire.

POP ART AND MINI OPERAS

By 1966, the Who had begun to move away from their Mod image. They began billing themselves as a Pop Art group (more Townshend art school agitprop). Rather than following Mod fashions, they began to design and wear their own clothing based on the bold, simple, geometric and iconic images that artists like Andy Warhol and Roy Lichtenstein were using. This was the era of the Who's bullseye shirts and Union Jack coats.

Singles were the main rock and roll medium in 1966; "album rock" was still a few years off. And the singles the Who released in '66-67 are still the benchmark by which aspiring pop bands measure their work.

Many consider these records to be Townshend's finest moments (much to the mature Pete's undying chagrin). Townshend had been deeply influenced by Bob Dylan, who, in the mid Sixties, freed pop music lyrics from simplistic "baby, I love you" clichés. But while writers like Dylan and John Lennon went after abstract intellectual themes in their lyrics, Townshend stuck resolutely to the notion that pop songs should be about things that kids can relate to. He just put a wry twist on conventional pop themes. In "Substitute," the guy gets the girl, but only because the girl can't get the guy that she really wants. So the poor slob in this song goes around in a tortured state because, even if other people are fooled, *he* knows that, in the girl's eyes, he's only an inadequate stand-in. *Very* Townshend. On another level, the song is about Townshend's own discomfort with his new status as a pop star and Mod icon, his anxieties over his own "authenticity," his class consciousness...the whole churning mass of neuroses that are Pete's artistic stock-in-trade.

Musically, the song is based around another Townshend signature, the I, V, IV chord progression over an open-string tonic (D in this case). This wistful pattern reappears constantly in later Townshend compositions such as "Pure and Easy" and "Cut My Hair."

"I'm a Boy" is the best song about androgyny ever written (years before the Glam era, too), and it's also probably the funniest. It's all about some hapless little shaver whose mother wanted only girls, so she refuses to acknowledge that he's a boy and makes him wear dresses. But any kid whose parents ever forced him to be something he isn't can identify with the song. Musically, the tune sounds deceptively simple. The minor-key bridge is actually based on a fairly complex chord structure that ascends gracefully back to the song's poppy major-key verse and chorus. It's Pete's succinct and essential lesson in How to Write a Bridge.

"The chord structure in 'I'm a Boy' and the opening chords in 'Pinball Wizard' were directly influenced by a piece of music by [*17th century English composer*] Henry Purcell," Pete once noted, "which I'm sure a lot of our fans will flinch at."

"Pictures of Lily" pioneered another standard Townshendism and all-around heavenly pop move: the chord progression based around a descending major scale. The song also offers a classic early example of the Townshendian key modulation in the chorus (from C to A in this case)—one more pop songwriting essential. "Pictures of Lily," moreover, is probably the best song ever written on the topic of beating off.

In short, Pete Townshend was (and is) a brilliant innovator of the pop song as a storytelling vehicle. Where he was heading with his innovations came into sharper focus on the Who's second album, *A Quick One*. The title track, "A Quick One While He's Away," is Townshend's—and the world's—first rock mini-opera. Running some 10 minutes in length, this slight tale of infidelity and ultimate forgiveness isn't too far removed from many conventional operatic plots. The "opera" format freed Townshend from the conventional verse-chorus-bridge pop song structure, while still allowing him to build the bright poppy musical themes at which he has always excelled. Lightweight, fun and gimmicky, "A Quick One While He's Away" was the harbinger of greater things to come.

A Quick One is perhaps the most democratic Who album. There are two songs by Keith Moon, two by Entwistle and one by Daltrey. Entwistle's contributions—"Boris the Spider" and "Whiskey Man"—established the bassist's macabre sense of humor and his ability to play a cool rock solo on the French horn. In the United States, the *Quick One* album was released as *Happy Jack*, the title of another one of its tracks. This was the first Who single to make a significant dent on the American charts. The first time this song came on my suburban teenage radio, I had a temperature of 104 and was a bit delirious. I truly thought I was going mad. After I'd recovered, I realized that the drums on "Happy Jack" really *do* sound like that.

By the time *Happy Jack* hit, the Who had finally made it over to the States. Lambert and Stamp managed to get the group on one of New York disc jockey Murray the K's package shows at the Brooklyn Fox theater. (Cream was the other new English band on the bill.) The band covered a lot of American turf in 1967, on tour with Herman's Hermits and on their own. The Who and the Jimi Hendrix Experience were the two explosive acts that rocked the influential

Monterey Pop Festival in June of 1967. It had only been about a year since a then-unknown Hendrix, just arrived in London from America, had walked into Marshall's music shop and demanded to buy the same kind of Marshall amp that Pete Townshend used. He had to be told that Pete had moved on to Hiwatts by that point.

1967 also saw the release of the band's third album, *The Who Sell Out*. One of the all-time great rock albums, the disc includes the Who's first forays into psychedelia. "Armenia City in the Sky" is a *tour de force* of trippy backwards guitar work. The album's big single, "I Can See for Miles," was pivotal in making the power chord a central part of the rock guitar vocabulary. Townshend's brash solo—a single E note rapidly double-picked for a space of some 10 bars—was a wry sendup of the growing vogue for drawn-out, self-indulgent guitar solos.

Townshend's drive to expand the rock song format continued on *Sell Out*, one of the first concept albums. The songs are linked by glitzy jingles and musical tags from Radio London, the illegal pirate radio station that operated from a boat off the British coast during the mid Sixties. Some songs take the form of commercials written for actual products—Heinz baked beans, Odorono deodorant, etc.—and performed by the Who. Townshend, Moon, Entwistle and Daltrey's album cover photos were also done as advertisements (Daltrey, who sat in a tub of ice-cold Heinz baked beans, later caught pneumonia), complete with hilariously smarmy ad copy.

Sell Out truly upset many among the growing legion of barefoot, sprout-eating, self-righteous hippies, who stood in bovine opposition to anything that was "commercial, man." With his Pop Art background, Townshend was more inclined to view advertising as a valid 20th-century art form. The Who publicly declared their love for commercials, and recorded radio ads for everything from Great Shakes canned milkshakes to the American Cancer Society. And so it went throughout the late Sixties. Townshend's alliance with the hippy "counterculture"—which was quickly becoming America's mainstream youth culture—was always an uneasy one, at best.

Sell Out concludes with another fine Townshend mini-opera,

"Rael." Although the plot is obscure—something about the Red Chinese, apparently—the work contains the musical themes that were to become the "Undertake" for *Tommy*. A staple of the Who's live shows for years, this ethereal-yet-powerful guitar piece again finds Townshend moving high-string chord shapes over tonic bases on the open lower strings.

Who fans had to content themselves with a few singles and some repackaged albums (the *Magic Bus* album in the US and *Direct Hits* in the UK) during 1968. But word of something big was starting to spread in Who circles. A growing tide of gossip and speculation hinted that the band was at work on a project far grander than anything that even they had attempted before.

TOMMY

The New York premiere of *Tommy* in 1969 was a banner event in a year full of auspicious rock happenings. The Fillmore East was a stately, if slightly tarnished, old theater in Manhattan's bohemian East Village. It seemed the ideal venue for the unveiling of the Who's new opus. Nobody was certain what to expect. The printed program distributed at all the Fillmore shows had been supplemented with a complete libretto for this performance. A ripple of electric energy surged through the crowd as the Who took the stage and slammed into the majestic opening chords of the overture. They played straight through the hour-plus musical work while the Joshua Light Show flashed incandescent images above the stage—not the usual acid blobs, but images drawn from the story itself, shattered mirrors and flying doves that seemed to swoop out into the charged atmosphere above the audience's heads. By the time the final chords had subsided, one thing was clear: rock music had been elevated to a new artistic level. But, as if to reassure everyone that it still was rock and roll, the band reappeared after an intermission and tore the place up with a raucous set of old Who hits.

By the next morning, it seemed like everyone had bought a copy of *Tommy* and was avidly discussing the record. "What did it all mean?" "What actually happens in the end?" As he'd done on a smaller scale in the past, Townshend had once again woven about half a dozen of his favorite themes into one piece of musical storytelling. His newfound devotion to the teachings of Indian guru Meher Baba is reflected in the story of the deaf, dumb and blind boy's spiritual awakening. And poor Tommy was definitely a kid who'd been messed up by his mum; the opera is a kind of dark retelling of "I'm a Boy" in that sense. And in Tommy's rise to superstardom and subsequent fall from mass adulation, it's not hard to see Townshend's perennial discomfort with his own fame and his growing obsession with the relationship between a rock star and his audience.

Tommy demonstrated Townshend's growing ability to handle a lengthy composition that was compelling from beginning to end and generously laced with songs—"Pinball Wizard," "I'm Free"—that could stand on their own as hit singles. Other late Sixties groups tried to elevate rock to the level of art by inserting increasingly longer and more intricate instrumental solos in the songs. They tried to turn rock into jazz. Townshend chose to expand the rock song form itself—a far more organic and ingenious approach.

IN THE SEVENTIES

When you've taken rock music to a new plateau, what do you do for an encore? The Who chose to go back to basics, releasing a bruisingly tight, no-nonsense concert album. *Live at Leeds* reflects what a great live band the Who had become in the six or so years they'd been together at that point, and it still stands as the definitive live rock album. Some of the songs go back to the Who's early days in the London clubs, but the sound reflects the new, heavier aesthetic that was coming into vogue in rock at the dawn of the Seventies.

On stage, Townshend had abandoned the Fenders he'd played in the late Sixties (he stopped playing Ricks live about '67) in favor of the meatier sound of Gibsons—first SGs and later Les Pauls. *Live at Leeds* underscored the favorable impression the Who had made at the Woodstock festival the previous year. Between their exposure at Woodstock and the tremendous commercial success of *Tommy*, the band's place in the States was finally assured; they were showing a profit for the first time in their career.

In keeping with the new vibe of the Seventies and with their own maturity, the Who had long since discarded their Sixties dandyism. Townshend began sporting a scruffy ascetic's beard, plain white overalls and workman's boots, like some socialist leader. And indeed, Pete was now striving to put a wildly ambitious piece of populist theory into action. He called the project *Lifehouse*. The idea—or part of it, anyway—was to do a series of concerts at London's Young Vic Theatre for a small, select audience that would return to the theater night after night. Townshend was hoping to create a closer bond between artist and audience than had ever existed before, where the distance between the two would blur and ultimately disappear.

Pretty trippy, eh? Not surprisingly, it didn't work; the invited audience just kept yelling for Who oldies. But while the *Lifehouse* project was never completed, it did supply some killer songs for the immensely popular *Who's Next* album in 1971 and Townshend's first solo record, 1972's *Who Came First*. *Lifehouse* has continued to obsess Townshend down through the years; themes from the project also crop up in his solo album, *Psychoderelict*.

Who's Next is the Who's most popular album. Is there a rock fan of any age who doesn't know "Won't Get Fooled Again"? Roger Daltrey's hyper-Wagnerian primal scream near the song's conclusion has become the club call of party dudes everywhere. But in the song's context, it's more of a scream of frustration than euphoria. "Won't Get Fooled Again" is another classic Townshend statement on the futility of revolutions—in politics, in rock, in youth culture—and the inevitability that any hero selected for mass adulation will always turn out to be a disappointment.

Who Are You reflects the Who's new emphasis on a heavier sound, as well as Townshend's growing fascination with synthesizer technology. Pete later explained that the synth pattern in the FM rock staple "Baba O'Riley" was generated by one of his *Lifehouse* concepts. He had planned to select audience members and feed their biographical data into a synthesizer: "height, weight, astrological details, beliefs and behavior, etc… The synthesizer would then select notes from the pattern of that person. On ['Baba O'Riley'] I programmed details about the life of Meher Baba and that provides the backing for the number."

Townshend's next project was nearly as ambitious as *Lifehouse*, but far more successful. Released late in 1973, *Quadrophenia* was the Who's second double-disc concept album. It rocks much harder than *Tommy*, but as always it's crammed with Townshend ideas and obsessions. Still striving to enfold real life into his art, he hit on the idea of using the Who's four violently disparate personalities as a structural device to advance his story of Jimmy, the disenchanted Mod kid. He wrote a musical theme for each band member and the themes are woven throughout the album, embellished with plenty of fluid guitar riffing.

By 1973 rock had become a bloated, boring commodity. How cool of Pete to choose this very moment to recall the pre-hippie innocence of Mod. *Quadrophenia* is an elegiac record. Songs like "I've Had Enough" and "The Punk Meets the Godfather" reflect Townshend's growing weariness with the whole process of stardom. Pete had long since begun to feel trapped by what he'd created with the Who—the obligatory guitar smashings and hotel-room trashings.

The mid to late Seventies were a rough period for the Who all around. Keith Moon's substance abuse had ceased to be charming or amusing (if it ever was that) and had begun to damage the drummer's health; he collapsed on stage at several shows. Townshend's own problems with alcohol were beginning to become chronic, turning him into a bitter, self-deprecating and generally unpleasant figure. (On stage at a mid-Seventies orchestral performance of *Tommy* in London, he made a self-loathing mime of wiping his ass with the libretto.) Meanwhile, the Who were having trouble presenting Pete's newer synth-scored, complex narrative songs on stage. Backing tapes and awkward spoken explanations of *Quadrophenia*'s storyline had begun to hobble the Who's awesome live power. All four members of the Who had begun putting a good deal of their energy into solo albums; Daltrey and Moon had budding film careers as well.

All of this turmoil is reflected in 1975's *The Who by Numbers*.

There are a few good songs, but the overall feeling of the record is brittle and strained. It was the first disappointing Who album ever. Townshend's "However Much I Booze" pretty much tells the whole story. Luckily, the Who were able to rally their creative energies for *Who Are You* in 1978. Some of the songs ("Guitar and Pen," "Music Must Change") are a bit "show tune," reflecting Townshend's growing love affair with the musical theater. But most of the songs, including the title track and Entwistle's bruising "Trick of the Light," are among the hardest rocking songs the Who ever recorded.

THE MUSIC MUST CHANGE

Who Are You turned out to be the Who's swan song. A month after the record's release, Keith Moon was found dead in his London flat, killed by an accidental overdose of the pills that had been prescribed to help him control his drinking. Rock had lost its foremost jester, its chief Dionysian celebrant. The Who, meanwhile, had lost their drummer. They chose to carry on for two more albums (*Face Dances* and *It's Hard*) with former (Small) Faces drummer Kenny Jones and keyboardist John "Rabbit" Bundrick. The last two albums contain some fine tunes, but it's difficult to call them "Who albums" in the same sense that the term had been used since 1965. Townshend half-acknowledged as much in a 1989 *Musician* interview with Charles M. Young, saying that the Who was no longer "the name of a familiar group of musicians, because once Keith died that was dead. It's become a kind of ideology—a sense of personal emancipation as opposed to political or economic emancipation. We who are in the Who should know that it's impossible to invoke that other kind of music without Keith. So I felt the band without Keith was a new band."

When that new band decided to call it quits in 1982, the Who became a memory—a legend. In 1989, Mssrs. Entwistle, Daltrey and Townshend got together with a group of ace musicians to celebrate that legend in a series of moving concerts commemorating the Who's 25th anniversary. Then they went back to their everyday lives: A bass virtuoso who's a regular figure at NAMM shows. A capable actor and one of the finest rock singers/song stylists still practicing the craft. And a successful writer, literary editor and composer for the musical stage, who currently has a hit called *Tommy* on Broadway and another called *The Iron Man* in London's West End.

In 1993, I attended Townshend's *Psychoderelict* concert in Los Angeles—a typically ambitious hybrid of rock performance and legitimate theater that brought actors and musicians together on the same stage. In the lobby, I was amazed and delighted to discover that Who crazies still exist. There was that same vibe: complete strangers approaching one another, saying, "Hey, did you hear that Entwistle's here tonight? Did you know Pete's gonna release a version of the record without the spoken bits?"

During the performance, I experienced a sensation I hadn't felt in at least 15 years. Having attended literally thousands of rock shows and seen bands go through their predictable paces, building to one tediously inevitable climax after another, I suddenly realized that, at this show, I actually didn't know what the hell was going to happen next! There was that same anticipation and uncertainty that one felt at Who shows long ago: the sense that the whole thing could at any moment disintegrate into total garbage—or be absolutely brilliant. And there was Pete Townshend up on the stage, his hair gray and thinning, but still pushing the envelope, taking chances, trying to stretch the limits of what can be done with rock and roll. Thank you for that, Pete.

Guitar World, August 1994

The Long Run

Welcome, once again, to "Hotel California." Eagles guitarist Don Felder offers a candid appraisal of the band's great past—and his high hopes for their "resumption."

By Alan di Perna

FIVE TRAILERS ARE drawn up in a tight cluster outside Stage 14, like so many covered wagons huddled together to meet an Apache attack. The vehicles seem tiny and oddly vulnerable amid the airplane hangar-sized soundstages and sprawling asphalt expanses of the Los Angeles rehearsal complex the Eagles have chosen as the staging point for their massive, much-publicized reunion world tour. They're the sort of trailers you see on film shoots: paneled 8 x 12 enclaves equipped with kitchenette and telephone, designed to give celebrities some privacy, a place apart from the riggers, roadies, soundmen and other clattering proletarians of the vast, microcosmic metropolis known as show business. There's one trailer per Eagle, and each one is exactly identical in size and design—just the sort of separate-but-equal democracy you'd expect in a band notorious for its tense personality clashes and protracted artistic feuding.

In the trailer nearest the soundstage, Don Felder is on the phone. He's talking to one of many guitar manufacturers who are vying to have him play their wares on his band's highly visible trek around the globe: "Yeah, I really liked that last one you sent me.

Don Felder & Joe Walsh of the Eagles

Kind of like an Explorer, but brighter, you know? Can you send another one of those?"

For a man of 47 and the father of college-age kids, Felder looks good. His hair is graying but it's still quite luxuriant, falling forward over his brow like a high stretch of California surf. He's got an infectious, insinuating laugh, the sort of laugh that grows slowly from a wheeze to a roar, drawing you into the joke, making you a co-conspirator in whatever bit of lore Felder happens to be retailing at the moment.

Don Felder is the Eagles' secret weapon, their most often overlooked asset. He's the guy who played that searing guitar solo on "One of These Nights." He's the one who wrote the music to "Hotel California," with its sinfully caloric layers of guitar harmonies, and who played the first part of the legendary solo so often—and mistakenly—attributed entirely to Joe Walsh. Felder was a key figure in the Eagles' transition from the soft-edged country rock of their first two albums to the harder-edged rock sound that brought the band its greatest success. He's an impressively well-rounded musician. During the current Eagles tour he'll be holding down pedal steel and mandolin duties while also adding his fair share to the guitar work of Joe Walsh and Glenn Frey. It takes a versatile, adaptive musician to match the supple lyrical wordplay of Don Henley and Glen Frey and the quintet's soaring vocal harmonies.

The guitarist is clearly excited about the tour and about the forthcoming new studio album from the Eagles. He proudly announces they've already got four tunes in the can, including one called "Learn to be Still," that Henley co-wrote with Tom Petty drummer Stan Lynch. And Felder seems especially fond of the special edition of MTV's *Unplugged* that the Eagles recently taped.

"It was the weirdest experience. When the five of us get together and play those songs, it's like nothing's changed. Like the Eagles never stopped working together. You're up there, and with the exception of being able to see the first two or three rows, everything is all black around you. It's like being in a vacuum—a time warp. And I had the sense that you could take that little time capsule and shove it 20 years in either direction—forward or back—and I'd still be up there, playing those songs. It was a very unusual sensation: like deja vu and days yet to view."

The Greek philosopher Heraclitus noted that you can never step in the same river twice. And the Eagles have been as changeable and free-flowing as any river. Band members have come and gone and the group has altered its artistic course on several occasions, moving in harmony with the prevailing musical landscape. The Seventies have gone and come back again with a vengeance. People and times may change, but Don Felder's never been the kind of guy who's afraid to get his feet wet.

GUITAR WORLD: Tell me the story of "Hotel California." The song that is arguably the Eagles' biggest hit originated with you, didn't it?
DON FELDER: Yes. I had just leased this house out on the beach at Malibu—I guess it was around '74 or '75. I remember sitting in the living room, with the doors all wide open, on a spectacular July day. I had a bathing suit on and I was sitting on this couch, soaking wet, thinking the world is a wonderful place to be. I had this acoustic 12-string and I started tinkling around with it, and those "Hotel California" chords just kind of oozed out. Every once in a while it seems like the cosmos parts and something great plops into your lap. I had a Teac four-track set up in one of the back bedrooms and I ran back there to put this idea down before I forgot it. I had one of those old rhythm ace things that Roland or somebody made. I remember it was set to play this cha-cha beat, so I started it up, set the right tempo and played the 12-string on top of it. I didn't do any more to it then because I was also working on "Victim of Love" at the same time. I had about six or eight song ideas I was working up. But a few days later I went back and listened to that 12-string thing with the cha-cha beat, and it sounded pretty unique. So I came up with a bass line. A few days later I added some electric guitars. Everything was getting mixed down to mono, ping-ponging back and forth on this little four track. Finally I wound up with a cassette that had just about the entire arrangement that appears on the record, verbatim, with the exception of a few Joe Walsh licks on the end. All the harmony gui-

tar stuff was there, as was my solo on the end.

GW: At what point did Henley and Frey get involved in the writing?

FELDER: When I gave Henley the cassette, it had eight or 10 different song ideas. He came back and said [*lowering his pitch in imitation of Henley*], "I really love this one track on your tape. The one that sounds like a matador or something…like you're in Mexico." We worked it all up and went into the studio and recorded it. When I wrote the song, it was in E minor—just regular, open, normal chords, in standard tuning. And we recorded it the first time in E minor. We made this killer track. All the electric guitars were big and fat and the 12-string was nice and full. Then Henley comes back a week later and says, "It's in the wrong key." So I say, "Well what do you need? D? F sharp?"

GW: Hoping you could varispeed the tape.

FELDER: Right. But he said, "No." So I sat down with him and started trying to figure out the key, and it turned out it had to be in B minor! So out comes the capo and it goes way up on the seventh fret to get the thing into B minor. We re-recorded the song in B minor and all of a sudden the guitar sounds really small. [*wheezing with laughter*] And the whole track goes [*making "small weenie" gesture with thumb and forefiner*]. "Oh no!!! What *happened*!!??" We decided it just wasn't as good as the first track. So we went back and tried it again in B minor. This was our third recording. Luckily, we came up with a better version in B minor.

GW: Did you stay with the capo scenario for that third recording?

FELDER: Oh, I had to, yeah. I recorded the acoustic guitar on that track through a Leslie. They took a D.I. out of the console with a mic on it and a stereo Leslie, so you get this swirly kind of effect. Then I went back in and did most of the guitars, except for the stuff where Joe and I set up on two stools and ran the harmony parts down.

GW: There are two sets of harmony guitar parts on the record: one that comes in at the end of the first verse and then an "answer" harmony that enters at the end of the second verse.

FELDER: You know it well! Yeah, Joe and I set up and did those together. It was a lot of fun working out all the little details.

GW: What about the solo section in the end? Who has the first solo?

FELDER: I do. Then it's Joe. Then we trade lines and then we go into the lead harmonies. But it works the other way on the acoustic version we just did. I let Joe have the first solo.

GW: When you play the song live, do you still have to capo up for the 12-string part?

FELDER: Yeah. I have a doubleneck Gibson—a six string and a 12-string—that I use to cover all my parts live. So on the 12-string neck I capo at the seventh fret. And it sounds okay. You know, even on the record—maybe because I've been hearing it for 20 years—that part sounds all right to me now. But it's not as nice as the E minor version. Even when we'd finished "Hotel California," I wasn't convinced that it should be a single. I thought it was okay as an album piece because all those guitars were a lot of fun. But when Henley said, "I think it should be our single," I said, "Are you kidding? The song is six minutes and change. They're not going to play anything over three minutes-30 seconds on the radio. Here we've got something that's twice their usual program length. It starts off quiet and it's got this quiet breakdown in the middle..." I was very skeptical, but I just yield to the wisdom of Guano, which is Henley's nickname. [*Guano means "bat dung" in Spanish—GW Ed.*]

GW: Guano?!

FELDER: Yeah, the Sonic Bat. He can detect anything that's even microtonally out of tune. He's got the Sonic Bat Radar.

GW: Did he come up with the entire lyrical concept for "Hotel California" right away?

FELDER: Pretty much, yeah. I think he and Glenn had this idea—kind of the fantasy of California. It's supposed to be kind of a microcosm of the world. But I wouldn't want to speak for them. The line, "You can check out any time you like, but you can never leave," was based on Jackson Browne's first wife, who committed suicide. In other words, you can check out—die—but you're still in the cosmos somewhere. You're not going to get out of that karmic phase of it. The way Glenn and Don tend to work together is Glenn is great at conceptualizing. He'll say, "I can see this guy driving in the desert at night, and you can see the lights of L.A. way off on the horizon…" Henley gets the picture and goes from there. He was an English literature major. He writes really great prose. He can take those little snapshots and put them into just two or three lines and it's just…wow! I try and do the same thing with a lick here and there.

GW: What was your musical background like when you joined the Eagles? Did you come more from the country/bluegrass side of things, or more the rock side?

FELDER: Well, I should take you back a step and say that I grew up in Gainesville, Florida, which was a very small town then. And there were a lot of people living there at the time who went on to be successful musicians. Stephen Stills [*Buffalo Springfield, Crosby, Stills, Nash and Young*] and I had a band together when we were 14. We made records. We went around in the back of people's pickup trucks and station wagons, playing at radio stations.

GW: What was that band called?

FELDER: The Continentals. [*ironically*] Really cool, eh? Then Bernie Leadon [*a founding member of the Eagles and the band's original lead guitarist*] moved to Gainesville for his junior and senior years in high school. Bernie came from a heavy country music background. He didn't even own an electric guitar when I met him. And I knew every Elvis Presley lick! I had really gotten into rock and roll and r&b, tryin' to listen to WLAC late at night when all the horrible white stations went off the air. You could hear people like B.B. King! Which is where my roots are, really.

So Bernie and I actually put together two bands, which we finally merged into one. One band was sort of a fraternity/high school prom dance band which played the Daytona strip along with the Allman Brothers, who were the Allman Joys at that time. [*Allmans drummer*] Butch Trucks also had a three-piece band. And little Tommy Petty, who was just a snot-nosed kid, had his band going down there. All of us in that area kind of knew each other.

Bernie and I also had a bluegrass band. Bernie was already a master at all that stuff—a killer five-string banjo player. I wound up learning how to play mandolin and flat-top acoustic guitar.

Reciprocally, I took Bernie to the music store, bought him a Gretsch electric guitar and taught him rock and roll. So way back in high school we were kind of laying the groundwork for what we'd be doing together in the Eagles, mixing country and rock.

We went our separate ways after high school, though. He went to L.A. and I wound up in New York, where I had a jazz-rock fusion band. And all the time Bernie kept calling me, saying, "You ought to move out to L.A." But it seemed so far away and the whole psychedelic thing out there seemed a little too strange for me. But then Stephen Stills happened with his band [*Buffalo Springfield*] and Bernie fell into some things [*Leadon played with seminal country rockers the Flying Burrito Brothers before joining the Eagles in 1970—GW Ed.*], so I said, "Well okay, I'll go to L.A." So by the time I got to L.A., I had a background in almost everything: country, rock, jazz… I'd even played gigs at Holiday Inns with a gut string guitar, playing movie themes.

GW: So you and Bernie were old friends. But how well did you know the other guys in the Eagles when you were called in to play slide on "Good Day in Hell," your very first session with the band in 1974?

FELDER: When I was living in New York, I'd go jam with them when they came through town. I'd built a relationship with them in the days when they were still kind of a small band playing 2,000 to 2,500-seat halls. It wasn't like sitting in with the Rolling Stones. So when they were doing *On the Border*, Glenn recalled that I played a little slide and they asked me to come play on "Good Day in Hell." The next day they called and asked me to join the band. And I said, "Well I don't know…" 'Cause every time I talked to Bernie, it sounded like the band had just broken up. And I didn't want to join a band that was going to break up every day. [*laughs*] I mean I was very excited about their offer. But it felt like I was joining a band that was crumbling apart.

GW: So it never felt like the Eagles were a rock-solid thing that would go on forever.

FELDER: No. To this day it doesn't feel like that. That's just the nature of this beast.

GW: Once you did join, there were three guitar players in the band: Glenn, Bernie and you. What was your approach to devising arrangements for all those guitars?

FELDER: Well, the arrangements were already pretty complex, and the band was having a hard time reproducing them live. There was a lot of bluegrass stuff on the first few records and Bernie obviously couldn't cover all of the instruments live. So when he played banjo, I would play mandolin. Or when he played pedal steel, I'd play flat-top acoustic—just like we used to do in high school. Even on the more rock-oriented studio material, they would double- or triple-track Glenn or Bernie's parts. If you listen to those early parts, Bernie played a B-string-bender, Tele-type thing and Glenn played his harmony lead parts on top of that. And somebody needed to take one of those three or four parts on stage in order to make it sound like the record. It's difficult to play "Already Gone" without three guitar parts. And one of the successes of this band in performance is that we sound exactly like the record—the vocal harmonies, the guitars, everything.

GW: Did all that guitar work tend to be cut live in the studio? Like "Take It Easy," for example—those dueling, intertwining leads...

FELDER: A lot of it was done live; I think we overdubbed only a couple of little things on that one. In fact, a lot of our tracks were cut live. We just set up and played.

GW: What do you recall about coming up with those interlocking rhythm guitar parts on "One of These Nights"?

FELDER: That was a unique situation. I added those parts after the record was done. It was originally a piano-based song, and we cut it with Glenn playing piano; he also did the harmony guitar parts in the beginning. But the song just didn't groove, so [*producer*] Bill Szymczyk figured out how we could make the thing scream a little. We added a couple of rhythm guitar parts. And I'll never forget doing the solo for that song. Don and Glenn were at a radio interview. They were going to call into the studio, live, from whatever radio station they were at, and Szymczyk and I were supposed to do this phone interview and then play them the solo we'd recorded, live on the air. So Szymczyk and I really set them up. We recorded a solo that started out like the one on the record, but halfway through, inserted two or three out-of-tune notes and a couple of mistakes. As the solo progressed, it just got worse and worse. [*laughs wildly*] And then we recorded the real one—the one on the record. But when Glenn and Don called, we played them the dud solo. It started off and they're saying, "Hey, that sounds good." And as soon as they finished those first couple of comments you could start hearing these, mmm, errant notes. And the next thing you know, everybody's laughing. That's one of the things I remember most about that solo.

GW: It's an interesting solo. Do you remember what inspired it?

FELDER: Every time I write a solo, I think I'm a sax player. Horn players have to be melodic. One member of that jazz fusion band I had in New York played soprano sax really well. We actually worked up some solos that we played in unison, which really helped my sense of phrasing and soloing. And since "One of These Nights" is kind of a rock version of an r&b-style song, I figured the solo should sound like a sax. And since we didn't have a sax player, I just did my best on guitar.

GW: How did Bernie Leadon's departure from the Eagles in 1975 affect the group's guitar sound and overall approach?

FELDER: When Bernie left, he bequeathed me the…burden [*laughs*]…of maintaining both the things he did: the country/bluegrass side and the rock side. At the same time, all through *On the Border*, *One of These Nights* and *Hotel California*, I was trying to push the band a little bit away from that very light, delicate, early acoustic material and into a sound that was more radio-playable. Stuff that could fill up larger venues and sell massive amounts of tickets. You know, more rock and roll. And everybody jumped on it. That's kind of where Glenn wanted to go. And Henley, he could sing the New York phone book and sell a million records, so he was really interested in that too.

GW: So it made a lot of sense to choose a real rock player like Joe Walsh as Bernie's replacement.

FELDER: Yes. Even prior to Bernie's official departure, Joe started getting involved in the band the same way I did, by coming around and hanging out, playing slide at rehearsals and screwing around. So when Bernie gave notice that he was leaving, Joe was the prime candidate to replace him.

GW: At the time, it surprised a lot of people to hear that Joe Walsh was joining the Eagles. He had a pretty solid solo career. And he had established himself with the James Gang as a real rock guy. Joe Walsh and the Eagles just seemed like a very unlikely combination in 1975.

FELDER: Yeah, well, Irving Azoff managed Joe and he managed us. Joe was always around. He opened some shows for us. We got to be friends. You know, I went out and did a couple of solo things with him. We did an album together and a TV show. Kind of [*breaks into the Rodgers and Hammerstein tune*] "Getting to know you, getting to know all about you..." Because that was the key: how well could Joe and I work together? The answer, it turned out, was really well. It's a delight to play with that guy. I've always really enjoyed that. I've missed it.

GW: On songs written solely by Henley and Frey, how much were the other band members involved in the actual, "hashing it out" creative process?

FELDER: I'd say not so much in the composition of the lyrics, melody or even the chord charts, but definitely in the arrangements. It's like Don and Glenn would set the table: "Here's the song, here are the lyrics. Now you bring something to the party." And everybody would add their insights, whether it was a solo or a pedal steel part, that would bring the song alive.

GW: Did the band ever become enmeshed in Don and Glenn's famous creative feuds?

FELDER: You know, the feuds that took place in the band were never based on individual egos. They were always conflicts over what was right for the material, or the best artistic approach to something. The feuds grew out of a concern for the quality of what was being produced. I think that was part of the strain—the criteria we set for what we were trying to achieve created a mountain that was difficult to climb. Even though we created the mountain ourselves! And I think that's why records ended up taking two years to make. It took a lot of coating off everyone's nerves to go through that level of creative struggle.

GW: There was a three-year period between *Hotel California* and *The Long Run*, during which you changed bass players.

FELDER: We pleaded and pleaded with Randy [*Meisner*] not to leave the band. But he just felt it was time for him to attend to his personal life—mainly his family. His kids were in their teens and they had literally grown up with their father gone all the time, first with the Rick Nelson band, then Poco, then the Eagles. He just reached a point where his heart told him to stop. We pleaded with him to continue and offered to change our schedule and do less work, but in the end he did what he had to do.

GW: How did Timothy B. Schmit's arrival change things?

FELDER: Well, Timothy had replaced Randy in Poco when Randy left Poco to join the Eagles. And when Randy's departure from the Eagles was announced we said, "Okay, let's list on one finger all the people that we know who can sing that high and play bass that well. Mmm, who might that be?" Timothy was the only logical choice. And he brought a great personality into the band.

GW: Let's take a giant step forward in time. What led to this reunion of the Eagles?

FELDER: It's not a reunion of the Eagles. It's a *resumption*. I only use that word because that's the one Henley and Frey have selected. And it really offers a pleasant perspective on what's happening—that this isn't a one-time get-together tour as much as it is a resumption of this group of people writing and recording together.

What directly led to this resumption was doing the Travis Tritt video. [*The Eagles backed Tritt on his video for "Take It Easy," the country rocker's contribution to* Common Thread: Songs of the Eagles—*GW Ed.*] That was the first time we all actually got together and played. It was like, "Can we all stand together in the same room and smile and play and have a good time? Or is it going to be too strange?" And it turned out to be great fun, like a high school rock band getting back together for a 20-year reunion and playing "Louie Louie." I think we only played "Take It Easy" once or twice. We just played a bunch of old songs and jammed and it was a lot of fun. It had the kind of innocence that we had back when we just played and wrote songs without the pressure of having to top our last 20-million-selling album.

GW: So all the less pleasant aspects of the Eagles' past history were just so much water under the bridge?

FELDER: Nobody really harbored any personal resentments. It was more a matter of not wanting to step back into the intensity of what would be demanded of us as the Eagles. But we've stepped back in, and here we are working on three projects at the same time We're trying to finish the television show that we videotaped for MTV. We're in the studio writing and recording.

So far, we've finished four new studio tracks for a new album. And we have a world tour starting in eight days. So it's like, "Aaaggghhh, we've done it to ourselves again!" But we're having a good time—laughing, and trying to take it with a lot more grace than we did last time. If we pace ourselves better this time than we did last time, we'll be all right.

GW: Is it true that there was a planned Eagles reunion that didn't work out?

FELDER: Yes. I would say that from the day we put this band on hold [in 1980], everybody in the back of their minds knew how wonderful it would be to play together again. Don and Joe and Timothy and I have all stayed in contact. And finally, about two-and-a-half years ago, it reached a point where everybody was talking to everybody else again. Don and Glenn had reconciled a few differences and wound up writing some songs together and were actually in the studio for three weeks. But nothing really came of it. The cosmos just wasn't in proper alignment for it to happen at that time. Either emotionally or musically, it just wasn't right.

GW: Would you say now is the right time? There has been a tremendous resurgence of interest in the Seventies and "classic rock" has never been more popular.

FELDER: I couldn't tell you. I don't know how it all came together in the first place. I don't know what caused it to break up. I don't know why we're together again right now. I just know I'm really enjoying it. I suppose it's nice to be a classic.

Guitar World, October 1994

Smash Hits

Pete Townshend, destroyer of guitars and musical convention, offers the final word on the Who's tumultuous three-decade career.

By Alan di Perna

PETE TOWNSHEND LEAPS to his feet. He clasps his two hands together and starts waving them frantically over his head. He looks a tad demented, particularly against the stately backdrop of the posh, empty Bel Air Hotel ballroom that his record label has commandeered for interview purposes. Pete is re-enacting a scene from the making of the Who's second album (*A Quick One*, released in the U.S. as *Happy Jack*) in 1966—illustrating how he persuaded the band's elegant but technically clueless manager that the only way to get a Leslie effect live was to swing a fragile, $12,000 studio microphone over your head.

"Basically that record was a scream from start to finish," Pete says, as he resumes his seat. "Running around the studios banging bass drums, playing pennywhistles, going out in the street and coming back in with the poor engineer trying to follow us with a microphone. It was a good, good period for the Who. Everybody in the band wrote a couple of songs for the record, including Roger. That album was when we realized that studios were the *greatest places*."

It does the heart good to see Pete Townshend *enjoying* the memory of the Who. He's so often been bitter on the topic, burdened by the weight of having been the guitarist and architect of the

World's Greatest Rock and Roll Band. Jealous, even of the way the Who have tended to upstage the mature Townshend's fine solo work. But today, Pete's in a mood to celebrate the Who; and when he wants to be, Townshend is the ultimate Who fan.

What has got the guitarist in such a great mood? It seems to be the release of the new 30th anniversary Who box set, *30 Years of Maximum R&B*, and a live video compilation of the same name. Together, these releases make a sumptuous feast for veteran Who lovers and novices alike. A video rarity like the live performance of "Water" from 1970 captures a moment in the Who's thunderous live act that might otherwise have died with the memory of the last grizzled Who follower. The four-CD box set is similarly littered with hitherto unheard gems, studio outtakes, bootleg obscurities, and of course the hits—clean, new remasterings of the powerhouse rock songs on which the Who's mass reputation so deservedly rests: "I Can't Explain," "My Generation," "I'm a Boy," "Happy Jack," "I Can See for Miles," "Pinball Wizard," "Won't Get Fooled Again," "Baba O Riley," "The Real Me" (the little-heard single version), "Long Live Rock," "Slip Kid," "Who Are You," "You Better You Bet"...you get the picture. The box set went through several versions before earning the Who's full approval. "It really is quite good," Townshend pronounces.

Nothing quite prepares one for the blueness of Pete Townshend's eyes when they engage yours in conversation. A few shades lighter than a summer sky, it's a soft yet intense blue, accentuated, somehow, by the stone-washed blue denim prison jacket and plain gray T-shirt Pete is wearing for his round of interviews. It's a blue that telegraphs a restless intelligence and spirituality. A blue that offers a startling, instant insight into the man who, after all, wrote "Behind Blue Eyes." A tall guy, Townshend carries his height self-consciously when he first enters a room, as if embarrassed by it. In his youth, he molded that awkward self-awareness into the voice of a generation. In the Sixties, Townshend pinpointed, personified and made great rock out of the inarticulate rage and erupting sense of self that are a universal part of the teenage condition. That's why the Who's music is as vital today as it was then.

Along with Bob Dylan and John Lennon, Townshend is part of the original triumvirate of rock and roll intellectuals. But more than those other two guys, Townshend has always been a musician's musician, the son of two professional musicians, deeply steeped in jazz, classical and other musical styles that lie beyond the pale of rock. No mere basher, Pete Townshend has thought as long and hard about melody and harmony as he has about everything else in life. But always in the service of rock. He may have elevated rock to the level of narrative art with *Tommy*, but he used good, honest power chords to do it. He is the man directly responsible for the invention of the Marshall stack. Townshend's pioneering use of feedback and other forms of creative guitar abuse had a profound and direct influence on Jimi Hendrix, giving him the basic guitar palette he used to make his own stunning contribution to rock. Wherever there's been a major upheaval in rock over the past 30 years—from psychedelia, to punk, to power pop, to today's noise guitar bands—something of Pete Townshend's relentlessly experimental, amp-frying, neck-splintering spirit has been in attendance.

GUITAR WORLD: How does it feel to see the Who turn 30 this year?
PETE TOWNSHEND: Well, in a way, what's turned 30 is the name. [*laughs*] And it's interesting to see that it still has value. But increasingly, ever since I've had the box set in my hands these last few weeks, I've got a sense that, more than ever, the Who is something that *was* rather than something that *is*. The creative life of the Who was about 18 years, from 1964 to 1982. There's been talk about the hundreds or millions of reunions and revisits we've had. But in the years that followed 1982, we've only done a couple of things together. So in a way, it's 30 years of repackaging! [*laughs*] But, for once, this is repackaging that's worthy of the name, I think. The box set really is a great package. I'm very proud of it, very moved by it. And in a way I feel very released by its release. I feel it's given me an opportunity to look at the band with the kind of perspective that I don't think I had even five or six years ago.
GW: What sort of insights have emerged from that?

TOWNSHEND: No great revelations, particularly. But certainly a feeling that the band had an experimental side which was fairly impish, impudent and adventurous. I've often been perceived as somebody who is very serious about rock and roll and perhaps sometimes even serious about myself. And that's been some sort of black ticket for the Who. I think the box set offers a more realistic view of the band, and of rock. Rock is very, very important and very, very ridiculous. A good example is Roy Orbison in the "Dream Baby" years—going on [*British TV's*] *Top of the Pops* in a black leather cowboy hat, but with that incredible voice, that fantastic guitar playing and that beautiful composition.

That was the sublime and the ridiculous mixed together. Or, as I said earlier, the important and the ridiculous. And that's the prevailing feeling you get from the Who. We didn't take ourselves entirely seriously, but neither did we buck the issues.

GW: Where did you first get your interest in the pop song as a storytelling medium?

TOWNSHEND: Well, you heard the first truly great pop songs and you were hooked, as far as I was concerned. "Cathy's Clown," "Hello Mary Lou," "Three Steps to Heaven"—songs of that quality, a lot of which came out of a Nashville-based songwriting tradition which I suppose was started by somebody like Hank Williams and developed into a more elegant style of…not so much storytelling, but what I call *vignetting*. Creating little vignettes, little views, sushi-like slices of life. And I just loved that music—the way the guitar was used as an orchestral instrument. So from the time I was 10, 11 or 12 and started to hear that kind of great American pop music, I was hooked into it. There was Buddy Holly, who actually created characters, like Peggy Sue, you know. I think that's when I got into the pop song.

A few years later, when I was about 15 or 16, I started getting seriously into r&b. As so many people did, I started to move away from the idea that the pop song was an important medium in any sense. But I rediscovered the pop song fairly quickly. You know, today I read an interview that Roger [*Daltrey*] did in Britain, where he said that he fought really hard against the idea of the Who being a pop band

almost up until *Tommy*. That was something I wasn't really aware of. From my point of view, when British kids who were in bands discovered r&b, what they discovered was a new way to write pop songs which was purely British, in much the same way that the songs I mentioned earlier were purely American.
GW: A way of adapting that musical tradition.
TOWNSHEND: Yeah, possibly because [r&b] came from a bleaker lifestyle. From our point of view in Britain, America in the Fifties was a very, very affluent country. You know, when I was eight or nine years old, I'd never seen chewing gum, never had a glass of cold milk, never seen frozen peas, never ridden in a car… And so the American servicemen we knew had this mysterious lifestyle. They had fridges with ice cubes. The kids had toys. I mean it was just bizarre. So for us in Britain, we probably responded to the message of the underclass that blues created. Because we felt like an underclass. Not compared to America. But an underclass compared to the people that had a sense of purpose through being in the military or being good Christians or whatever.
GW: When you were 13 or so, were there any guitarists you would have killed to sound like?
TOWNSHEND: The first guitarists I listened to were country players and pop players. People like James Burton playing with Rick Nelson. Burton is probably the most important guitar player in American music, in some ways. And he's still very undervalued in that respect, but only because he was with Rick Nelson, who is also completely undervalued as an artist and is now tragically dead. [*Nelson died in 1985.*] Tragically, because I think by now we would have woken up and realized that just because he was on a TV show [*Ozzie and Harriet*] doesn't mean to say that he was a schmuck. His records are fucking great. And he really was a great artist who knew what good music was, and he surrounded himself with great musicians. And God, he was beautiful, too. Had it all, really. But where was I?
GW: James Burton…
TOWNSHEND: Yeah, that kind of guitar player was extraordinary to listen to because he was the first guy I ever heard make a normal gui-

tar sound like a pedal steel, bending those strings, which was also something that came out of the blues and connected blues up with pop: the bendy-string phenomenon. It must be hard for guitar players today to even understand the difficulty of bending a string in 1962. The string sets they sold back then only came in one heavy gauge. But Burton hit on the idea of using two second strings instead of a second and a third, and that made bending much easier. So the second was usually very slack, and usually much too loud because it resonated too much and was tuned too low. So the string balance would be bad.

I also studied Chet Atkins, another country player, and I'm very good at reproducing his fingerpicking style. It might surprise people, but I can do all that stuff. Maybe not as well as what's-his-face [*Mark Knopfler*] from Dire Straits, but I can play it.

And I listened to Wes Montgomery, Barney Kessel and Johnny Smith a little bit—the guitar players of my father's music era, really. [*Pete's father, Cliff, was a successful dance-band saxophonist in Britain.*] That kind of stylish lounge jazz guitar playing. I suppose Wes Montgomery was the top gun. There's a certain lyricism to what he did that I try and shoot for in my solos. And then later, when I got into the blues, I started listening to guitar playing in a different way. I loved John Lee Hooker for the visceral style of his early electric recordings. And then there was a whole rush of other guitar players. Jazz players like Kenny Burrell, who played with [*organist*] Jimmy Smith. And, going back to Kenny Burrell's influences, people like Charlie Christian.

But really, I wasn't a guitar purist. To me, the guitar was always a second instrument, bizarrely enough. I wanted to be like my father: a saxophone player. And when I couldn't get a note out of a reed, he suggested I try what was then his second instrument, guitar. So I always felt like I was playing a second instrument, a not-very-important instrument, but one that had been appropriated by rock and roll because it was sexy and by the blues because it was cheap. You could make one. In fact, the first guitar I ever played had been made for my best friend by his father. And the very fact that I was able to get a tune out of this thing, which was strung with piano wire, made my father decide to help me progress on the guitar.

I've got two strains to me. One side is the pure music lover/musicologist/aficionado of music, which grew out of my life with my father, who was a superb musician and very highly valued in his own business. But there's another side of me that got into the idea of rock and roll—its socio-political function, if you will, more than its musical content.

So the guitar for me has always been a gun. And the only thing you could do with a machine gun in the Sixties was break it across your legs, and that's what I did. I suppose that I do sometimes sit down with an acoustic guitar and try to use the guitar as an instrument of love and communication. But even the way I play acoustic is very aggressively rhythmic. My best work is rhythmic and machine gunny.

GW: That jazz side emerges on compositions like "Sunrise" [from 1967's *The Who Sell Out*]. The chord changes are quite opulent, harmonically.

TOWNSHEND: There's a kind of Mickey Baker influence there, really. He's another guitarist I listened to—a side man in the Stan Kenton band or something like that. Occasionally he used to play a solo, but what was lovely about him was his chord work. And also his instruction books [Mickey Baker's Complete Course in Jazz Guitar, *(Lewis Music)*], which showed you how to translate the normal kinds of triads and groups of chords from the popular songs of the day into chords that had more interest and more harmonic tension.

GW: One hallmark of your style is the way you shift chord shapes around on the high strings while sustaining the open D, A or E string. "Substitute" is perhaps the earliest example of your doing so. Where does that come from?

TOWNSHEND: It might have come from the fact that, for a long time, I couldn't afford strings. So after I'd broken a couple of strings, I used to take the strings that were left and group them together in the middle of the guitar and make up chord shapes around them. So I think that I was actually working in a kind of early bluegrass style of harmonic playing, where you're playing as many as two or three strings open, with a dulcimer-like technique—but then trying to make it sound like rock and roll. I was certainly inventing new fingerings, those fingerings being very simple. But also remember that the first band I had with John Entwistle was a traditional jazz band [*the Confederates*] and I played banjo. So I started listening to banjo players, and to bluegrass playing in particular.

GW: And bluegrass five-string banjo has that drone string.

TOWNSHEND: Exactly. When I was very young, I spotted an important link: I was 18 or 19 years old, listening to Ozark Mountain music and Baroque music at the same time. And I thought, "This is the same stuff!" If you go back to their roots, there's only about 50 years between the styles. You know, Ozark music was a bunch of Swedes that got on a boat and went to America and colonized a mountain. A lot of banjo music, a lot of hillbilly music, is Swedish folk music. That song by Abba called "Arrival" [*he sings the melody*] is a combination of Northern European Christian Baroque music and hillbilly changes. And I really locked into that. I got a real heart buzz from that kind of Northern European stuff—the feeling that there was something stately about it, as well. And I think I was always trying to find some way to bring that into my playing with the Who. I still find that delightful—to find a new way of playing a group of chords where there can be a sympathetic note that runs throughout.

GW: You've said that the chordal structure for the bridge to "I'm a Boy" and the intro to "Pinball Wizard" were inspired by [*English Baroque composer Henry*] Purcell.

TOWNSHEND: Yeah. Purcell did this very short piece called "Symphony upon One Note." It's a very plaintive piece, almost like the [*20th-century U.S. composer*] Samuel Barber composition "Adagio for Strings." Only the Purcell piece was written in 1600 or something. And throughout that whole piece runs a single bowed note. I found that a stunning thing to call upon while I was in the process of writing. I analyzed every single chord in the piece and found ways to play them on guitar. And, yeah, I used a group of those chords in "I'm a Boy."

GW: What's the real story of the guitar solo on "I Can't Explain"? It's sometimes attributed to Jimmy Page. Other reports have it that you and Page both cut very similar-sounding solos, and no one is sure which one made it to the final mix.

TOWNSHEND: The solo? No, the solo's me. Jimmy doesn't play like that.

GW: Thank you. You know, there are those who still insist it's Page.

TOWNSHEND: Jimmy was there at the session to play lead guitar, but no, he didn't do the solo. There was a [session] drummer there, too; I can't remember his name. Keith Moon just threw the guy's drums out the door. But Jimmy was a friend of mine. We'd had a mutual girlfriend. There was a girl who worked for our manager, Kit Lambert. I was going out with her around the time that we made that record. And she'd gone out with Jimmy before and was still, you know…kinda hooked on him—for a little longer than I was comfortable with. Anyway, she was much older than us. We were 19 and 20 and she was about 30. And a fucking sexy woman! She'd obviously fucked him to death and then proceeded to fuck me to death. And we had her in common. We were both kind of cross-eyed with this woman. So when Jimmy showed up at the studio, we just started to talk about what we always talked about, which was her. "What's she going through? Has she called you? Has she called me?" And then I said to him [*in affable tones*], "What are you doing here?" He said, "I'm here to give some weight to the guitar. I'm going to double the rhythm guitar on the overdubs." And I said, "Oh, great." And he said, "What are you going to play?" "A Rick 12," I told him. And he said, "Oh, okay, I'll play a…" whatever it was. It was all very congenial. But meanwhile, Keith was over in the corner, telling the drummer, "Get out of the fucking studio or I'll kill ya! On a Who record, only Keith Moon plays the drums!" That kind of stuff. And the backing vocals were done by some surf band.

GW: The Ivy League, yeah.

TOWNSHEND: I think [*producer*] Shel Talmy didn't have much money and didn't have much understanding of what the band was about. As far as he was concerned, we were a phenomenon that would come and go and be finished in a month.

GW: Were you sort of meant to be his next Kinks?
TOWNSHEND: That's right, yeah. Well, we were. He recorded "My Generation." He got a great sound.
GW: Your discovery of feedback has been well documented. But what about other "found" sounds on guitar that you pioneered in the early days—like flipping the toggle switch rhythmically or scraping the mic stand across the strings? Were those things as accidental as your discovery of feedback?
TOWNSHEND: No, they were very considered. They were all part of that art school tradition I'd got, of breaking the rules. I was at an art school where the course was dedicated to breaking the rules and I just drafted that into my work as a guitar player. Most of the techniques I used were very virulent, violent and aggressively expressive. Because, as I said, I was in this mode where the guitar was a weapon. And, wonderful though my Fender Pro amp sounded, it wasn't loud enough. So I went out and bought a Fender Bassman as well and plugged into both. And, wonderful though that was, it wasn't loud enough either. So I went to Jim Marshall's [*then a music store in London*], threw down my Fender Bassman and said, "I want that, twice as loud." And, almost like Krupps, the military manufacturer, Jim Marshall's eyes sort of lit up and he said, "I will supply this man with the weapon he requires." And from that came the Marshall stack and the big amplifiers of the Sixties.

The toggle switch thing was literally to make the guitar sound like a machine gun—*dah dah dah dah dah*—when it was feeding back. And when I bought my first Rickenbacker, I packed it with paper and found I could actually produce feedback on select harmonics, which was quite extraordinary. You can hear it briefly on "Anyway, Anyhow, Anywhere." And I could reproduce it live. I could actually do that by moving the guitar in relationship to the speakers and get harmonics. That was extraordinary to me, to be able to reproduce that live. And as long as I kept that guitar—which was briefly, unfortunately—I could do it. It was a stunning example of how we were able to reproduce very difficult studio recordings live. Not that our records sounded very good, anyway.

GW: Were you playing through Marshalls with your Rickenbacker 12-string by the time you recorded singles like "Anyway, Anyhow, Anywhere" and "I Can't Explain"?

TOWNSHEND: No, that was probably a Fender Pro with the internal speaker disconnected and the amp running into a 4 x 12 cabinet. Or else a Fender Pro and Fender Bassman. I might have had a Marshall by then, but I don't remember that I used them in the studio. You know, I never liked them. I liked the cabinets. But I wasn't really happy until Sound City started to make amplifiers. They became Hiwatts. I was much happier with the slabby sound they made. Marshall didn't exactly copy the Fender Bassman. They found they couldn't do it because of the way the power rail was constructed, so the treble was overweighted by the bass when you went into deep distortion. And somehow, in the HiWatt design, they found some way to improve the power rail feed to the treble side, much in the way that Boogie has done it now, by cascading power rails.

GW: Exactly when did you change to Hiwatt?

TOWNSHEND: Very quickly; I only used Marshalls for a short period of time. It was by the time Jimi Hendrix hit the U.K., which was 1967, pre-Monterey. He came to see me at IBC Studios and asked me what kind of amplifiers he should buy. Well, he didn't actually say anything. [*Hendrix manager*] Chas Chandler asked me what sort of amplifiers Jimi should buy. And I said, "Well, I like Hiwatts—or Sound City, as they were then called—but he might prefer Marshall." And Jimi said, "I'll have one of each." For the first two dates that I saw, he was kind of using both. And I think he preferred Marshall. But anyway, around '67 is when I switched to Hiwatt.

GW: Did you have a lot of opportunity to hang out with Hendrix? Jam with him?

TOWNSHEND: No, I would never have dreamed of jamming with him. Get out of here.

GW: Because there's an interview segment with Roger in the new video [*30 Years of Maximum R&B Live*] about a jam he witnessed under a stage somewhere. Hendrix was playing and so was [*Mamas and Papas vocalist*] Cass Elliot.

TOWNSHEND: That was at Monterey. But I wouldn't...I wasn't jamming. Jimi was on acid. And he stood on a chair. And I was trying to get him to talk to me about the fact that I didn't want the Who to follow him onto the stage. John Phillips [*also of the Mamas and Papas, and an organizer of the Monterey festival*] was there. I don't remember if Mama Cass was. And I was saying to Jimi, "For fuck's sake, Jimi, listen to me. I don't want to go on after you. It's bad enough that you're here. It's bad enough that you're gonna fuck up my life. I'm not gonna have you steal my act. That's the only thing I've got. You're a great genius. The audience will appreciate that. But what do I do? I wear a Union Jack jacket and smash my guitar. Give me a break. Let the Who go on first." And he was kind of, I thought, teasing me. You know, playing the guitar and ignoring me. But Brian Jones told me later on that he was just fucking completely whacked on acid. So John Phillips flipped a coin and it came down in my favor, and I said, "Right. We go on first." And that has become apocryphally told as a story where I was arguing with Jimi. I was shouting at Jimi, yes, because he was ignoring me. [*laughs*] But I wasn't angry with him. I loved him very much. I got to know him in L.A. [*after Monterey*] I came to L.A. and spent some time here, and Jimi was hanging out here, and suddenly—maybe it was a different bunch of drugs he was using—he was very affectionate and friendly to me. And he'd started to acknowledge some of the things that I'd done to help his career. Such as they were. I don't mean to imply that I'd done all that much. But the Jimi Hendrix Experience were on Track Records [in England], which is the Who's record label. And we helped them with early dates and stuff. And, obviously, I was a stone supporter of his work. I was like a press machine on his behalf. And then he died. [*pauses*] So I never got real close to him. And I certainly never played with him.

GW: Your backwards guitar work on "Armenia City in the Sky" is phenomenal, especially given the recording technology that existed in 1967. What was the inspiration for that? What do you recall about recording that?

TOWNSHEND: Nothing. [*laughs*] I suppose by then I was pretty adept at recording—certainly more so than the so-called producers and engineers that we worked with in the studio. So I was probably quite adept at backwards recording because I was doing it at home. I was certainly the first person I knew of, outside jazz, after Les Paul, to have a fully equipped multitrack recording studio at home. I think I helped break the ground for the idea that the artist's technical understanding of the medium he works in is important. That it's like, for example, a painter knowing that there are certain acids or oils or pigments in the paints they use that will make the paint lay on in a particular way. It was important for musicians to learn what goes on in a studio. So that when you came up with an idea, you knew it was possible, rather than having the man in the control room tell you, "Yeah, we would have an atomic bomb explosion on the fucking record, but unfortunately we can't do it, shithead. So get back out there and do as you're told." Which was very much the tone of the recording sessions that we were first presented with. On our first album, I was only allowed into the control room to hear playbacks, because [*engineer*] Glyn Johns had told Shel Talmy I was interested in recording. John, Roger and Keith didn't get in.

GW: So when you broke with Shel Talmy, and your managers, Kit Lambert and Terrance Stamp, became your producers, you got the creative freedom you wanted?

TOWNSHEND: It wasn't that we wanted creative freedom; we wanted to have fun with the studio. Kit Lambert knew nothing about recording. I mean, we wanted to see what happened when you sawed a tape machine in half. The answer was, you got a big studio bill! We went straight in at the deep end, you know? "What happens when you plug this into this...?" BANG!!!

GW: After going to those kinds of sonic extremes on *A Quick One* and *The Who Sell Out*, the guitar on *Tommy* seems like a move away from the big amps, big volume, big feedback sort of stuff. Was that an intentional shift?

TOWNSHEND: Well, it was a shift that was very much in key with—in the same universe as—the shift in my songwriting approach at that time. Which was a move away from the way the Who had been performing and writing pop songs. We'd been nominated by our audience, in a way, to express their own inarticulacy—if that's not a contradiction in terms. But we suddenly found ourselves in a vacant place, lost in the world of Jimi Hendrix and Cream. Cream had come over to the U.S.A. with us for the first time, with loud amplifiers and psychedelic shirts. These were, to some extent, new bands. Compared to them, the Who were an older band. So we were feeling quite out of touch, thinking, "We're not selling singles anymore and neither do we fit into this new psychedelic era. We're not an experimental band like the Pink Floyd. We're not a guitar-based blues band like the Cream. We don't have the kind of extreme genius of Hendrix. What do we do?" And I started to look at *composition* as a big issue.

In writing *Tommy*, I was very meticulous about making sure the composition and the harmonies were very structured and clean. I think it was maybe the first cohesive piece in which I used quite a lot of piano, really. That was probably the first time that I voiced guitar to piano chords in a big way. "Pinball Wizard" was written on guitar, but "Amazing Journey" was written on the piano. "I'm Free" was actually written on a Lowery organ and voiced for guitar afterwards. "Sally Simpson" was written on guitar, but a lot of the other stuff was written on keyboards. The guitars came afterwards. So I think a lot of care went into the way that the guitar was used to reinforce what I had on the piano.

GW: It's a much more orchestral use of guitar.

TOWNSHEND: By that time, I was working in almost a new medium—a new way of writing. I was less conscious of "this has got to be a little vignette," and more conscious of "this has got to be a series of vignettes which add up to something." And if it's not through-composed [*a classical music term for a piece of music that has no repeating themes*], it's got to be through-integrity.

GW: So that was a case where the superstructure came first, before the individual songs?

TOWNSHEND: Yes.

GW: The *Who's Next* album emerged out of another extended conceptual piece of yours, *Lifehouse*, which you ended up discarding.

Was it simply a matter of taking the best songs that came out of *Lifehouse* and using them for *Who's Next*?

TOWNSHEND: By the time that album was recorded, for the third time in my life, with Glyn Johns at Olympic Studios, I had very little interest in it. I'd been fucking damaged by the *Lifehouse* project. I'd come up with this fantastic idea, sold it to Universal Pictures, got a budget together, came back to London and convinced Frank Dunlop down at the Young Vic Theatre that this was going to be the great follow-up to *Tommy*, worked with all kinds of extraordinary people in looking at computer programs, quadraphonic sound systems—and then realized that the Who's managers were using hard drugs. I had a double album's worth of songs, which were just demos for *Lifehouse*, examples of what might actually happen. Because it was going to be a film about a concert, through which there would be woven a number of different stories. And the Who's job was simply to do the concert. That was very difficult, because I was being somewhat duplicitous, saying "You just be the band, guys, and I'll concentrate on the rest of it. No need for you to really know what's going on here." But they kept pressing; they wanted to know what was going on. And the more I tried to explain it, the more I realized I was Einstein to their cavemen. They just didn't get it. Today, the sort of things I was talking about then have become like child's play. Ideas like virtual reality, for instance. And Oliver Stone has made a movie about the moral and ethical implications of something like experience on the internet. It just seemed to me to be basic art school stuff, which they were not getting. Nobody was getting it.

And, in the end, I had an actual nervous breakdown. So by the time we were in the studio making *Who's Next* we had great music, and we were playing great because we'd recorded the album something like 15 fucking times! Glyn Johns had a very easy job. He made the record in two weeks. It sounded very fresh, somehow. And then he said, "I think this should be a single album." I said, "But we've got 26 songs!" But he persisted, "Well I think it will be better as a single album." And that's what we got. And it was better as a single album—for commercial reasons. But then [*in mock pretentious tones*], I'm a composer, you know.

GW: You began using synthesizers during that period. Did that alter your approach to guitar in any way?

TOWNSHEND: Well, there was the promise early on of the two things becoming one. I was involved with A.R.P. in the development of the first guitar synthesizer, which was bizarrely called the Avatar [*which in Sanskrit refers to an incarnation of God on earth*] because I used to follow [*Indian spiritual master*] Meher Baba, who was one of the many avatars. Well, I still do follow Meher Baba, but a number of other people have decided to call themselves avatars as well since he died. Anyway, A.R.P. made me a guitar interface. So when my A.R.P. 2500 studio synthesizer landed in the middle of the recording studio, it came with a guitar interface. It was only a single-string interface, but I was playing with note-tracking and envelope-following synthesizer devices in 1971. I was also trying to create crude computer programs at the time by writing systems on paper which would then dictate the way, for example, I might cut up a piece of tape. Or use a number of musical motifs, which would then be repeated in series. It was very much that [*avant garde composer*] Terry Riley-style of composition that was happening at the time. I was starting to look at ways in which music could be used to very literally and accurately reflect certain statistical information about a human being. [*The synth part to the song "Baba O'Riley" was created by programming biographical statistics about Meher Baba into a synthesizer.*] So I was right in there with the other people who were doing early computer music. But at the same time, I was bangin' away at rock and roll and drinking lots of brandy.

GW: A productive combination, apparently.

TOWNSHEND: Well, it produced a great album, and it was a great time for the Who. *Who's Next* is a great record; there's no question about it. But what you hear on the album is a bunch of demos, really, for a much bigger idea. *Lifehouse* will almost certainly be a CD-ROM one day, because that's the only way I could cover all the ground that we went over in preparing the project. I mean, I had meetings with [*avant garde composer*] Karlheinz Stockhausen and with Roger Powell, who was an engineer with A.R.P. at the time. This was before he joined Todd Rundgren. We'd just brainstorm ideas. We actually invented a machine that would play guitar notes backwards. It was a helical wheel with a [recording] tape wrapped around it. The top part of the wheel revolved forwards and the bottom part revolved backwards. There was a group of record heads on one side and a group of playback heads on the other side. You would play a note and the note would travel from one side to the other. Immediately after you played the note, it would be reproduced backwards. And as far as I can remember, it worked!

But anyway, those are the kinds of things I was exploring, and it would be great to reexplore some of that. For me it was also bound up with some ideas from Sufi [*an Islamic sect*] literature and modern science: how the spiritual effect of music, the energizing effect of music, can be explained with modern laws of physics. The way we are affected by vibrations and how the world is made up of vibrations. This is the side of me I mentioned earlier—the pure music lover. For me, *Lifehouse* was a way of inhabiting the world I love most, which is trying to understand why music is so poetic. Why music is so spiritual. Why, at its most violent and nihilistic, rock music is capable of spiritual uplift. It was something that I was grappling with. And out of that came *Who's Next*.

GW: At the other end of the spectrum, tell me about the Who's turn to a harder rock sound around the years '69, '70 and '71.

TOWNSHEND: You know, all that happened was we had *Tommy* out there, we were out on the road a lot and we became a really extraordinary machine. We were a fucking great band. We were briefly called The Greatest Rock and Roll Band in the World, and we were. There was no question about it. I used to wake up on the stage every night and think, "Oh my God, I'm riding this horse again!" It just got to be so extraordinary. We just got very good at what we did.

GW: While other guitarists of that era did lots of blues-based, riff-oriented soloing, the Who were doing more thematic improvisations on stage—little musical segments, chordal things, melodies that all wove into one another. Was all that spontaneously created on the stage?

TOWNSHEND: Yeah. I could play anything and John would follow me. Absolutely anything—even atonal stuff—and he could follow me. We can still do that to this very day. He jumped up on stage with me at the Wiltern Theater last year, when I brought *Psychoderelict* to L.A. He was halfway into a bottle of claret and he stood up there, and everything I did, he was right on top of me. Not behind me. He was on *top* of me.

GW: What moved you at the time of *Quadrophenia*—in the depths of rock's post-hippy, early-Seventies doldrums—to look back to the [early-Sixties] Mod scene?

TOWNSHEND: I actually felt that I'd lost my original brief as a writer, as a result of being introduced to stadium rock and being one of the main proponents of stadium rock. I'd lost the specific sense of writing for Roger's voice within the Who, and of giving him words to sing that expressed the feelings of inarticulacy, dislocation and frustration of the audience that we grew up with. I felt I'd lost that. I used to look out into an audience of 86,000 people and think, "What do they want me to do? I don't know. There's just too many of them." So, in *Quadrophenia*, I went back to examine what happened. And to address the fact that the Who, as four members, each a facet obviously voted onto the stage by an individual—Jimmy, in the story—had abandoned that individual, just as everything else in Jimmy's life abandons him. I wanted to try and work that out. And I think I did reestablish that connection, and then realized there was no way I could speak to those people anymore. Because I was too rich, too successful, and I'd spent too much time in America and not enough time in the Goldhawk Social Club in Shepherd's Bush. So it was over for me. It was a bitter pill, to use a cliché. And when *Quadrophenia* failed to be a good piece for the Who on stage, that was an extra slap on the wrist for me. 'Cause I suddenly felt, "Well, this revisiting Mod looks like nostalgia, or going over the same ground again."

It was a good album for the Who, and an important album. But the place where it worked best, strangely enough, was America, where, though it wasn't a huge success, the people who latched onto it found it to be very important in their lives. For them it's one of those rock albums that you can't imagine not having had in your life—because of that feeling of abandonment that comes when you're about 16 or 17 or 18 and somehow all the rugs are pulled out from under you. And you throw yourself down. Abandonment leads you to a spiritual question, a spiritual opportunity. You know, "Love Reign O'er Me," sitting on the rock thinking "What happens now?" I didn't provide any answers, of course, but *Quadrophenia* really would stand up to revisiting, I think. In fact, I've been thinking about that quite a lot.

GW: Fast forwarding in time, how did the post-Keith Moon Who affect your guitar playing?

TOWNSHEND: In a really good way. Not because of Keith's not being there. But having to put a new band together enabled me to bring into the Who something I'd always wanted, which was another harmonic element. And I discovered John "Rabbit" Bundrick while working with Ronnie Lane on *Rough Mix*. As soon as he played with me, I realized he was absolutely unique among keyboard players in his understanding of guitar voicing. He knew what notes were not being played. My voicing on guitar is very important. Often there'll be two-note or three-note chords at most, whether I'm playing six strings or not. The fingerings are all about trying to cover so that you've never got four-note chords: an inference of complexity where often there was none. And Rabbit was so locked into that. I'd play a chord, he'd restate it, and I could play over it. So my guitar playing changed because I felt liberated by that. I think my solo playing improved. I became more expressive. As I practiced, I became slightly faster. It was not a great time for the Who, unfortunately, but a good time for me. [*dismissively, after a pause*] Well, we made a few good cuts....

GW: On which Who album are you happiest with Roger's vocal interpretation of what you had written?

TOWNSHEND: Well, actually, the most difficult was *Who by Numbers*, which happens to be one of his favorites. I wrote these very personal, difficult songs and he sang them incredibly well. He wasn't at all in the same place as me, emotionally. I was very disaffected, becoming very alcoholic, very perturbed about Keith using extraordinary drug cocktails which I knew would get him in the end, and maybe having my first marriage problems; I don't know. But I was very unhappy in the Who at that time, and I think that came out in the work. What was extraordinary was the way Roger took that unhappiness into his own work and sang it. I just think that's incredible.

GW: Do you have any plans to work again with Roger and John, either as the Who or in any other context?

TOWNSHEND: No. No. The opportunity is there in kind of a veiled way, 'cause they've got this band they're doing, Roger's "Music of Pete Townshend," which is his orchestral experiment. But no, I actually really feel that I've finally let go. I think I haven't been entirely honest about this in the past. You know, I said no and then decided, "Well, I don't have to say no. I might change my mind." I've been playing around with it. And of course the people it's been hurting most haven't been the fans or the record company, but really Roger and John. They've been drumming their fingers, waiting to see whether the whim will take me to go and work with them. So I finally said to them, "Well, listen, go ahead and do what you like. I'll be there for you. I'll come with the oxygen, but I'm not going to go on the stage." I enjoyed my solo tour last year very much. At Jones Beach, in New York, I discovered that I could go out like Bruce Springsteen and run around for three and three quarter hours and do a show where, for weeks afterward on the streets of New York, people were stopping me, grabbing me by the shoulders and saying "That was the best fucking rock and roll show I've ever seen in my fucking life! Do it again!" But having done that, I proved something to myself. Some demons have been cast away. I proved that, despite my thinning hair and graying beard, my lungs are still good and I can still do it. But I don't necessarily want to. For the first time ever, really, this month, this past couple of weeks, the Who really does feel like it's over. You know, the box set has got quite a lot to do with it, I think. The fact that I liked it so much and I've come back to look at my relationships with Roger and John. I had a really good conversation with Roger, and I hope to have a conversation with John on the same subject. I think for the first time I've said to them both, "Fuck what anybody thinks. You're still the Who. I'll be there for you if you want to do something. I'll write some songs if you like. I'll be there in the studio. But I'm not gonna do the road work." I don't want to go to fucking China...go to Columbia and get fucking shot. You know, give me the Bel Air Hotel, Los Angeles, or my home in Twickenham, which looks much the same. [*Flashing his "wicked" grin.*] I'm rich and famous and that's what I've got and I'm sticking with it. I don't have to do that fucking Harlem Globetrotters shit anymore. I suppose I could mention Keith Moon and say it would never be the same, but I don't think that's what it's about. I think that when Roger, John and I are together, there's enough of us present for there to be a quorum, as they say, and you sense Keith almost by his absence. But I just *don't wanna do it*, you know. I went out in '89 [*for the Who's 25th Anniversary Tour*] pretty much for the money and ended up loving it, 'cause it was such a cruise. But I think for the first time ever I can tell myself—and be really honest—that even if I had not a single penny in the bank, even if I were about to go to jail for bankruptcy, I still wouldn't do it. So partly with that in mind, and partly due to the fact that *Tommy* keeps me busy—with productions happening around the world—I know I've got plenty to do. But I am getting used to the idea that I have indeed finally let go.

Guitar World, February 1995

Peace of Mind

Musical trends may come and go, but Tom Scholz, Boston's reclusive rock man, couldn't care less.

By Alan di Perna

ALONG THE WOODED highway that leads north out of Boston stands a dingy red brick building. This unassuming structure houses Scholz Research & Development, birthplace of the Rockman and site of rehearsals for Boston's upcoming world tour. The first Boston tour since 1988, the dates herald the release of Boston's latest opus, *Walk On*. It's only the fourth Boston album since 1976, but then Tom Scholz moves to an internal clock very different from the chronometer that governs most people's lives. Like the Vampire Lestat, he seems to regard the passing decades as the briefest blinks of the eye.

A tall, lantern-jawed man, Scholz seems cramped in his company's tiny reception area. Surprisingly youthful, he looks much the same as he did in '76. Though the New England autumn is well under way, Scholz is dressed in thigh-length sweatshorts, a T-shirt and windbreaker. But then again, what else would a confirmed basketball sicko wear to work, particularly when he owns the place? After a vigorous handshake, Scholz's first act is to offer coffee.

"It's still morning for me," he laughs, "Even though it's late afternoon for everyone else."

Tom Scholz is a nocturnal creature. He's the quintessential crack-

Guitar World Presents CLASSIC ROCK

Tom Scholz of Boston

pot Yankee inventor—late 20th Century style. An American original, he does things his own way. Let the rest of the world be danged. Sometime in the mid Seventies—having scored a Masters in mechanical engineering from the Massachusetts Institute of Technology (M.I.T.) and slaved in countless bar bands—Tom Scholz found his métier: analog audio and what would come to be known as classic rock. He has resolutely stuck with both while the rest of the world frittered its way through disco, synths, punk, digital, new wave, MTV, hair bands, grunge and CD-ROM.

Like Mr. Edison's lightbulb, Mr. Scholz's brand of rock and roll has proved an enduring invention. How many bong hits in how many carpeted vans parked in how many middle-American driveways have been sweetened by some Boston track or other? Tom Scholz's name has become synonymous with exquisitely layered guitar confections and, of course, with his invention, the Rockman, that tiny blue headphone preamp which changed the way rock records were made and spawned a whole guitar style of its own.

Scholz is the kind of guy who thinks nothing of designing and building a whole new studio to record an album. Which is exactly what he did to create *Walk On*. As always, Tom played 90 percent of the instruments on the disc, writing most of the material as well. His labor-intensive work habits are the main reason why there have only been four Boston albums in a period of 18 years. But like a bag of prime bud, a little Boston goes a long way.

Armed with a mug of half decaf and half hazelnut-flavored rocket fuel, Scholz leads the way into Boston's rehearsal room. The space is cluttered with vintage Hammond organ pieces, drums and Rockman amplification gear of every stripe. Planting himself on a spindly director's chair, Tom Scholz prepares to offer a piece of his highly iconoclastic mind.

GUITAR WORLD: The Boston sound hasn't changed much over the years.
TOM SCHOLZ: No. It can't. [*laughs*]
GW: You've never been one to bow to trends.

SCHOLZ: Well, it's easy not to, because I don't know what they are. I never listen to current music, except when I'm out shooting pool or when I go to the basketball court in the summer. Somebody always has a blaster going, or their car door's open with the radio on. There was a period of time a few years ago where I went to this one pool club that I liked. And they played...not dance music, but maybe you'd call it Top 40; Madonna and so forth. And after getting exposed to that once or twice a week for six months, all of a sudden I found I was starting to write dance music. I said, "Wow, this is scary." I had to deprogram myself. So I went to Boston Billiards, where they play rock and roll.

Boston has always been non-current, right from the very first album [*Boston*]. When that record came out in 1976, everybody said to me, "Wow, it's too bad that you didn't have this last year. Disco is the happening thing now. The radio stations are dropping rock and roll." And every time I've gotten a record done, there's always been some new thing that's the in style. But I feel that people just like good music. And without being egotistical, I think Boston makes good music. I wouldn't put it on tape if I didn't think it so. I know people who went to see the Elton John and Billy Joel tour who also buy Red Hot Chili Peppers albums. You can like Smashing Pumpkins *and* bands from the Seventies.

GW: When Nirvana's "Smells Like Teen Spirit" came out, everybody said, "The chorus sounds just like Boston's 'More Than a Feeling.' " Do you hear a similarity between the two songs?

SCHOLZ: You know, I don't want to insult them, but I don't know that song. I've heard some of their tunes played in pool clubs and I like them. But if that song does sound like "More Than a Feeling," I take it as a major compliment, even if it was completely accidental. I don't mean to imply that they borrowed it from me, 'cause I simply don't know.

GW: What did you get interested in first—music or electronics?

SCHOLZ: Good question. I was always a Junior Engineer type. I made model airplanes and cars. I was into go-karts at a pretty young age. On the other hand, I've been into classical music since I was three or four. I'd sit in front of the huge speaker that my parents had—it was mono then—and blast out their classical collection. I think my mother let me do that because she was glad to have me out of her hair and know where I was at the same time. So I've been doing both things since I was very young.

GW: What was your first instrument?

SCHOLZ: Piano. I had lessons and learned how to play classical piano. Actually, I got through a few fairly well-known pieces; not that I can play them now. In fact, I can't read music anymore, either. But I used to, back when I was in fifth or sixth grade. Then I quit the piano and didn't start again until I heard the Kinks, the Who, the Yardbirds…the English rebellious-type bands. That's when I got into rock and roll. I started learning how to play keyboards by ear. I'd try to play the rock songs I liked on piano. And that turned into playing organ in bands, which is what got me into guitar. I always thought that the way the guitar player was playing wasn't as good as what I heard on the records—this was strictly cover bands. So I decided to try guitar myself. I've been trying ever since! [*laughs*]

Keyboards were a snap. I can stay away from those things for years and then come back and play just fine. But guitar is a constant struggle. It's like basketball. If you don't do it every week you lose it.

GW: Do you practice regularly?

SCHOLZ: No. I practice very irregularly. I'm torn between so many other things that I choose to do or have to do. I end up spending an enormous amount of time working as a producer, recording engineer and songwriter. And I play all the other instruments on Boston records. So between bass, keyboards, drum parts and just simply playing guitar parts in the studio, I get very little time to practice the thing. I'm trying to make up for that now. We're getting ready to go out on the road in 10 days. I don't want to be the weak sister. *Walk On* has some very demanding parts, both on guitar and keyboards.

GW: How soon after *Third Stage* did you begin writing material for *Walk On*?

SCHOLZ: I started right after we stopped touring, in 1988. I also decided to build a new studio at that point. The old one was getting too outdated. I had a concept for putting a studio together that would make it possible for me to bypass most of the time that was required by production work. The idea was for me to be able to go into the studio and be a musician and an arranger and songwriter, as opposed to an engineer and producer.

In a typical studio situation, you might spend eight hours trying to get a guitar or drum sound. I wanted to find a way to get past all that screwing around. So I took my best shot at a production sound for all the instruments that I like to use—drums, bass, Clavinet, Hammond organ, a bunch of electric guitar sounds, acoustics—and preset those sounds in all the equipment that was required. And I built some other gadgets where I could select one or the other at will. For example, if I'm working on an organ track for one tune, and I want to try a guitar idea for something else, I can push two buttons, put on the guitar and roll tape, play and get a real good, finished, master sound.

GW: Is this all accomplished via Rockman modules?

SCHOLZ: Yeah. My studio is wall-to-wall blue—all Rockman units, because the Rockman stuff is obviously designed to get a sound that I like. Everything ends up going through Rockman modules sooner or later. The guitars certainly do. I'll fool around a little with a tube amp here and there, but 99 percent of it is Rockman stuff, straight-in, direct. The keyboards are all processed through Rockman Sustainers, Rockman preamps and the Rockman choruses. The Rockman chorus is certainly part of my secret for getting that widely dispersed stereo sound where you can't find its center. I first became fascinated with that kind of really wide stereo spectrum when I heard the song "Hocus Pocus" by Focus. That had a lot to do with the kind of production I went for in Boston.

GW: Since your new studio is optimized for you to work alone, is it one big room? Or did you go with a conventional control room/recording room design?

SCHOLZ: No, there's no separate room this time. By the end of *Third Stage*, that separate room was nothing more than a place to store junk. Who needs it? I feel lost if I go in a commercial studio and I have to go off in a separate room and play something. In fact, I tried that with a piano track for *Walk On*, and it reminded me of why I make records by myself; trying to explain to another person where the punch point is going to be and what isn't right about the headphone mix is just too time-consuming for me. The way I record, I don't have to communicate with people, and it saves an incredible amount of time. If I tried to do one of those Boston records in a normal studio situation, forget it. I'd only finish one record in my life. That would be it. I'd have to retire after that. I wouldn't have time for a second one.

GW: You were one of the first to blur the line between musician and engineer/producer.

SCHOLZ: Yeah, I did the basics and even a few of the vocals for the first album in the basement of my apartment house. I knew I could not do that working in a studio with an engineer running stuff. And I also didn't think I could perform the things with somebody else there watching. I got used to doing it by myself.

GW: Are you a shy kind of performer?

SCHOLZ: Oh, yeah. In the studio. I'll be the first to admit that most of what I do is horrible. I think most of what I do sucks. But I'm very tenacious. So I'll keep trying. I like to do things in unconventional ways. All you have to do is tell me, "Oh, that's not how you record that." Or, "That's not the way you're supposed to play that chord." I'm just so naturally rebellious that that's like waving a red flag in front of a bull. Any way you tell me I shouldn't do something, that's the way I'm gonna do it. Just because you said I shouldn't.

GW: Are any tracks on a Boston album ever recorded simultaneously, for example bass and drums?

SCHOLZ: No. I do it all piece by piece. And on the tracks where somebody else plays, I usually do that by remote control. Like if Dave [*Sikes*] is going to play bass on a track, I'll just give him a copy of the basics without the bass, so he can try some bass lines in his own studio. If there's anything I like, I'll dub it onto the master. I find that's better than working one-on-one with a player in the studio. I find that people do better work if they don't have to worry about what some other person thinks of what they're playing while they're doing it. Eventually I started working with [*guitarist*] Gary Pihl that way, too. It's gotten to the point where he doesn't even come into my studio anymore. He got used to doing it by himself, too. I'd still be the producer, because I'd sort through all the takes and see where I thought it was going. Sometimes I'd say something like, "This one starts great. Keep going with that kind of energy." Or, "Back off and be smoother there." The only person I work one-on-one with is the singer. And he's always singing to a tape track. So there are never two things being done at once.

GW: Does Gary play any solos on the album?

SCHOLZ: Oh, sure. Some nice stuff, as a matter of fact. He played that blistering solo in the middle of "I Need Your Love." He also played some of the solos in the bolero section of the *Walk On* medley. He plays that guitar thing that goes over that whole bolero part. That's just one of my favorites.

GW: Do you have a lot to do with his tones?

SCHOLZ: No. Except that he uses Rockman equipment. He has his own guitars and sets his own sounds. As the producer on the record, I will add effects to it and so forth. Like in the bolero section of *Walk On* and in the "I Need Your Love" solo, I added some delayed doubling that's also swept with a real old Rockman chorus. I love Rockman choruses. We don't make them anymore, so this isn't a product plug. But you can't get that kind of chorus out of any digital piece of equipment; it's just physically impossible. Digital equipment causes phase angle changes across the spectrum.

GW: It's inherent in the encoding and decoding.

SCHOLZ: Yeah. You can't do it. So the Rockman chorus is very lush and full, probably because it's analog. Also because it has a huge pre-delay, which is what made it so expensive when it was on the market. So, anyway, we use that for certain things. Naturally I have tons of those sitting in the studio.

GW: What's the source of the transient shimmer that is so much a part of the Boston sound?

SCHOLZ: Dumb luck. Air.

GW: It's a hard thing to pin down. One moment you'll think, "Oh, it's the reverb."

SCHOLZ: No, the reverbs are all old. There's almost no digital processing at all. In fact, the reverb is almost 100 percent an old EMT Gold Plate. The echoes are all those analog Rockman echoes that we used to make a while ago. I just stocked up a bunch of those when they went out of production. 'Cause I love the way they sound. They're very close to tape echoes. In fact when I did *Don't Look Back* and some of *Third Stage*, I had a separate tape machine running all the time so I could use real tape echo. I built a little gadget that would rewind the tape when it got near the end of the reel so I could keep going with the echo. So, no, I don't think it's the reverb. I think it's the miking and the processing on the electric instruments as they go to tape in the first place. I do pay really close attention to the high end of the instruments. The dynamics of the high harmonics are the key thing. If they're too "peaky," you end up with a grating sort of sensation, as opposed to that airy sort of feeling. But thank you for noticing.

GW: You don't have much use for digital in general, do you?

SCHOLZ: Well, no. Although I do like it for problem solving. Like if there's a noise or something you have to remove from the recording, or if you need to move a guitar part to some other point in time and there's no other way of accomplishing it, then digital editing can come in handy. But first of all, I don't like the way digital audio sounds. Well, let me qualify that. I thought that the less-expensive digital equipment and the original high-end stuff was all pretty hideous. Nowadays you can get some extremely good-sounding digital things. I don't think even I could tell the difference from analog. But now we're talking about really expensive equipment. And for simple storage of the music itself, I still prefer analog tape because of what it does to the sound. I don't like digital because you get these nasty phase changes when you store sound on most digital equipment. I also don't like the fact that there is no limiting—no tape compression. There is no distortion, except for really horrible distortion.

Of course, you can protect yourself from that, but we're talking about things that are a lot of work and take a huge amount of equipment just to do the same thing that a very inexpensive analog tape deck does when you push it hard. You can use that compression and tape saturation to your advantage. I do.

GW: So it's fair to say that analog tape compression is essential to your guitar sound?

SCHOLZ: Absolutely. In fact, I've had to design a special circuit to simulate it when we play live.

GW: So what's the thickest layer on the new album? The maximum number of guitar tracks?

SCHOLZ: Oh, I lose count. I just keep going until I like it. Sometimes it's one guitar playing a part, but not very often. I'm sure there are places where there are six or eight guitars playing the same rhythm part. And there's a million places where there's three guitars playing the same lead line—even a pretty quick, intricate lead line. Those get a little tricky. If I have a part that has a really good feel to it and I decide I want to double it, I have to be very careful to have that same exact feel. You can't let the timing stray off by very much, or you lose the notes. Some of them are pretty short. But there are a lot of places where there are three guitars playing a single lead line. And of course, the guitar harmonies usually have two or three parts.

GW: So each part in the harmonized lines will be made up of more than one guitar track?

SCHOLZ: That's right. If I want a really big, full sound I'll put three on. If I want it to sound simple, but also make sure that you can't identify where the guitar is coming from—so you don't concentrate on it—I'll put on two lines and spread them out on different sides. If it's something I really want the listener to pay attention to, I'll just put it there by itself with maybe a little echo or chorusing or something. But obviously there are a lot more of the other. I like the big sound. It's more like Rachmaninov and Tchaikovsky when it's really big.

GW: Were you into Brian May?

SCHOLZ: No. I wasn't. I mean, I think he did some really neat things. But it's somewhat different. I like brute force. I'd add another guitar playing the same part because I wanted an absolute cement block wall of sound. I wanted it to be overwhelming.

GW: Have your techniques for achieving the Boston "wall of sound" changed much over the years? Or are you still doing a lot of the same things you did on that first album?

SCHOLZ: It's almost identical. There are things about the production of the first album that I didn't like. I always felt the deficiencies in the production of that first album were obvious. If you compare it with the *Walk On* CD, the sound of *Walk On* is so much bigger. I would love to go back and remix that first album the way that I'd like. But at the time, it was actually the best I knew how to do. I was still very much in a learning stage.

GW: You had demoed a lot of those songs earlier, right?

SCHOLZ: Oh, sure. I'd been writing those for years. I think "Fourplay" was written in 1969. They'd been around for a long time.

GW: When you double- or triple-track a guitar part, do you EQ or process each track differently?

SCHOLZ: No. I use the same sound because I'm looking for the same effect. Technically, it's known as "random phase cancellation." It's so much more complicated than what you can achieve with just chorus. It's what's called an uncorrelated signal. If you do it again with a different sound, you can't duplicate the original signal. So you get some phase cancellation of fundamentals and harmonics that are in your chord or your note. But so much more of it is not the same; every single note is different. When I'm doubling a part that I like, I'll play it many many times, listening to get the best effect on each chord and each note. I experiment with everything from tuning to timing. Tone changes radically from note to note when you're playing guitar. You can make huge adjustments simply by the way you pick the note, without changing anything in the recording.

GW: It's very performance driven.

SCHOLZ: It is. After I've done something like that on tape, then I'll have to go back and listen to it closely, to discover what it is about the effect of the two that I want to bring across when I play it live. I don't do all the solos exactly like the recording. I used to do that, but now I'd rather not. There are key places, though, where I really love what's happening on the record. So I have to figure out exactly what was going on and duplicate that technique on stage.

GW: When it's time to record a solo, what's your usual plan of operation?

SCHOLZ: First I just play along with the basic tracks blasting in my phones. I don't think about what I should play or how long the part should be; I just turn it on and start playing. And I always leave myself plenty of open tracks. The first time I get something that has some magic to it—a feeling that I think does something for the song—that's it, it's done. My tapes have tracks all over the place. Channel 13 might have the lead in the end of the first verse, channel 18 might have the lead in the break… Sometimes I have to spend hours and days trying to reorganize it so I can mix the total thing afterwards.

GW: Do you do any comping of solos? Taking a few bars from one take and a few bars from another?

SCHOLZ: Yeah, once in a while. Not very often. But I often end up changing the music underneath the solo. I'll subtract bars, add bars or change the chords or the bass line. That's true with the lead vocals too. If I hear something that sounds good but won't work with what comes next on the underlying instruments, I'll go back and change the arrangement on the rest of the song. Which is as time-consuming as it sounds. It involves rerecording as many as eight tracks of instruments.

GW: You're not doing MIDI sequencing.

SCHOLZ: No, it's all taped, so any editing I want to do is with a razor blade and splicing tape. If I want to increase the length of the arrangement, first of all I have to cut the master, which doesn't bother me at all. I have 100 splices in most masters these days. I run at 30 ips and I use 3M M79s [*analog 24-track-recorders*], the only machines where you cannot hear splicing. In fact it's very hard to find the splices on a scope.

I can splice with reckless abandon—and I do. I'll also do anything to the underlying chord progression that needs to be done, once I start into a solo or a vocal part. Take that long organ solo in the middle of "Walk On." That started out only being about 16 bars. That whole thing about two-and-a-half or three minutes worth of accompaniment—never existed. I just started playing on the organ and decided, "Oh well, I have a lot more to do here. So I had to make the backing track longer. Then I had to introduce some variety into it, to make it different. I just kind of kept going with it.

GW: Are you working with only one 24-track machine?

SCHOLZ: I use two, but in a very unusual way. Years ago, I did the usual thing. I got a synchronizer and locked the two tape machines together. But for a lot of reasons, I didn't like doing it that way. What I do now is put the basic tracks on one 24-track first. Then I'll put a mix of the basics down on two tracks of a second 24-track machine. On a separate track—or tracks—I'll have a snare drum, hi-hat or some timekeeper from the drum set.

I then record all the vocals on the second 24-track machine, using up however many tracks I want. I do the same thing with the singer that I do with my guitar solos: I have him try a lot of different things. I'll end up with a whole second tape full of vocal parts and maybe some different lead guitar parts. I then dump that stuff back to the original 24 track master. By this point, I will have already sorted through and selected the tracks I want to use, and mixed them all down. So what I dump back onto the master is very concise: lead vocals, harmonies and any additional lead parts I want to use. To do the transfer, I just sync up the two machines by hand. I don't use a synchronizer anymore. I'll put the snare drum from one tape in one ear and the snare drum from the other tape in the other ear.

GW: And you do it manually?

SCHOLZ: Yeah. I do it better than any robot synchronizer. Way better. If you ever make the mistake of putting correlated signals like, say, left and right cymbal overheads on two different tracks of those two different machines, you'll hear just how horrible a job synchronizers do. The phasing is just all over the place, while the synchronizer is trying to hunt and stay locked on. Some are better than others, but they're all pretty wide of the mark.

GW: You don't use any kind of pilot tone?

SCHOLZ: Nothing. I just run the two machines and use the drums as my guide, keeping them in sync by hand. I make very small speed corrections as the tape runs. I'll use the variable speed control on one tape deck for gross changes. But for small changes, nothing works better than a thumb on the supply reel.

GW: So you're riding it in real time.

SCHOLZ: Yeah, using the drums as my guide. I like to keep the cymbals in the earphones. Those provide the best clue for phase changes. Also, when you have the two machines synched properly, the snare drum will be right in the middle of your head, in your headphones. If the timing goes off, you'll hear the snare move very slightly. The timing we're talking about is very tight, so I can usually get it where I want it. I can also use this technique if I want to make some timing adjustments. Like, if the singer was late on a note or something, I can set it up with an offset, by ear.

GW: Wow!

SCHOLZ: That's part of the art of it. These days people will do similar things on digital systems, where they have a visual display and move events by milliseconds. It's still an artistic thing when you do it that way, but somehow it's a little more fun when it's tape-based. You never do it the same way twice, of course. And with all these analog processes you only get one shot. That's a consequence that doesn't usually exist when you're working with digital storage. You can back up and go back to what you had. But once you erase something on tape, it's gone forever.

GW: Do you feel like that kind of analog tape manipulation is becoming a lost art?

SCHOLZ: Oh, yeah. No one does that anymore. They don't even make the tape that I used for the last two projects anymore.

GW: Scotch 226.

SCHOLZ: Yeah, I had to go buy up a bunch of their remaining stuff. The 996 [*3M's newer tape stock, which replaced 226*] is an amazing tape, but it's just not my cup of tea.

GW: Why did you first devise the Rockman?

SCHOLZ: It was a combination of wanting to get a practice amp and also wanting to take a shot at putting all the things I like about a guitar sound in one place. I found that all those things could be packaged in a tiny unit, even with the technology available back in 1981. So that gave rise to actually putting it on the market and making it available as a headphone amp. Because it was small enough to go in a guitar case. And back then, guitarists didn't have stereo sound systems on stage, so there was nothing to plug it into anyway. I figured I would produce it as a headphone amp. People could hear what the box could do in the headphones. Then, a lot of people went from there and took that little headphone amp and made records with it. In fact, I knew of about 20 or 30 records that had been recorded using that original Rockman headphone amp before *Third Stage* was ever completed and released to the public. *Third Stage* has Rockman stuff all over it, some of which were more advanced reincarnations of that little headphone amp.
GW: So on the first two Boston albums, you were just using miked cabinets?
SCHOLZ: Yeah, it's all miked on the first two albums. And a little bit on the third one, too. But mostly Rockman. The fourth album is virtually all direct.
GW: Do you prefer the sound of direct guitar, or is it a convenience thing?
SCHOLZ: Both. It is a huge convenience. I can go back six months later and change a guitar part and reproduce the exact same sound of the track. You could never do that with miked cabinets. Never. I've tried everything. I set up the mikes with three coordinates, so I could get them in the same place within an inch or so. I tabulated different settings on the equipment—all this stuff. Forget it. It's never the same twice. I thought I had the bases covered pretty well. I had old Ampegs and Marshalls and Fenders. I had regulated voltage power supplies: big boxes supplying regulated AC at a certain voltage level. And it was still totally unpredictable. You'd get a great sound one day and the next week it would sound horrible. As a producer, the Rockman stuff lets me forget about all those hassles. It frees

me up to be a musician, rather than hassling with getting guitar sounds and wondering if they're all right.

But I also really like the sound of direct. I did a lot of tracks on *Walk On* where I recorded direct with my Rockman modules, and then tried the same part through a tube amp with processing and so forth. I almost always ended up keeping the Rockman track. Plus the Rockman allows me to do things I could never do with a tube amp. I can turn the guitar down and it will get very, very clean and still be bright and loud. I can swell smoothly back into a distortion part and back out. That's impossible on a tube amp.

GW: The one type of gear you don't mention in the liner notes for *Walk On* is your electric guitars!

SCHOLZ: Didn't I put that in there? It should be in there. It's real easy, anyway, 'cause it's all Gibson Les Paul. That's the only electric guitar that I use. Oh, there's one or two parts where I fooled around with a Jackson a little bit, but that's it. If that's not mentioned, it was an error of omission. I'll have to look at it. I wrote it. Ooops.

GW: Do you have a lot of Les Pauls?

SCHOLZ: One of my Les Pauls is the first good electric guitar I bought. And I bought another one when I got the deal to make the first Boston album—to have a backup for the studio and playing out in clubs. I went to some second-hand guitar shop and saw another gold top Les Paul. It sounded just like mine so I bought it. It was cheap, like $350 or something. I didn't get another guitar for years. But somewhere on a tour in 1977, I realized that I should get a third guitar. I needed two on stage, and I started worrying about what would happen if something should happen to one of the guitars I had. So I went into a music store, saw some Les Pauls and said, "Oh, that one looks nice." I picked it up and the neck was totally different from my two Les Pauls. It was a big thing. It sounded good but I couldn't play it. I ended up trying like 12 guitars in the shop, and I freaked: "None of these are Les Pauls that I know. What's going on here?" Now, those two Les Pauls that I bought are the only two Les Pauls that I ever played in my life. And it turns out that both of them were only made for like six months in 1968. It was this one model that had the same kind of neck as a '57 Les Paul. The pickups were single-coil and it was a one-of-a-kind thing and they probably only made a few hundred. And I had learned how to play on these guitars that had necks radically different from all the others.

So no, I don't have a lot of Les Pauls, because I can't find any I like. Except, I now have one that Gibson made for me.

GW: Have you modified the pickups in any way?

SCHOLZ: I had to go to humbucking DiMarzios, simply because of the hum problems with the single coils.

GW: You can play all the instruments on Boston albums. Why do you sometimes choose to have other players come in?

SCHOLZ: For a fresh perspective on a part. That's the only reason. Gary plays a lot differently than I do. So, usually what I'll do is run him off a tape of something I've done without telling him what, or even where, I think additional guitar parts should be. And he'll come back with things that never would have occurred to me. I think it's better to have more than one performer's interpretation of the music on a 45-minute CD. It helps keep the listeners' interest. I hate the idea of somebody just skipping to a few favorite cuts on a Boston album and not listening to the rest of it. I always try to make the album so that someone will want to hear the whole thing.

GW: Do you conceive the album as one continuous piece of music as you're writing it?

SCHOLZ: While I'm working on them, the songs are all separate ideas. But in the back of my mind, I'm always thinking of the album as a whole. I'll end up throwing away a lot of song ideas because they don't fit in with the whole thing. And I do some sequencing of songs as I go along [*arranging the songs in the order that they will appear on the album.*] Traditionally, producers would record a bunch of songs and sequence them in the end. But I try to do that while I'm going. Because a lot of decisions—for instance, what key to play a song in—can make a huge difference in the final result. If you have some idea of the song order ahead of time, you can make a change starting from one song into the next. It will make the next song very effective. Or, if you don't do it right, it can destroy the effect of the next song. It's the same thing with instrumentation, arrangement, the level, tempo...all sorts of things. I try to have an idea of all of that as I'm recording. But all things do not end up the way I plan them. An awful lot, fortunately, happens by accident.

GW: What takes longer, writing the material or recording it?

SCHOLZ: Recording it. The arrangements are very time-consuming. Songs themselves are hard to come by—they're valuable things. So I agonize over the arrangement and recording of them.

GW: Did "We Can Make It" really go through 87 versions, as you say in the liner notes?

SCHOLZ: Probably more. I picked that number out of the blue. Frankly, there were lots of songs that went through 87 or more different versions.

GW: What kind of console was *Walk On* mixed on?

SCHOLZ: It's a real old, small Auditronix 501 that's been totally ravaged and modified inside and out. I like the EQs. It's only got 26 channels, so I had to add some outboard mixing. Things were getting tight with channels. But I'm recording alone most of the time, so I don't need a monitor mix. I have one mix and it's the board mix for the song. The monitor mix system has been turned into auxiliary sends. There's all sorts of rewiring that's been done to expand it to do the things I need to do. I have a real old Fadex automation system.

GW: I remember those. They're from the late-late Seventies.

SCHOLZ: Yeah. Old. And it's very troublesome. But it does something that no other fader system that I've been able to find will do. I can rearrange and cut tape with absolute impunity, because this particular fader system doesn't depend on any sync tones. I can't really use sync tones or anything like that on tape because I always change my mind and make the verse twice as long or something.

GW: And once you cut the master, that's it for the sync code.

SCHOLZ: Yeah. And unfortunately, so much of the equipment that's built today relies on SMTPE code. So I can't use it.

GW: Do you mix very consciously for FM radio compression?

SCHOLZ: I try to. But I finally realized you can't second guess them. Whatever you do, they'll find a way to screw it up.

GW: Each station miscalibrates its gear differently.

SCHOLZ: It's hopeless. I always cringe when I hear a song I produced coming over FM radio. It's never the same. Sometimes they're just demolished and sometimes they're okay. But it's never what it is on the CD or the tape.

GW: And yet Boston is heralded as one of the ultimate FM rock radio bands. That sound seems so suited to the medium.

SCHOLZ: Yeah. [*laughs*] By the time I'm done with a mix, it's exactly the way I want it. I mean I understand why FM has to limit the dynamics. Most people are listening in their car or as background music in their house. If you put on a tape of *Walk On* in your car, if you're in any kind of normal driving situation, you won't be able to hear the quiet parts. But unfortunately that's the way it has to be because the quiet parts are there to make the loud parts more dramatic.

GW: When will we be seeing the next Boston album?

SCHOLZ: I know that I can't do one faster than two or three years. On the other hand, I've got this new studio worked out really well. So it's possible that it could be as early as '97 or '98. I do have several starts on songs that I'm really excited about. Ordinarily, if you were to ask me that question I'd say "Geez, I don't know." But I've already got some things on tape, so I'm getting excited early about the next one.

Guitar World Presents CLASSIC ROCK

Neil Young

Guitar World, September 1995

Journey Through the Past

Neil Young is the ageless chameleon of rock. In this history of his long and distinguished career, *Guitar World* traces his evolution from hippie icon to Godfather of Grunge.

By Marc Weingarten

MIDWAY THROUGH NEIL Young's 1976 arena tour with his longtime musical cohort Stephen Stills, Young abruptly jumped ship. There had been no warning, no apparent provocation. Young left Stills, his old pal from Buffalo Springfield and Crosby, Stills, Nash & Young, high and dry, with nothing but a note for consolation: "Dear Stephen, funny how some things that start spontaneously end that way. Eat a peach. Neil."

A strange story, were it not for the fact that it pretty much typifies the way Neil Young has willfully thwarted his career at every turn. Why else, for instance, would Young follow up *Harvest*, his biggest selling album, with *Time Fades Away*, a sloppy, aggressively uncommercial mess of a record? Or spend 10 years flitting from one disparate style to the next so quickly that not even his most ardent fans could keep up? The answers are right there in his records, all 40 of them—for Young, stardom has always taken a back seat to his art.

And it is Neil Young's singular art, not record sales or his fans' well-meaning adulation, that has sustained him and kept him going for 30-plus years. He's the accidental rock star, an icon without any discernible image except that of a musical chameleon.

It is a testament to Young's renegade, searching muse that, in addition to writing a handful of definitive air-guitar anthems ("Cinnamon Girl," "Into the Black," "Southern Man") and some of rock's most enduring ballads ("Helpless," "After the Gold Rush," "Heart of Gold"), he's also penned heinous clunkers like "Kinda Fonda Wanda" and "Ocean Girl." But the misses are just as essential to Young's aesthetic as the hits. His failures are often far more interesting than other artists' successes.

Mistakes also play a key role in Young's guitar playing. By emphasizing instinctual "feel," off-kilter phrasing, and dissonance, Young forever liberated lead guitar from the technoid ghetto and pointed the way for like-minded contemporary players like Pearl Jam's Mike McCready, Sonic Youth's Thurston Moore, Pavement's Steve Malkmus and Dinosaur Jr's J Mascis.

But it is Young's strange and circuitous musical journey—a journey that has seen him record and play folk, country, rockabilly, new wave and blues—that remains his greatest legacy. The man himself pretty much summed it up in a 1985 interview: "I just hate being labeled. I hate to be stuck in one thing. I just don't want to be anything for very long. I don't know why. I just want to keep moving, keep running, play my guitar." He hasn't stopped moving yet.

EXPECTING TO FLY (1955-1968)

As with so many artists of his generation, Neil Young's discovery of music coincided with the birth of rock and roll. As a hockey fanatic growing up in Winnipeg, Ontario, Young's initial exposure to American popular music came via local radio. "It was about 1955, I guess, when I really became aware of what was going on," Young told an interviewer in 1982. "I knew that I wanted to play, and that I was into it. 'Maybe' by the Chantels, 'Short Fat Fannie' by Larry Williams,

Elvis Presley, Chuck Berry...those were the first people I heard. The radio was right by my bed; I used to just fall asleep listening to it."

The Squires, Young's first semi-professional band, were modeled after twangy instrumental groups like the Ventures and the Shadows. Young Neil was especially taken with the Shadows' guitarist Hank Marvin, attracted to his pioneering use of the tremolo arm, which would become a trademark of his own technique. The Squires cut one single for V records, a local Canadian label, "The Sultan," backed with "Aurora." Both songs were highly derivative, Young-penned instrumentals; both stiffed. By 1965, the Squires were no more.

Which suited Young just fine. By that time, he had gotten wind of the epochal folk music explosion then coming out of the States. Inspired by the plain-spoken poetry of artists like Bob Dylan and Phil Ochs, Young abandoned rock and roll completely and began working Toronto's coffee-house circuit. (It was during this time that Young met a fellow Canadian folkie named Joni Mitchell.) Again, Young ran into fierce indifference. "There was a review of one of my shows in a newspaper and it said my songs were all like a cliché," Young recalls. "Toronto was a very humbling experience for me. I just couldn't get anything going."

Gigless and penniless, Young hooked up with local bass player Bruce Palmer and a flamboyant American singer-guitarist named Ricky James Matthews (who later became funk superstar and convicted felon Rick James), switched gears once again and formed the Mynah Birds, an r&b-flavored rock band. Although the Mynah Birds managed to sign with Motown in 1964 and cut an album's worth of material, none of those recordings ever saw the light of day. Shortly after the band's first and last brush with success, Rick James was busted for draft evasion, and the Mynah Birds were history. Young and Palmer promptly sold the band's equipment and, perhaps out of mourning for the departed Mynah Birds, bought a hearse. In this distinctive vehicle, they drove to Los Angeles in hopes of landing a few local gigs. "I had to leave a lot of friends behind," Young told an interviewer in 1994. "I almost had no conscience, I was so driven to make it."

Young got more than he bargained for when he ran into Stephen Stills and Richie Furay, a couple of local players he'd met in Canada. Recruiting Dewey Martin, an out-of-work drummer who had briefly played with country artists the Dillards, the four promptly formed a band called the Herd. Then fate intervened.

"We were living on Fountain Avenue, in Los Angeles, and workmen were tearing up streets to do resurfacing," Richie Furay told writer Mat Snow in 1994. "They were using these big steamrollers to flatten it all out, and they had a nameplate on the side—just two large words: Buffalo Springfield."

Out went the Herd, stampeded by the cool new name. Young's contributions to Buffalo Springfield's three albums (*Buffalo Springfield*, *Buffalo Springfield Again* and *Last Time Around*), like his solo albums, vary in style, theme and musical texture. Buffalo Springfield's "Burned" and "Flying Close to the Ground Is Wrong" described bad acid trips, the approach of the two songs certainly going against the prevailing counter-cultural ethos of LSD-enhanced psychedelic bliss. "Nowadays Clancy Can't Even Sing," with it's decidedly un-Top-40-like use of metaphor and allegory, served notice that even at this early stage in his career, the nascent songwriter was already pushing the boundaries of his art. The lilting country-rock of "I Am a Child" laid the foundation for Seventies Nashville-cum-L.A. bands like the Eagles and Pure Prairie League, while "Mr. Soul," with its incessantly militant drum pattern and scorching guitar solo, provided the sonic template for Young's subsequent work with Crazy Horse.

Although it appeared on *Buffalo Springfield Again*, "Expecting to Fly" was really Neil Young's first song as a solo artist; he had temporarily quit the band when the track was recorded. "There were a lot of problems happening with the Springfield," Young told writer Nick Kent. "There were a lot of distractions, too. Groupies. Drugs. I remember being haunted suddenly by this whole obsession with 'How do I fit in here? Do I like this?' " A stately, evocative track featuring a lush orchestral accompaniment arranged by Phil Spector alumnus Jack Nitzsche, "Expecting to Fly" was to be the first of many neo-symphonic excursions Young would embark on during his career.

Buffalo Springfield's third and final album, *Last Time Around*, was merely an afterthought; the band had split up prior to its release, due in no small part to Young's desire to move on. "Everything started to go too fucking fast," Young recalls. "We were getting the shaft from every angle, and it seemed like we were trying to make it so bad and were getting nowhere." Of course, every member of the Springfield eventually *did* get somewhere, with other musical partners—Stills with Crosby and Nash, Furay with Springfield clones Poco, and Jim Messina (who replaced Bruce Palmer just after *Buffalo Springfield Again*) with Kenny Loggins. Only Young ventured out on his own. He would reap the richest musical rewards.

THE LONER (1968-80)

Had Neil Young chosen the path of least resistance for his solo career, he could have easily cashed in on his Buffalo Springfield credentials and made his first solo album "Mr. Soul Redux." Instead, Young went back into the studio with Nitzsche and recorded *Neil Young*, a wildly eclectic album that bewildered critics and Springfield loyalists alike. Neil Young had country and classical instrumentals, a lugubrious ballad called "Last Train to Tulsa" that droned on for nearly 10 minutes, a few lovelorn ballads, and "The Loner," a more conventional rocker built around one of Young's great monster riffs.

"That was the farthest thing from my mind, what people would think of it," says Young about his first album. "Songs were coming really fast and I was just grabbing them all and...getting them out." Neil Young was all over the map, made nary an impact commercially, and gave no indication whatsoever of the direction Young was to take with his next album.

In late 1968, during the time that Young was brooding over whether to leave Buffalo Springfield, he could frequently be seen checking out a local Los Angeles bar band called the Rockets. The Rockets were hardly a world-class outfit; drummer Ralph Molina and bassist Billy Talbot had been playing for less than a year, and though guitarist Danny Whitten occasionally wrangled some session work (Young had met him during the recording of Buffalo

Springfield), he was no studio slick. And that's exactly what appealed to Young. He loved the Rockets not for their technical proficiency—they had none—but for their instinctual, spontaneous approach to playing. After the fussed-over fastidiousness that had engulfed him during the sessions for his first album, Young was eager to make some no-holds-barred, guitar-driven rock. So in 1969 Young recruited the Rockets, renamed them Crazy Horse, and recorded his second album, *Everybody Knows This Is Nowhere*.

There is a feverish energy to *Everybody Knows* that is only hinted at by Young's previous recordings, and it all sprang from a certain guitar transaction made by Young with Jim Messina prior to the *Everybody Knows* sessions. "When I traded Jim Messina my orange Gretsch for that black guitar...boy, I really scored big," Young told Cameron Crowe. "That's my biggest memory of that time. *Great* guitar."

That guitar, a 1956 Les Paul, enabled Young to get the spiky, gritty tone that has become his signature. On extended guitar showcases like *Everybody Knows*' "Cowgirl in the Sand" and "Down by the River," Young, apparently liberated by the sonic possibilities of the Les Paul, unleashes a fire-storm of knotty, minimalist solos while Whitten counter-punches with crafty chordal flourishes. "Cinnamon Girl" contains Young's most transcendent solo—a single, repeating note. On *Everybody Knows*, Young had stripped his music down to the bare essentials, and the effect was galvanizing.

Everybody Knows was an artistic breakthrough, but it took a brief stint with Crosby, Stills & Nash for Young to enter into the mainstream. Although Young and Stephen Stills had engaged in some titanic ego clashes during their days with the Springfield, neither could deny the magic of their previous musical collaborations. So when Stills became a superstar, it only seemed fitting that Young should join the fold. "Steve and I play really well together," Young told Cameron Crowe in 1975. "People can't comprehend that we can both play lead guitar in the band and not fight over it. We have total respect for each other's musicianship. We bring out the best in each other." Young's contributions to CSN&Y's second album, *Deja Vu* (particularly "Helpless," a bittersweet ballad about his childhood), exposed his music to millions of new converts and paved the way for the success of his next solo album, *After the Gold Rush*.

HEART OF GOLD

On *After the Gold Rush*, Young tempered *Everybody Knows'* guitar squall with elements of folk and country balladry, albeit with a decidedly Young-ian twist. Despite the chiming, tuneful nature of the melodies, there was a pervasive undercurrent of melancholy in Young's lyrics. So while *Gold Rush* featured ebullient rockers like "When You Dance (I Can Really Love)" and love songs like "I Believe in You," it also had "Southern Man," a powerful anti-bigotry broadside and "Tell Me Why," a sober-minded meditation on mortality. Nonetheless, for Young's followers, it was ultimately the music that mattered. By seamlessly combining winsome acoustic material with raucous guitar rave-ups, Young was able to appeal to fans of both styles, giving him his first Top Ten album.

That brilliant acoustic/electric blend wasn't Young's original idea. He had hoped to make *After the Gold Rush* an all-electric Crazy Horse collaboration, but scotched the idea when he discovered that Danny Whitten had gotten hooked on heroin while Young had been touring with CSN&Y. "There was no reason," Billy Talbot later recalled. "In those days, people just started shooting right up. Didn't snort nothin'. He just shot some speed, the next day some smack, and from then on he was a junkie."

Following the release of *After the Gold Rush*, Young suffered a slipped disc, the effects of which would leave him at least partially incapacitated for a couple of years. During his convalescence, Young organized a group of Nashville session musicians dubbed the Stray Gators and recorded *Harvest*. While the new album contained a couple of vitriolic rockers in "Alabama" and "Words," for the most part Young stuck to the shambling, languorous balladry that had made *After the Gold Rush* a breakthrough success. Not surprisingly, *Harvest* became the biggest selling album of his career. Both the album and its first single, "Heart of Gold" (featuring backing vocals by Linda

Ronstadt and James Taylor), catapulted to Number One.

With the enormous success of *Harvest*, Young's transformation from cult artist to big-time rock star was complete. For his first arena tour in 1973, Young decided to draft the Stray Gators and Danny Whitten to accompany him. By this time, however, Whitten was too strung out to even think about music. "We were rehearsing and he just couldn't cut it," Young told Crowe. "He couldn't remember anything. He was too out of it. Too far gone. I had to tell him to go back to L.A. He just said, 'I've got nowhere else to go, man. How am I gonna tell my friends?' And he split. That night, the coroner called me from L.A. and told me he'd OD'd. That fucking blew my mind. I loved Danny. I felt responsible."

Devastated, yet committed to the tour, Young hit the road. But anyone expecting to see a greatest-hits revue was in for quite a shock. Whitten's death, combined with Young's disintegrating marriage to actress Carrie Snodgrass and the nightmarish hassles over his first film, *Journey Through the Past* (Warner Bros. had agreed to release the film, then reneged at the last minute), had driven Young to self-destructive excess. He was now drinking heavily and delivering raucous, tequila-drenched performances—none of which featured a single recognizable song—in a weary, tremulous croak of a voice. "Neil was sort of dribbling out of the side of his mouth on that tour, the mood was so down," recalls longtime manager Elliot Roberts.

Young culled highlights (or low lights, depending on one's point of view) from the tour for *Time Fades Away*, his follow-up to the Platinum-selling *Harvest*. "I imagine I could've come up with the perfect follow-up," Young told Cameron Crowe. "But it would have been something that everyone was expecting. Nobody expected *Time Fades Away*, and I'm not sorry I put it out. I'd rather keep changing and lose a lot of people along the way. If that's the price, I'll pay it."

That summer, Crosby, Stills, Nash & Young roadie Bruce Berry OD'd, sending Young into a further tailspin. It was the second drug-related death of a close friend in less than a year, and in an attempt to somehow come to grips with the twin tragedies, Young holed up in his Topanga Canyon ranch in Los Angeles and began frantically writing songs. He then summoned Molina, Talbot, guitarist Nils Lofgren and steel-guitar player Ben Keith to record them.

"What we were doing was playing those guys on their way," Young told Crowe. "I mean, I'm not a junkie and I won't ever try it out to check out what it's like. But we all got high enough, right there on the edge where we felt wide open to the whole mood."

Young and the band recorded nine songs in two drunken nights for what would eventually become *Tonight's the Night*, considered by many to be one of the most harrowing, emotionally naked and downright spooky albums ever made. "*Tonight's the Night* is like an OD letter," Young explained. "The whole thing is about life, dope and death." Indeed, Young's scratchy, ravaged voice and the band's barely together playing on anti-drug dirges like "Tired Eyes," "Speaking Out" and "Mellow My Mind" give the album an aura of mournful, wasted despair. *Tonight's the Night* was so unflinchingly raw, in fact, that Warner Bros. waited almost two years to release it. In the interim, Young made another record with his on-again, off-again collaborator Stephen Stills (the listless *Long May You Run*) and recorded two solo albums—*On the Beach* and another, originally entitled *Homegrown*. The latter, a chronicle of Young's divorce, was highlighted by "Like a Hurricane," an epic, Crazy Horse-powered paean to Snodgrass featuring one of his most coruscating guitar solos. The album was eventually released in 1977 as *American Stars and Bars*.

Strange, surreal and unremittingly bleak, *On the Beach*—which featured the anti-air pollution protest song "Vampire Blues"—was Young's most pointedly political statement since "Ohio," the screed against the National Guard killings of four Kent State students, that he had recorded with CSN&Y in 1970. Musically, however, the album's tone was muted and somewhat diffuse.

Not until Young reunited with Crazy Horse for *Zuma* did he begin to rock out again. Recorded and released in 1975, this was the first official Crazy Horse album since *Everybody Knows*, and it more than made up for lost time. With new guitarist Frank "Pancho" Sampedro on board, Crazy Horse was able to regain the incendiary chemistry that had been lost when Whitten died.

After cranking it up with *Zuma*, quick-change artist Young returned to the homespun, laid-back acoustic style of *Harvest* with 1978's *Comes a Time*, an album that resonates with some of Young's most exquisitely beautiful songs. One track, "Lotta Love," became Young's first Top Ten hit since "Heart of Gold," but not until former back-up singer Nicolette Larson covered it.

Just when it seemed as if Young had settled into a comfortably mellow groove, however, he suddenly veered off in a radically different direction. By this time, punk rock was challenging the hegemony of the old rock hierarchy, and Young, alone among his sadly anachronistic contemporaries, embraced the revolution. As he told one interviewer: "As soon as I heard them [*rock's old guard*] saying, 'God, what the fuck is this...this is going to be over in three months,' I knew it was a sure sign right there that they were going to bite it if they didn't watch out." Emboldened by punk's elemental, back-to-basics approach, he recorded *Rust Never Sleeps*, his best album of the decade.

"It's better to burn out than to fade away," Young warbled on "My My, Hey Hey," the song that opened and closed *Rust Never Sleeps*. The line was at once a commentary on the creeping complacency that Young felt was rotting rock's old order and a ringing affirmation of the music's new vitality and relevance. As Young saw it, rock was now as much about the Sex Pistols as it was about Elvis ("The King is gone but he's not forgotten/This is the story of Johnny Rotten").

And if the scabrous, neo-punk thrash of *Rust Never Sleeps* tracks like "Powderfinger," "Sedan Delivery," and "Welfare Mothers" was any indication, Young and Crazy Horse weren't about to be written off as obsolete Jurassics any time soon.

After the twin triumphs of *Rust Never Sleeps* and a subsequent 1979 tour, it was painfully obvious that, among those rockers who had come of age in the Sixties, Young was about the only one who still had something meaningful to say or play. He had started the Seventies with a bang and ended them with a sonic boom. In 1979, both *Rolling Stone* and New York City's *Village Voice* voted Young the Artist of the Decade.

SAMPLE AND HOLD (1980-1989)

Even the most hard-core Neil Young fans regard the Eighties as Young's "lost" years, and have trouble reconciling the erratic (and frequently awful) albums of the era with his seminal Seventies output. But to disregard the genre-hopping Young of the Eighties is to not take the full measure of the artist. Neil Young simply has to follow his capricious creative instincts wherever they may lead him, critics and consumers be damned; he wouldn't be Neil Young if it were otherwise. "Neil Young from the early Sixties and early Seventies is like Perry Como," Young told an interviewer in 1982. "That's the way I look at it. If I was still taking it that seriously, I'd be where Crosby, Stills and Nash are today."

After starting out the decade recording *Hawks and Doves*, an odd and frequently inscrutable amalgam of love songs and populist sloganeering, Young once again teamed up with Crazy Horse for *Reactor*. An uninspired return to the raunch-and-roll of *Rust Never Sleeps*, *Reactor* seemed more like a regression than a step forward. But then things really started getting interesting.

As primal punk mutated into the cold, metallic, keyboard-driven sounds of New Wave, Young followed suit with *Trans*, an album—his first for Geffen Records—that almost exclusively featured synthesizers and digitally processed guitars and vocals. "This new technology has opened up a whole new thing for me," Young told David Gans in 1982. "This is the most free expression I've been able to have, because it's so technical. I love the machines, and I think the machines are where it's at." Young, rock's unpredictable provocateur, was at it again. But this time, there was a method to his madness.

TEACH YOUR CHILDREN

In 1981, Young's second wife, Pegi, gave birth to a son afflicted with cerebral palsy. Remarkably, Young had now spawned two children with the disease by two different women (ex-wife Carrie Snodgrass had conceived his first son, Zeke). *Trans*' electronically generated vocals had evolved out of Young's "search for communication with a severely handicapped non-oral person"—his own son.

Wiping the slate clean of any easy-to-grasp musical references, Young alienated all but the most stalwart members of his audience with *Trans*, particularly when he toured behind the album. Not only did Young dare to play *Trans*' squonk-pop in its entirety, but he digitized and deconstructed old war-horses like "Down by the River" and "Mr. Soul" as well.

"The Eighties are here," Young told *Rolling Stone*. "I've got to just tear down whatever has happened to me and build something new." Although Young actually made that statement in 1988, the sentiment it conveyed was clearly close to his heart from the decade's outset. He's continued to reinvent himself throughout the Eighties, even as his record sales continued to dwindle. *Everybody's Rockin'*, his follow-up to *Trans*, was a straight-ahead rockabilly album featuring a pompadoured Young on the cover. *Old Ways*—recorded with a band of country musicians Young dubbed the International Harvesters—was his third neo-*Harvest* album, as gently pastoral as *Trans* was harsh and bloodless. All of the aforementioned albums were critically lambasted and sold only a fraction of what Young had been accustomed to.

Old Ways was Young's most user-friendly release since *Rust Never Sleeps*, but Geffen, weary of Young's abrupt stylistic detours and sagging commercial fortunes, thought otherwise. Shortly after he delivered the album, Geffen sued Young for making "unrepresentative music." "I handed in [*Old Ways*] and they sued me," Young told Bill Flanagan in 1985. "They said, 'We don't know what you're doing. We're scared! We want Neil Young!' That was confusing to me because I thought I *was* Neil Young. But it turns out that when I do certain things, I'm *not* Neil Young."

Frustrated and bogged down by the $3 million lawsuit, Young recorded two more albums for Geffen before returning to Warner Bros. Although they look and sound like more conventional "Neil Young" albums, *Landing on Water* and *Life* were really corporate concessions made expressly to appease Geffen and release Young from his contract.

"It was the worst period of my working life," Young told writer Greg Kot in 1990. "I felt I was being manipulated and I began manipulating back. It was all so anti-creative. Making music became a hassle."

Back at Warner Bros., Young was once again free to make records as he saw fit. Controversy continued to dog him, however. The 1987 release *This Note's for You* was yet another genre exercise, with Young fronting a big brassy blues band called the Blue Notes. But it was a video for the title song, not the album, that ruffled powerful feathers this time.

The Julien Temple-directed clip, a stinging commentary on the increasingly cozy relationship between rock stars and corporate sponsors, featured, among other commercial parodies, a send-up of the infamous Michael Jackson "hair-on-fire" Pepsi ad. Not too surprisingly, MTV, fearful of insulting its own sponsors, banned the video. When Young offered to re-edit the video and delete the bogus commercials, MTV still refused to air it.

"It's sort of like dealing with spineless twerps," Young told *Rolling Stone* at the time. He got the last laugh, however, when the clip, mock commercials and all, won MTV's Best Video of the Year award. Young was back in the public eye, but his comeback had only just begun.

RAGGED GLORY (1989-95)

By 1989, the thunderous sound of Young and Crazy Horse had influenced a new generation of artists who had been weaned on their older brothers and sisters' worn copies of *Decade*, the 1976 three-album retrospective of Young's career. Guitar-driven bands such as Dinosaur Jr, Sonic Youth and the Pixies—all of whom appeared on a 1989 Neil Young tribute album called *The Bridge*—were hailing Young as the forefather of alternative music. But instead of graciously accepting his elder statesman status, Young proclaimed he "wasn't ready to be embalmed yet," and came roaring back with renewed fervor.

Freedom, Young's triumphant 1989 return to form, combined anthem-rock ("Rockin' in the Free Word") and acerbic social commentary ("Crime in the City") with anarchic noise-rock ("On

Broadway," "Eldorado") just as effectively as *Rust Never Sleeps* had done 10 years previously. *Freedom* promptly became Young's best-selling album in a decade and started him on the road to an artistic and commercial rebirth.

1990's *Ragged Glory* paired Young with Crazy Horse for the first time in five years. A primal, snarling showcase for rock's ultimate garage band, the album featured some of Young's most impassioned, caterwauling guitar playing in eons. The release of the raging, infernal *Ragged Glory* also coincided with the emergence of grunge, a Seattle-based sub-genre whose best practitioners—Nirvana and Pearl Jam, in particular—credited Young with pioneering grunge's sound (loud, crunchy guitars) and style (flannel shirts, ripped jeans). After a decade of musical fits and starts, Young—the newly christened "Godfather of Grunge"—was back where he belonged, playing with the band that had spurred him to his greatest triumphs.

"I can't do this with anyone else," Young told Stephen Holden, referring to his longtime cohorts in Crazy Horse. "I don't think of my guitar solos as guitar solos, because when we play we're like a big band jamming and taking long rides together." With the one-two punch of *Freedom* and the Platinum-selling *Ragged Glory*, it was indisputably clear that Young was once again a musical force to be reckoned with.

Since *Freedom* revived Young's career, this timeless, ageless iconoclast has been anything but complacent. The Nineties have already seen him explore elegiac country (*Harvest Moon*), return to the meditative, ramshackle ugliness of the *Tonight's the Night* era (*Sleeps with Angels*) and kick-out-the-jams grunge (*Mirror Ball*). In between those projects, Young has toured with Booker T. and the M.G.'s, stolen the show at Bob Dylan's 30th anniversary concert, earned an Academy Award nomination (for his musical contribution to the film *Philadelphia*) and been inducted into the Rock and Roll Hall of Fame. What's next? There's been talk of a massive, multi-CD retrospective of his career and an autobiography, but don't hold your breath. If history is any indication, not even Young knows where he's headed.

Guitar World, November 1995

American Beauty

Guitar genius, hippie prince, King of the Dead—
Jerry Garcia was many things to many people.
Guitar World pays tribute to one of
the most influential musicians of our era.

By Blair Jackson

FORGET FOR A moment the dilapidated VW vans plastered with colorful decals and bumper stickers. Forget the legions of long-haired, tie-dye-wearing, pot- and patchouli-scented fans lost in that formless, serpentine dance-trance. Forget the smiling pictures of "Captain Trips," resplendent in an American flag hat and paisley velour shirt. Instead, *listen.*

Listen to the crystalline notes as they ascend in a bright spiral, then blast into deep space, scattering like cosmic debris. Listen to the melancholy cry of six strings singing about life and death, love and loss, memory and regret. Listen to the joyous dance of life in a thousand buoyant strums and bright melodic filigrees. Ten years, 20 years, 50 years from now, it's going to be Jerry Garcia's music—and not the day-glo Deadhead sideshow—that most people will remember.

The clichés come so easily: "counter-culture guru," "rock legend," "Pied Piper of the Haight," "tragic outlaw figure," etc. There is truth in all of these. But when the day is done, Jerry Garcia was really just a working guy who loved to play music. Celebrity and deification were unfortunate by-products and distractions for this gentle, self-effacing man whose strongest addiction was music, not

Guitar World Presents CLASSIC ROCK

Jerry Garcia of the Grateful Dead

drugs, and whose legacy is a body of music that is breathtaking in its scope.

The Grateful Dead's music was a crazy-quilt of different styles and influences. They drew from folk, bluegrass, old-timey, blues, r&b, ragtime, rock and roll, modern classical, jazz, Indian, electronic and just about any other style you'd care to name. Their musical heroes were people like the Beatles, Bach, Bob Dylan, John Coltrane, Bill Monroe, Howlin' Wolf, Merle Haggard, Ornette Coleman, Stravinsky, Chuck Berry, Edgar Varese and Willie Dixon, and they wore their influences proudly. At the same time, they assimilated those influences, improvised around them, and magically blended them into their own thoroughly original amalgam. Where does a song like "Help on the Way" come from? "Tennessee Jed"? "China Doll"? "Days Between"? These are unique slices of the Dead's peculiar oeuvre, impossible to categorize precisely except to say that they are Grateful Dead Music, with all that implies.

Even outside of the Dead, Garcia's appetite for music was voracious and all-consuming. The Jerry Garcia Band's repertoire came from Motown and Trenchtown, Chicago blues and Southern gospel, Irving Berlin and Mick Jagger, Hoagy Carmichael and Van Morrison. Then there was the acoustic music he played with mandolinist David Grisman: old mountain tunes, sea shanties, ageless ballads, a few Dead tunes and cool jazz numbers like Miles Davis' "So What" and Milt Jackson's "Bags' Groove." In the last year of his life alone, Garcia's studio work included adding guitar to a song on fellow-traveler and occasional GD member Bruce Hornsby's latest album (*Hot House*); cutting a version of the venerable pop standard "Smoke Gets in Your Eyes" with the Garcia Band for the superb film *Smoke* (directed by Wayne Wang, a one-time Garcia roadie); incomplete tracking on a new Dead album, and, in what was his last session, laying down "Blue Yodel #9" for an upcoming Jimmie Rodgers tribute album. Who knows what other irons were in the fire at the time of Garcia's sad demise?

Garcia grew up in San Francisco and lived his entire life in Northern California. He was named after composer Jerome Kern and was the son of clarinetist and band leader, Joe Garcia, whose drowning death during a family vacation was witnessed by a five-year-old Jerry. Around the same time, he lost part of the middle finger on his right hand when his older brother Clifford accidentally hit it with an axe. His mother, Ruth, remarried and tried to pick up the pieces for Jerry and Clifford, running a San Francisco bar frequented primarily by sailors and soldiers.

"I grew up in a musical household and took piano lessons as far back as I can remember," Garcia said in a 1993 interview. "The first time I decided that music was something I wanted to do, apart from just being surrounded by it, was when I was about 15. I developed this deep craving to play the electric guitar.

"I fell madly in love with rock and roll. Chuck Berry was happening big, Elvis Presley...I really liked Gene Vincent, the other rock guys, the guys that played guitar good: Eddie Cochran, Buddy Holly, Bo Diddley. At the same time, the r&b stations were playing stuff like Lightnin' Hopkins and Frankie Lee Sims, these funky blues guys. Jimmy McCracklin, the Chicago-style blues guys, the T-Bone Walker-influenced guys, that older style, pre-B.B. King. Jimmy Reed actually had hits back in those days. You listen to that and it's so funky. It's just a beautiful sound, but I had no idea how to go about learning it.

"When I first heard electric guitar, when I was 15, that's what I wanted to play. I petitioned my mom to get me one, so she finally did for my birthday. Actually, she got me an accordion and I went nuts—'Agggghh, no, no, no!' I railed and raved, and she finally turned it in, and I got a pawnshop [*Danelectro*] electric guitar and an amplifier. I was beside myself with joy.

"I started banging away on it without having the slightest idea of anything. I didn't know how to tune it up; I had no idea. My stepfather tuned it in some weird way, like an open chord...I played it that way for about a year before I finally ran into a kid at school who could actually play a little. He showed me a few basic chords, and that was it. I never took any lessons. I don't even think there was anybody teaching around the Bay Area. The electric guitar was like from Mars, you know. You didn't see 'em even."

While still in high school, Garcia decided to pursue his interest in drawing and painting, and this indirectly led to a shift in his musical interests. "I was an art student at the California School of Fine Art, which is now the San Francisco Art Institute, and I was taking a Saturday class, and my teacher played a four-string banjo and a little guitar," Garcia said in 1991. "[One day] he was playing a Big Bill Broonzy record. I was 16 or 17...I knew what it was but I'd never heard anyone play blues on an acoustic guitar, and it knocked me out."

Garcia dropped out of high school and enlisted in the Army, hoping to perhaps see more of the world. Instead he was stationed at San Francisco's Presidio, where he quickly learned that heavy discipline and regimentation were not for him: he went AWOL several times, and felt more at home hanging out in San Francisco's North Beach area—then still the center for the once-thriving Beat culture—than in his barracks. About the only positive aspect of being in the Army for him was that he met a few people who turned him on to country guitar styles.

"After I got out of the Army," he said in 1990, "I fell in with [*future songwriting partner Robert*] Hunter, and we were influenced by the folk scare—the Kingston Trio and that kind of stuff. I didn't know how to find my way into that kind of music 'til I met some people who were more involved with it, like Marshall Lester, who was a friend of mine from when I was 10 to 13. By now he was a college guy, and he turned me on to bluegrass music and old-time string band music. He played a little frailing banjo and introduced me to the [*blues fingerstylist*] Reverend Gary Davis. I heard that sound and I just had to be able to make it."

Garcia moved to the Peninsula (south of San Francisco) and lived hand-to-mouth for a few years, practicing the banjo and guitar night and day and playing in a succession of local string bands with fanciful names like the Thunder Mountain Tub Thumpers, the Sleepy Hollow Hog Stompers and the Black Mountain Boys. The endless hours of woodshedding in this wholly acoustic musical environment paid dividends that served Garcia for the rest of his career. His lifelong love of the clearly articulated note came in part from his passion for the banjo. And his devotion to improvisation was fueled by watching great country and bluegrass players.

"I get my improvisational approach from Scotty Stoneman, the fiddle player, who is the guy who first set me on fire—where I just stood there and don't remember breathing," Garcia recalled in 1991. "He was just an incredible fiddler. He grew up in bars and was a total alcoholic wreck by the time I heard him, in his early thirties, playing with the Kentucky Colonels [*featuring noted flatpicker Clarence White—later to play with the Byrds—and mandolinist Roland White*]. I went down to hear him the first time at the Ash Grove in L.A. They did a medium-tempo fiddle tune, and it's going along, and pretty soon Scotty starts taking these longer and longer phrases—10 bars, 14 bars, 17 bars—and the guys in the band are just watching him! They're barely playing—going ding, ding, ding—while he's burning. The place was transfixed. They played this tune for like 20 minutes, which is unheard of in bluegrass.

"I'd never heard anything like it. I asked him later, 'How do you do that?' and he said, 'Man, I just play lonesome.' He probably died of drinking hair tonic; he was another one of those guys... But his playing on the records he appears on—mostly anonymously—is this incredible blaze. He's like the bluegrass Charlie Parker."

Garcia was so deep into bluegrass that he spent a month in 1964 traveling through the South and Midwest with his Black Mountain Boys bandmate Sandy Rothman, recording various bluegrass bands. When Garcia returned to the Bay Area, however, he joined a bunch of his musical friends and formed what was actually a less serious group than many he'd been involved with: Mother McCree's Uptown Jug Champions, which included a scary-looking but soulful teenage blues singer and harmonica player named Ron McKernan—who'd already been dubbed "Pigpen" for his unkempt appearance—and a 16-year-old novice guitar player (actually a student of Garcia's at Dana Morgan's Palo Alto Music Shop) named Bob Weir. Also playing with the group from time to time were future Grateful Dead soundman Bob Matthews, and David Parker, who was to become the group's financial associate. This rag-tag bunch played a cool mixture of folk, blues and jug-band numbers in local clubs. But, by 1965, the Beatles had shown what fun being in a rock and roll band could be, Dylan had plugged in, and Pigpen was looking to get down with some amplified Chicago-style blues. Garcia, Weir and Pigpen recruited a young drummer named Bill Kreutzmann to join their new electric band, dubbed the Warlocks, and when Dana Morgan, Jr., son of the music store owner, couldn't quite cut it on bass, they brought in a one-time jazz trumpeter and "serious" music composer named Phil Lesh—even though he'd never played bass before.

The band cut its teeth playing in small clubs, bars and even a pizza parlor down on the Peninsula, playing mainly r&b and blues covers, as well as a few amplified folk and jug tunes. They often played five sets a night and built their following slowly—first driving out the regular patrons with their skull-splitting volume and weirdly elongated tunes, then bringing in their own audience of misfits and thrill-seekers. Around the same time, the Warlocks hooked up with *One Flew Over the Cuckoo's Nest* author Ken Kesey and his commune, the Merry Pranksters, becoming the de facto house band at their LSD parties, the infamous Acid Tests. "It wasn't a gig, it was the Acid Test," Garcia once said. "Anything was okay. It was far-out, beautiful magic. We had no reputation and nobody was paying to see us or anything like that. We weren't the headliners, the event was. Anything that happened was part of it. There was always the option to not play... The freedom is what I loved about it. When you're high, you might want to play five hours, but sometimes you might want to stick your head in a bucket of water, or have some Jell-O or something."

The group had already been smoking pot for a while, but LSD, which was legal until October, 1966, is what really blew the doors open and influenced the band to stretch out in weirder directions. Garcia, the guitarist, was being influenced by a number of different artists during this period, from Mike Bloomfield, whose incendiary blues playing fueled the music of Dylan and Paul Butterfield, to saxophonist John Coltrane. "I never copped his licks or sat down, listened to his records and tried to play his stuff," Garcia told an interviewer in 1981. "I [was] impressed with the idea of flow, of making statements that sound like paragraphs. [Coltrane would] play along stylistically with a certain kind of tone, in a certain kind of syntax, for X amount of time, then change the subject and play along with this other personality coming out. Perceptually, an idea that's been important to me in playing [*which also derives in part from Coltrane*] has been the whole odyssey idea—journeys, voyages, adventures along the way."

In December 1965 the Warlocks became the Grateful Dead and the group shifted its focus to San Francisco, where like-minded bohemians and psychedelic pioneers were quickly turning the Haight-Ashbury district into a hip mini-city with its own music, businesses and support services. The Dead were just one of a slew of bands that lived in the area, but from the beginning they were among the most popular—always guaranteed to get the crowds that drifted in and out of the various San Francisco ballrooms up and dancing, whether it was with a 15-minute version of Martha and the Vandellas' Motown smash "Dancing in the Streets," a peppy rendition of Howlin' Wolf's "Sitting on Top of the World," or their half-hour workouts of Wilson Pickett's "Midnight Hour," with Pigpen leading the charge. During this period and through the recording of the Dead's Warner Bros. debut album in early '67, Garcia played a red Guild Starfire, with a single cutaway and two pickups, through a Fender Twin Reverb amp. From the outset, Garcia's guitar style was marked by active motion in his left-hand fret-work—bending and shaping notes and dancing around the song's melody.

The band started writing its own material in earnest in late '67 and '68: This is the era that produced the ambitious "That's It for the Other One" (from *Anthem of the Sun*) and Garcia's first few collaborations with lyricist Robert Hunter, including "China Cat Sunflower," "Dark Star" and "St. Stephen." In '68 Garcia switched from the Guild to a Les Paul; then in '69 he moved on to a Gibson SG, which he used to shape the classic Garcia sound heard on what remains the watermark of the Dead's most psychedelic period, 1969's *Live Dead*. This double album (now a single CD) showcases Garcia and the Dead at the height of their improvisational powers, as they boldly navigate through 21 minutes of intense instrumental exploration on "Dark Star," build to one roiling, explosive climax after another on "The Eleven," and rip through Bobby Bland's "Turn on Your Love Light" like some crazy, funky bar band on multiple hits of LSD-manufacturer Owsley Stanley's finest.

As the Sixties drew to a close, Garcia added to his already rich sonic palette by playing acoustic guitar with greater regularity (a number of 1970 Dead shows featured an acoustic set, as well as songs that blended acoustic and electric instruments) and tackling the pedal steel guitar (a ZB model) both with the Dead and the country-rock Dead offshoot the New Riders of the Purple Sage.

"What I'm doing with the steel is I'm going after a sound I hear in my head that the steel has come closest to," Garcia noted in 1971. "I'm really a novice at it, but I'm not really trying to become a steel player." Novice though he was, Garcia's sound on the instrument was quite distinctive, and he lent his steel talents to several excellent albums between '69 and '71, including the Jefferson Airplane's *Volunteers* ("The Farm"), Brewer & Shipley's *Tarkio Road*, Paul Kantner's *Blows Against the Empire*, David Crosby's *If I Could Only Remember My Name* and, most famous of all, Crosby, Stills, Nash & Young's *Déjà Vu* ("Teach Your Children").

The fall of '69 through 1972 represents the Golden Era of Garcia's songwriting partnership with Robert Hunter: produced during this period were the studio albums *Workingman's Dead* and *American Beauty*, the solo *Garcia* (on which Garcia played all the instruments, except drums, himself), and the live *Grateful Dead* (better known as "Skull & Roses") and *Europe '72*. Between them, these albums cover a wide cross-section of American song styles, and contain many of the duo's best songs, including "Uncle John's Band," "New Speedway Boogie," "Black Peter," "Ripple," "Brokedown Palace," "Attics of My Life," "Wharf Rat," "Bertha," "Loser," "The Wheel," "Bird Song," "He's Gone" and "Tennessee Jed," to name just a handful. Garcia's guitar work in this era moved easily from twangy countrified picking—showing the influence of such masters of country's "Bakersfield

Sound" as Don Rich and Roy Nichols—to completely dissonant wah-wah inflected flights into outer space. Though the early Seventies saw the Dead frequently dubbed a "country rock band," it was also a period when they played some of their spaciest, most "difficult" music. Garcia's guitar of choice in this era was a '59 Fender Strat. He moved away from Gibsons because "I got bored with them," he said in '81. "I felt I really didn't have any place else to go on them. [The Strat] was more of a challenge. It wasn't that I wanted to lose the SG part of my playing, but my reasoning was along the lines of, 'I think that no matter what guitar I play, I won't have any trouble getting a sweet sound,' even though the most difficult thing to produce is a sweet sound."

As early as 1971 Garcia had been talking about having a guitar built for him, and by '73 this was a reality. A Northern California luthier named Doug Irwin built Garcia's first custom instrument, which he described as having the best features of both a Strat and an SG. "[Irwin] was working for a friend of mine, [and] I picked up a guitar that he had built the neck for at a guitar store and said, 'Wow, where did this come from? I gotta have this guitar!' " Garcia remembered a few years ago. "I bought the guitar and [upon discovering that Irwin had built the neck] I commissioned him to build me a guitar. He did, and I played this guitar [*nicknamed The Wolf because of its cartoonish hungry wolf inlay design*] for most of the Seventies. When he delivered it to me, I said, 'Now I want you to build me what you think would be the ultimate guitar. I don't care when you deliver it, I don't care how much it's gonna cost or anything else.' A couple of months later he told me it would cost about three grand, which, at the time, was a lot for a guitar, since it was the early Seventies. He delivered the guitar to me in '78, eight years later. I'd forgotten I'd paid for it. Whatever that guitar says to me, I play."

Since he first played The Wolf, Garcia played Irwin's guitars exclusively on stage, except from 1975-77, when he favored a bone-white Travis Bean. This was another fertile period for Garcia and the Dead—it includes the albums *Blues for Allah* and *Terrapin Station*. Not many changes in his playing style crop up during this era, though the introduction of some new effects (like the envelope filter that's so distinctive on "Estimated Prophet") did color his sound in interesting ways. Garcia's involvement with the insidious and addictive drug known as Persian (a heroin-like opiate that is smoked) began in the late Seventies, and while it's hard to gauge its effects on his playing, his songwriting output nose-dived from '79 until the diabetic coma that nearly killed him in 1986. "For a long time there I sort of lost heart," Garcia told me in 1988. "I thought, 'I don't know if I want to do this. I don't know what I want.' I felt like I wanted to get away from everything, somehow. But I didn't want to just stop playing, or have the Grateful Dead stop because that's what I wanted to do. I didn't even know consciously that's what I wanted."

For most of the Eighties, Garcia played an Irwin guitar nicknamed Tiger (again for its beautiful, distinctive inlay). When he became interested in incorporating a MIDI set-up into his arsenal in the late Eighties, Irwin came up with "Rosebud," and Garcia used that guitar, along with two lighter, graphite-necked models, until his death.

It's not surprising that Garcia embraced MIDI so enthusiastically—he was always an explorer on the lookout for new sounds and new ways of thinking about his instrument. So, beginning in 1989, songs that he'd played a hundred times with a certain tonality suddenly opened up for him in exciting new ways—"Bird Song" might have a flute line, "Shakedown Street" a soprano sax break, "Standing on the Moon" a breathy, undefinable choral quality and "Let It Grow" a Mexican horn part. And he employed a hundred other textural variations, from a light, shimmering musical shadow to full-out MIDI drums. The famous second-set "space" segment, in particular, became a MIDI playground for Garcia, Weir and Lesh.

Ask most hardcore Deadheads, and they'll probably admit that Garcia's playing during much of the last two years of his life wasn't as strong as it had been in the late Eighties, when he had recovered from the coma and was free of hard drugs. He produced his last great works—"Standing on the Moon" and "Days Between"—during this period. As his habit reasserted itself, from the middle of 1993 until his death, his on stage lapses and musical errors became more frequent, his playing often took on a listless quality for long stretches, and he seemed physically incapable of playing complex passages with any sort of precision. He had ongoing problems with carpal tunnel syndrome and just how much his slow but steady physical deterioration during this period affected his playing can only be guessed. Still, even on his final tour in June 1995, he was able to rise to the occasion—particularly on his moody ballads, which were always perhaps his strongest suit—and rip into a solo with an unbridled passion and grace that was something to behold.

Jerry Garcia was never the type of guitarist who topped guitar magazine reader's polls. He was always an ensemble player; a brilliant and distinctive instrumental voice, to be sure, but still just one bright thread in the complex weave of the Grateful Dead's sound. He was the antithesis of the flashy guitar extrovert, choosing to stand stock-still most of the time, letting his fingers do all the dancing and fancy moves. He hit more clams than your average pro, but that's because he was fishing for pearls, always looking around the next corner, following his muse and his bandmates into uncharted realms. Constant improvisation involves higher risk, but the payoff is worth it; the musicians and the audience are witnesses to the birth of music that is completely fresh and new.

Looking around the musical landscape he left behind, we don't see many Garcia imitators per se, but there is now a generation of players who have been, at the very least, influenced by his and the Dead's way of doing things—staying true to themselves, their music and their fans, record biz be damned. And, of course, the counterculture the band literally helped create 30 years ago has evolved into a strong and vibrant community. Garcia may be gone—and, as the song says, "nothing's gonna bring him back"—but it's already clear that his sweet song will reverberate forever.

"People need celebration in their lives," Garcia said in 1989, trying to explain the Dead's appeal. "It's part of what it means to be human. I don't know why. We need magic. And bliss. [We need] power, myth and celebration in our lives, and music is a good way to encapsulate a lot of it."

Guitar World, October 1996

Trick or Treat

The feast-or-famine story of Rick Nielsen and Cheap Trick, America's greatest power pop band.

By Tom Beaujour

I T'S A BRUTALLY hot day in Rockford, Illinois, and rock legend Cheap Trick is about to make a special hometown appearance at Lollapalooza '96. Most of the 35,000 being crushed against the stage weren't even alive during the band's late Seventies heyday, and are largely oblivious to the fact that they're about to witness one of America's greatest rock and roll bands in action.

Backstage, however, the air is pregnant with anticipation. Metallica's James Hetfield and Jason Newsted, Soundgarden's Kim Thayil and Matt Cameron, Joey Ramone and Rancid's Tim Armstrong and Lars Fredericksen have all forsaken the air conditioned comfort of their dressing rooms and tour buses to watch the band perform from the wings. And as Cheap Trick hits the sun-baked stage and tears through a rousing set, it becomes clear that all in the superstar audience are fans of the band's unique brand of amped-up power pop. Another artist who would certainly have enjoyed the show is the late Kurt Cobain, who once said, "Nirvana is a very heavy pop band—like if Cheap Trick were to have a lot of distortion on their guitars." When the all-too-brief set comes to a close with a roaring rendition of the classic "Surrender," Cameron

Guitar World Presents CLASSIC ROCK

Rick Nielsen of Cheap Trick

is visibly disappointed by the brevity of the band's set. "Fuck! That's it?" he pouts. "They didn't even play 'Auf Wiedersehen.' "

Truth be told, this is a rare occasion for Cheap Trick, who these days rarely get the opportunity to parade themselves in front of America's youth. Nor do they often share a bill with any of the current "alternative" bands they have so profoundly influenced. More typically, the Tricksters find themselves relegated to nostalgic classic rock package bills and smaller club dates attended by legions of aging, if rabid, fans. "Of course, once in a while it feels like a chore," says Nielsen of the band's incessant touring. "But do you think we would keep doing it if we didn't love it? Most people would have hung it up long ago."

It has been a long time—more than a decade and a half in fact—since the band released the seminal albums that would place them at the top of every power popster's list of influences. Combining an obsession with British Invasion melodies with a addiction to raw guitar power, Cheap Trick blew out of the Midwest with 1977's *Cheap Trick* (Epic), a fire-breathing album propelled by Robin Zander's over-the-top vocals and the ultra-tasteful rhythm section of bassist Tom Petersson and drummer Bun E. Carlos. But what truly set the band apart from their contemporaries were their quirky lyrics and, more than anything else, the eccentric persona of guitarist/mastermind Rick Nielsen. The quintessential guitar anti-hero, Nielsen was an absurdist, checkerboard-clad blur whose prodigious collection of baseball caps and geeky bow ties was matched only by his mouth-watering arsenal of guitars. "I would hear two things when we were starting out," Nielsen recalls. " 'Rick, whatever you're on, I want some!' and 'Whatever you're on, I don't want to know about it.' "

Following their debut, Cheap Trick produced four more stellar discs in the space of two years: *In Color* (Epic, 1977), *Heaven Tonight* (Epic, 1978), *At Budokan* (Epic, 1979) and *Dream Police* (Epic, 1979). And then suddenly, as the Eighties dawned, Nielsen and company lost their footing, recording a series of ill-conceived albums that did little or nothing to further the band's career or reputation. It's a tailspin from which the band is still trying to recover.

But the beauty of Cheap Trick, and what makes their devotees love them as one loves a delinquent child, is that there's always the outside chance that one day they'll get their shit back together. The band, too, seems intent on restoring their good name. At present, they perform virtually none of their weaker, late-period material and are in the midst of intense songwriting sessions, feverishly trying to recapture the magic of their early years. It's a goal which, in view of their continued prowess as a live act, seems well within their reach.

And just as the band sets its sights on the future, *Sex, America, Cheap Trick* (Epic/Legacy), a jam-packed four-disc box, celebrates their legacy. The box includes a healthy dose of greatest hits and misses, outtakes and previously unreleased gems, scrupulously documenting Cheap Trick's rocky two-decade-plus run for the money.

GUITAR WORLD: Many of today's young bands, like Smashing Pumpkins and the Posies, cite you as an important influence on their music.
RICK NIELSEN: We always hear about all these bands that like us. I think they like us because we're still around and because we've made every mistake possible. We've done good and we've done lousy, we've sold records, and we haven't sold. And through it all, we're still around and we actually can play and actually write songs.
GW: Do you hear your influence when you listen to those bands?
NIELSEN: Yeah, but I usually hear it more in the bands that don't admit it. [*laughs*] With the bands that do cop to it, I don't always quite hear the direct influence, although I have to confess that I don't scrutinize and listen to music all the time. It's too difficult to keep up with. I can barely remember the guys' names in Aerosmith! I don't have the passion to be an archivist.
GW: Cheap Trick recently played with Smashing Pumpkins in Chicago, at their record release party for *Mellon Collie and the Infinite Sadness* (Virgin, 1995). What was that like?
NIELSEN: It was cool. They were nice as pumpkins. Nice as could be. It was especially cool because they asked us. Billy Corgan and the rest of the band came to one of our shows—one that we were hap-

py to play, but which I thought was flawed in a number of ways. After the show, we talked for a while. Soon after that, I got a two-page letter from him that didn't mention any of the stuff that was wrong with the show. It just talked about what was right. It was one of the best letters—maybe *the* best letter—I've ever gotten from a fan. It seemed especially validating because people know who he is. It was inspirational to me. He knew my music more than I know his, and since then I've been trying to catch up.

GW: Setting aside the fact that Tom Petersson left the band for several years during the Eighties, Cheap Trick has managed to remain intact for more than two decades. What's held you together?

NIELSEN: Tom left? Oh, yeah. I guess I remember hearing something about that. [*laughs*]

We've stuck together because we're the best Cheap Trick band around. I don't think we know our total capabilities, but we *do* know our limitations. Is Bun E. the best drummer? No. Is Tom the best bassist? Am I the best guitarist? No. But together, it's pretty cool. As Cheap Trick, there's no four better than what we've got. Some guy could be flashier, but that would destroy our simplicity.

We value simplicity, but we're not slouches either. We know music well enough to throw in the occasional weird twist or left turn—a seventh chord to a major to a minor—cool little details that go by so fast that a lot of people don't even notice them. Most importantly, we're still banging around and we're still pissed off, which proves we're alive and which proves we care.

Once in a while, I feel like I've run the gamut, that I should move on and do something else, but every time I sit down with a guitar I'm like, "Hey, I really like this!" Some people might say, "Well, you guys certainly aren't the 'new thing' anymore." But I don't think that we're embarrassing—well, maybe a little. But not *too* much. [*laughs*]

GW: How did you come to adopt your goofy, almost court jester-like persona?

NIELSEN: As far back as when I was in high school, my nickname in the clubs was "the Screaming Chicken" because I used to smash and trash shit and jump around screaming. I didn't know any better.

I never wanted to be the best-looking person in the world. I never wanted to be the richest person in the world. I was never going to be the prettiest guy in town. I was never going to be the groovy guy with great, groovy hair and rock and roll lips. I was a songwriter, you know?

GW: Do you think that the persona hurt you in any way, that it eclipsed your skills as a musician?

NIELSEN: Well, really, what's a serious rock musician? Somebody who's so good that he completely ignores reality, and immerses himself in art for art's sake—with no concerns about whether it sells or not? If that's how you feel, go back to your room and play all you want! Be happy! Don't lay it on us!

Of course, by today's standards, anything I did back then seems tame. Now you've got to tattoo your head and have unicorn horns made out of horse penises coming out of your ears to leave any impression at all.

It was like, "Well, let's see...we could be the loudest band. No, that's already been done. We could be the smelliest band...nah. We could be the band that only swears...nah." The name Cheap Trick in itself came out of the fact that we were trying to have fun when everyone else was playing progressive rock and writing pretentious concept albums. We were like, "What the hell is that all about?"

Cheap Trick has always suffered from an identity crisis. When we made the first album, I had a dilemma and went to Tom and said, "This album has pop songs like 'Mandocello' and crazy stuff like 'The Ballad of T.V. Violence (I'm Not the Only Boy),' a song sung from the perspective of serial killer Richard Speck. I feel like I should use different songwriting names like 'Harvey Neat Song' and 'Dick Chainsaw Killer.' " He said, "Screw it. Your personality is that you have all that stuff inside of you. You shouldn't feel embarrassed about any of it."

GW: Unlike many power pop bands who just sing about broken hearts and puppy love, many of your songs, particularly on your first album, do have a darker side to them. For example, "Daddy Should Have Stayed in High School" is sung from the perspective of a twisted older man stalking little girls at the playground.

NIELSEN: "I'm 30 but I feel like 16." With those lyrics, I was trying to put myself in the place of a grown man who's consumed by lust for girls half his age. The song addresses the kind of dark thoughts that go through a lot of people's minds. It's like when you ask, "Well, do you ever think about suicide?" [*sarcastically*] "Gee, no, I've never heard that word!"

Writers for movies, TV, books or songs are free to mess around, and mess around with their own minds as well.

GW: Beneath its pop sheen, the 1979 single "Dream Police" seems to be a song about impending madness.

NIELSEN: I've been an insomniac all my life. For my physical well-being I pursue more sleep, but I often dream so heavily that I wake up exhausted! "Dream Police" is an attempt to take a heavy thought—a quick bit of REM snatched right before waking up—and put it into a pop format. I could have created some spooky, heavy, Metallica-like song to go along with those lyrics [*sings the chorus of "Dream Police" with a sinister rasp*], but then we'd have been Black Sabbath doing "Iron Man." When Ozzy sings something like that, you believe him, but from me? Come on! Our songs are half pop and half something else.

GW: When you made the first Cheap Trick album (*Cheap Trick* [Epic, 1977]), you were 30 and had already made an album with Fuse (*Fuse*, [Epic, 1969]). You must have had a pretty strong idea of what you did and didn't want.

NIELSEN: We never said this to one another, but essentially we wanted our album to sound like the cool B-sides of all the singles that we loved but that nobody had ever heard of. I remember that back in high school, we'd all take the same subjects, we all listened to the same radio stations and we all ate the same lunch—but I always wanted to know more than that.

I was one of the few people around here who would listen to this station from Little Rock that played the top ten English singles every Sunday night. The first time I heard Jimi Hendrix was on that show. I was out driving and pulled over to the side of the road when

I heard it. I was like, "I'm *not* going to lose this signal!" I didn't care where I was going or who I was going to meet. I was always addicted to the feeling that I was listening to stuff nobody else I knew had heard. When my friends had parties, I would always walk in with something that no one had ever heard of before. I'd be like, "Guys, I've got the latest whatever." Of course, I would listen to it first to see if it was any good. And if they didn't like it—all the better. You don't want your bands to be obscure, but you don't want people who don't get it to get it.

GW: Of course, it can become a problem if you've built your *own band's* music around stuff that most people don't get.

NIELSEN: [*laughs*] Yeah, but despite popular belief and the subsequent reality of it, we never deliberately made any record to be obscure. Although quite a few are.

GW: Did you pick Jack Douglas, who produced the first album, or was he assigned to you by the label?

NIELSEN: We decided that we didn't want some staff producer and went about the business of figuring out which records we liked. Well, the English producer guys who we liked were in England, so we figured we would never get them. And we weren't really big fans of Aerosmith but, man, that *Rocks* [*Columbia, 1976*] album—Jeez! Forget about it.

So we figured, "Jack Douglas: sells tons of records and gets great sounds—let's get that guy." Then he came to see us in Waukesha, Wisconsin, at this club called the Sunset Bowl. By that point we had built up quite a following and there we were, playing these goofy songs, jumping around and smashing ceiling tiles out of this ugly room. He said, "Yeah, I love you guys." It was like, "Wow! Somebody told us they like us! Sure, we'll have sex with them!"

Of course, our first choice had been John Lennon. I mention that in the liner notes to the box set. He was the "us" guy of the Beatles, the one who seemed to embody so much of what Cheap Trick was about. He didn't have the best voice in the world—but he had the best voice in the world. He didn't play great—but he played great. All of us could relate to him on some level.

We talked to our manager who said he would put a call in to his people. We didn't know any better, we believed that he could get a call through. Of course, we never heard back. So then four years later, when Bun E. and I were working with Lennon on the *Double Fantasy* [Geffen, 1980] sessions with Jack Douglas, we mentioned it to him and he said, "Oh, well, I would have done it!" Of course, given the situation that's probably what anybody would say, but I believed him and I still believe that.

GW: What was working with Lennon like?

NIELSEN: It was great. Jack had called us in because Lennon was trying to get a little bit of a harder edge on his stuff and he wanted us to supply it. Lennon liked the way I played. Once, while I was in the booth doing "Losing You," he said to Bun E., "Boy, I wish that I had had this guy when I was recording 'Cold Turkey' [*a song on which Eric Clapton played guitar*] because Clapton choked up on that."

GW: That's quite an accolade.

NIELSEN: Not bad, right?

GW: Getting back to the making of *Cheap Trick*, how long did that album take to record?

NIELSEN: Twenty days or so.

GW: Was it essentially recorded live?

NIELSEN: Yup. But we took the time to experiment, as well. We would take Tom's bass amp out into the stairwell and have it reverberating like mad. We were like, "Gee, that's noisy! Cool!"

GW: Do you remember the guitar and amp setup you used on *Cheap Trick*?

NIELSEN: I was probably using my Orange 80-watt 2 x 12 combo and some Sound City amps. In 1968, I went and bought either six or eight stacks of Sound City amps that I still have and use today. I was one of the first people in America to know about Orange, and also one of the first people to bring a Mellotron back to the United States.

As far as guitars go, I probably used some Fender Esquires, Telecasters, '57 Strats and Gibson Les Paul Juniors with humbuckers put in them. Back then, there were no "vintage guitars." These were still just used guitars. "Vintage" was a word that you used for wine—

maybe. They were like used cars. You could buy a Les Paul Junior back then for $200, so you didn't care about keeping it in original condition. If you thought the P-90 didn't sound quite right, you pulled it out.

GW: Were you consciously trying to make an album that was harsh and abrasive?

NIELSEN: It still wasn't what we had envisioned. But while you make an album, you sit there in the control room and listen on big speakers and it sounds cool.

It was wonderful. We just had so many ideas at that time. We went in and recorded 28 songs during those sessions. We recorded "I Want You to Want Me" and "Surrender" then, but we didn't use those versions. Not that we made things any better when we recorded them again, although I suppose that, in some ways, Tom Werman, who produced the next few albums, did make things more listenable—and in some ways more unlistenable. He toned us down so we could at least get listened to. A few people got the songs *and* the noise on the first album, but most people didn't get the songs *or* the noise. And that record wasn't even as heavy as we wanted it to be!

GW: Despite the fact that you worked with him on several albums—*In Color, Heaven Tonight* and *Dream Police*—you seem to have had a love/hate relationship with Werman's production style.

NIELSEN: Oh definitely. He hated the Sex Pistols, and we thought they were great. When *Never Mind the Bollocks* [*Virgin, 1977*] came out, I thought it was the ultimate. The Pistols were the storm troopers of England, and that album captured everything that we've ever wanted to do with our snarly songs like "Auf Wiedersehen" and "He's a Whore." We didn't want to depose the Queen like they did or anything like that, but we wanted to spit our rock venom. With Werman, that just wasn't going to happen. But when you're making a record, you're so happy just to be there that you let things go.

GW: Still, it must be difficult to continue recording an album if you're not happy with the way it sounds.

NIELSEN: What you have to realize is that, with any producer we ever worked with, be it Douglas or Werman or Roy Thomas Baker, we recorded innumerable heavy tracks. But it always got sort of lost in the mix. Our balls were usurped, you could say.

Name almost any song, and I recorded heavy guitar tracks for it. But then we'd get asked to add more decorative, prettier parts—this little ringing on top—and all of a sudden, the ringing was the gist and the basic track was lost. Before you know it, you're brainwashed, and everyone is telling you, "Don't worry, we'll fix it in the mix." It's never been fixed in the mix *ever*.

GW: The consequences of that sort of situation are glaringly apparent when one compares the dolled-up *In Color* version of "I Want You to Want Me" to the Who-like, guitar-driven version on the box set that you recorded with Douglas during the *Cheap Trick* sessions.

NIELSEN: The *In Color* version is so wimpy, it's unbelievable. It sounds incredibly sappy, especially when you hear it now. But back then, people weren't ready to hear us the way we really were.

It's not like the original version was the greatest thing in the world, but we wanted Werman to knock off only *some* of our warts. Some warts are badges and medals of the war you've gone through.

GW: During that period, you produced albums at an astonishing rate. *Cheap Trick, In Color, Heaven Tonight* and *At Budokan* were all released in the space of two years.

NIELSEN: The label didn't know what to do with us, so they kind of allowed us to have our way. We didn't cost them that much! [*laughs*] Nobody held a gun to our head. There was no formula for what to do.

Back then, there were two things going on in our minds simultaneously: we were shocked that anyone gave enough of a crap about us to put out our records. But we were also shocked because we weren't *selling* any records. We were humble and arrogant at the same time.

GW: It must have come as a relief then, when *At Budokan* finally took off.

NIELSEN: It was funny, though. That album was never intended for American release. There was no reason to put out a live album in America, where we had no hits at all.

At Budokan was geared to the hit singles that we'd had in Japan. I wish it had been a double album that included some of the songs like "Downed" and "Stiff Competition" that we put on *Budokan II* [*Epic, 1993*]. It would have shown a heavier side of the band to the world.

GW: It seems that you've made similar errors in judgment at several key junctures in your career. Does that have anything to do with why you recently split with Ken Adamany, your manager of more than 20 years?

NIELSEN: You know the old musician's cliché about leaving for "artistic reasons?" Well, we left for medical reasons; he made us sick. [*laughs*] That's a joke, of course.

He had one business philosophy, which was very good in certain ways. The good things that he did and can do are terrific, and the other things, well... Since the very early days there were projects proposed to us that we weren't allowed to do.

Just to give you an example, I was asked in 1979 or '80 to do a solo record. I should have made the time for that. It's not like I wanted to take two years off to do it. I wanted to do the album as quickly as possible but do it cool.

One song on the box set is sort of a vestige of that solo project—the version of "World's Greatest Lover" with me singing on it. It was a song that I had been goofing around with for a long time, that didn't seem to fit the Cheap Trick format. Then, of course, when we started working with George Martin on *All Shook Up*, it was like, "This guy can take this thing and do something with it." And with him at the helm, you didn't want *me* singing it. Let's be realistic, Robin's a little bit better of a singer than I am.

That song was written from the perspective of a guy sitting in a foxhole, and all his buddies are getting blown up all around him, in World War II, Korea, Vietnam—wherever. And he's sitting there writing this letter, trying to figure out how to say "I love you" to his girl back home before he gets killed. My original concept was to include lots of explosions and other sound effects, but obviously that detracts from the song, and the rest of the band didn't really get that.

The idea for the solo stuff was to use Robin, but also other vocalists. I had enlisted Bon Scott, who said that he would do it, Steve

Marriott from Humble Pie, Alex Harvey, Roger Chapman from Family, Roy Wood from the Move and I wanted to try to get Jeff Lynne from E.L.O.

I envisioned taking a few songs like "Auf Wiedersehen" that I thought had been overlooked on our albums because they weren't singles and trying them with a new spin. There were a lot of songs that we did that I'd have liked to resurrect, not because I'm lazy but because I believed in them.

So I was offered the opportunity to do this project and told that I couldn't. Well, there are no guarantees—it could have been a huge flop, but at least I would have gone out trying. And now, four fifths of those singers are dead!

GW: After working with Tom Werman up through *Dream Police* you chose three producers in a row: George Martin [*the Beatles*], Roy Thomas Baker [*Queen, Journey*] and Todd Rundgren [*Meat Loaf*].

NIELSEN: George Martin was the ultimate—the greatest producer. George Martin was my pal! The Guy had done everything and didn't need to do any more. Musically, he was the most knowledgeable person I had worked with, and someone I could emulate. Out of all the people we worked with, George was the one who came closest to doing what he said he would do. He did more than he had to for us. He could have phoned it in. [*laughs*]

All Shook Up [*Epic, 1980*] was recorded in Montserrat, at a studio the Stones had used. It's the same studio that you see in the Police's video for "Every Little Thing She Does Is Magic."

GW: Was it hard to take any sort of artistic stand when dealing with a producer of such enormous stature?

NIELSEN: No. Not at all. To him, there weren't any bad ideas, just ideas. You see, he didn't write the Beatles' songs, he rewrote them. I worked extra hard on the arrangements before we went in with George. I didn't want to show up with three chords and be like, "Okay, George. Fix it!"

George really pushed us to go the extra mile in our songwriting, arranging and playing. For example, we never would have attempted a song as complex as "Go for the Throat" without his encouragement. That song would have been tricky even for Rush to execute properly!

Also, we made that record during a very strange time for us, because Tom Petersson had one foot out the door.

I wish he had wanted to leave when we were working with Werman or Richie Zito—but not with *George Martin*. But that's where the cards had been dealt. So the whole time we were making that album, instead of talking about music, I was talking about relationships.

GW: Describe your experience making *One on One* (Epic, 1982) with Roy Thomas Baker.

NIELSEN: Roy Thomas Baker was probably the most extravagant, the most eccentric and the most fun. If he liked something, he would let us go all out on it. He'd be like, "Don't tone down the guitars! Be bombastic! Scream here!" But then, sometimes, you'd play him something and he'd just be like, "I don't like it." We would ask him what in particular he didn't like…was it the guitar, the third verse? He would never answer those kinds of questions. There was no constructive criticism or middle ground. It was either, "Yeah!" or "That stinks. Let's go to dinner." [*laughs*]

GW: How about working with Todd Rundgren on *Next Position Please* [Epic, 1983]?

NIELSEN: I got along great with Todd because we're both screwballs. But Todd had a very strange, rigid schedule where he would only work from noon until six. That gave us 18 hours a day to sit around and watch this one TV set that was in the house we stayed in. That wasn't much fun; we watched what Bun E. wanted to watch.

GW: Why haven't you ever produced an album yourselves?

NIELSEN: Why ask why?

GW: Did you ever ask to be allowed to?

NIELSEN: We used to lobby for it. I'd say, "Why Not? I don't get it. Where's this rule that we can't produce ourselves? It's not like we're doing something real bad." And rather than argue and argue, we would give in.

GW: It seems that your relationship with Epic Records in the mid-to late-Eighties can be summed by misspelling your name "Rick Nelson" on the back cover of *Standing on the Edge* [Epic, 1985].

NIELSEN: Why didn't that record do well? Well they couldn't even spell my name. The fundamentals were not tended to. On a check, they can call me "Mr. Mxyzptik" for all I care. But on the back of the album? It takes about one second to check something like that.

Of course, when the label forces you into doing something that you don't want to do, like making us record "The Flame" [Lap of Luxury *(Epic, 1988)*], and then it becomes a Number One hit, then you're happy about it. I've been up on our web site lately, and people have been saying things like, "I'm happy that Cheap Trick isn't playing 'The Flame' at their gigs anymore." And it's funny that now, after being forced into doing that song, I find myself defending it. It wasn't the scourge of the earth. I mean, I hated the song when it was presented to me, but that was only after I was told by people around me that I was a piece of shit, that I didn't know how to write anymore, and who the hell was I? Also, we only agreed to "The Flame" after I had rejected 12 or 15 other songs.

Our producer for that album, Richie Zito, who knows every song ever written since "My Boy Lollipop," refused to admit that the intro of that song was lifted directly from Spirit's "Nature's Way," which they had a huge hit with in 1970. That was the one song he'd never heard of!

GW: That must have been a very difficult time for you as a songwriter, being forced to perform other people's material.

NIELSEN: Well, it's a strange thing. People say, "Oh wow, your first record's great—you really know how to write." But then the record doesn't sell and before you know it...you lose your confidence. I cared so much about the band that I was willing to try anything. I didn't want to be a whore. I didn't want to sleep with *them*, I didn't want to be a stripper, but my kids were hungry! We agreed to it. It's hard to say no to those people in the big buildings in New York.

Guitar World Presents CLASSIC ROCK

Joe Perry of Aerosmith

Guitar World, April 1997

Classic Rocks

Aerosmith takes a disc-by-disc journey through the albums that made it America's greatest hard rock band.
By Alan di Perna

THE FIRST SONG that Steven Tyler, Joe Perry and Tom Hamilton played together was "I'm Down," a Beatles cover that Aerosmith would reprise 17 years later on their 1987 multi-Platinum "comeback album," *Permanent Vacation*. Back in 1970, the three young rockers were still years away from being even single Platinum, but the obsessive, energetic Tyler had his eyes on the prize—as always.

"A friend of ours who was roadying for Led Zeppelin heard that the Jeff Beck Group was looking for a singer," Joe Perry remembers. "Steven was without a band at the time, so he asked me and Tom to play on 'I'm Down' for a demo, so he could send a vocal to Jeff. We were in a club and they ran a little Wollensak tape recorder. That was way before cassettes."

Rock history might have turned out very differently had Tyler gotten the gig with Beck. But that humble demo session gave birth to Aerosmith, the definitive American hard rock band. 1970 was a void year in rock. Jimi Hendrix, Jim Morrison, Janis Joplin and Brian Jones were all dead. The Beatles had disbanded. The hippie dream was over. The forces that would define Seventies rock—metal, glam, funk, prog rock, fusion—hadn't quite crystallized yet.

Aerosmith would become one of the most important bands in that crystallization—shaping the sound, look and attitude of Seventies rock. They took a lot of shit from the critics at first. But many of the very traits deemed tacky and derivative by early Seventies rock critics (aging hippies, for the most part) are now venerated by children of the Nineties as the quintessence of cool.

Meanwhile, Aerosmith has transcended the decade that gave it birth. Rising from the ashes of drug addiction in the mid Eighties, the large-lipped Mr. Tyler and his band have become a classic rock icon, an American cultural institution whose signifying power has been tapped by everyone from Run D.M.C. to *Wayne's World*, from Beavis and Butt-head to Robin Williams in drag as Mrs. Doubtfire.

It's staggering to think that all this came out of an amateurish recording of "I'm Down." That fateful first session took place in Sunapee, New Hampshire, where Joe Perry and Tom Hamilton had assembled a series of cover bands with names like the Pipe Dream, Plastic Glass and the Jam Band to play for the summer tourist trade. Steven Tyler was a slick urban hipster by comparison—up from New York City where he'd played the Bitter End in Greenwich Village and hung around at the One Sheridan Square club, catching glimpses of Donovan and the Stones. Tyler, born Steven Tallarico, was already a pro. During the final years of the Sixties, he'd sung backing vocals on some singles by the Left Banke (who'd had a big hit earlier on with "Walk Away Renee"). As drummer and vocalist with his own group, the Strangeurs (later re-christened Chain Reaction), Tyler had even opened for the Yardbirds when that legendary rock band had Jimmy Page on lead guitar.

"Steven's bands were so fucking professional," Tom Hamilton recalls. "Joe and I would go to see them when they played up in New Hampshire, and it was always real hard to get in. The place was always packed."

Hamilton and Perry had decided to move down to Boston and take a shot at going pro themselves. For their drummer, they recruited Joey Kramer, a musician who'd grown up with Tyler in Yonkers, a New York suburb just north of the Bronx.

JOE PERRY: One night I saw Steven at a party and said, "Maybe we should hook up." He wanted to sing and not play drums anymore. So I said, "We got this guy, Joey Kramer, involved." And when Joey heard Steven was thinking about joining, he said he'd join too. So we all moved in together in Boston. Tom and I rented an apartment and everybody moved in.

STEVEN TYLER: And what a move-in it was!

PERRY: It was a rockin' place: 1325 Commonwealth Avenue, on the second floor. Open door. It was wild. Boston was such a great place to have a band because it's a college town. Everybody had so much energy, and all the freshman girls, and…it was just wild.

TYLER: You couldn't walk down the hallway, 'cause we'd lined the wall to the ceiling with amps. To get to the bathroom, you had to walk sideways—do the shuffle. That was the apartment. That's how it was. We'd bring all the gear up every night because we didn't want to get ripped off. We had it in an International Harvester flour truck owned by our roadie, Mark, who lived there too. Every night after a show, at three in the morning, we'd be lugging the shit up the stairs again.

AEROSMITH (Columbia, 1973)

That funky communal apartment witnessed the realization of several songs that would form the backbone of Aerosmith's self-titled debut album, including the all-time classic "Dream On," and "Movin' Out"—Tyler and Perry's first joint composition (in every sense of the term). Meanwhile, the band—who had taken on Brad Whitford to replace an earlier guitarist, Ray Tabano—had connected with the management team of Steve Leber and David Krebs, whose other client at the time was the New York Dolls. Initially, both the Dolls and Aerosmith were dismissed as Rolling Stones clones by the rock press. But subsequent rock history has more than vindicated both bands.

GUITAR WORLD: What other songs, besides "Dream On," did you write at that apartment?

TYLER: "One Way Street." Actually, I wrote them up in New Hampshire, in Sunapee, but that apartment is where I put "Dream

On" together with the lyrics and stuff.

TOM HAMILTON: I liked it from the beginning. I used to wake up hearing it, the piano was in my room, and Steven would be in there. He got up earlier than me. He'd come in and start playing it.

TYLER: I wrote the lyrics to "Dream On" in the Hilton at the airport [*in Boston*]. That was our managers' idea. Managers are all the same. They said: "We don't want you writing at home, you won't get anything done. Come down here and stay in the hotel."

PERRY: They wanted us to be away from our girlfriends, because they figured we'd be able to concentrate better. But either I wouldn't show up at the hotel, or I'd bring my girlfriend with me.

GW: What do you recall about putting together that great two-guitar arrangement for "Dream On?"

BRAD WHITFORD: The idea was just to transcribe what Steven was doing with his left and right hands on the piano.

TYLER: Joe played the right hand; Brad played the left.

HAMILTON: ...which became a pretty big part of how we arrange songs.

GW: Was "Movin Out" the first Tyler/Perry composition?

TYLER: Yes. I remember being overjoyed that I had some lyrics for that, and also that we put another hole in Mark's [*the long-suffering roadie*] waterbed. I was sitting on the waterbed trying to write these lyrics, and the pipe was lit. We were smoking pot; dropped seeds crackling all over the place. We closed the door and I just remember a stream of consciousness came out [*reciting lyric*]: "Tell me what you know and I'll tell you who to/Go see my friend and he'll set you free/Tell me what you need and maybe I can go too/No one knows the way but maybe me." Now what does *that* mean? Didn't matter. It was just great. It was one of those examples of where you start the song off low and you just jump up to the next octave.

GW: At times, it seems almost as if you conceive of your lyrics as rhythm riffs.

TYLER: That's because I was a drummer for eight years before I was in this band.

GW: Did Aerosmith ever share a bill with the New York Dolls?

PERRY: Sure. Many times. When we first played [*hip Manhattan night spot*] Max's Kansas City to get our record deal, we were so wet behind the ears. I'd never played New York. Steven had with a few other bands, but certainly not with the kind of band we were in. We were there, and the Dolls came up to watch us do a soundcheck, something they never did themselves. I don't think they were ever in tune. But they sure looked great.

When we came down to New York, the Dolls were the big thing, the media darlings. We thought all you had to do was play well and write good songs. But they were proving that all you had to do was look good. And they rocked out, too. I can't take anything away from them. I love their first two records. They had a rock and roll attitude that just wouldn't stop. And so we ended up going out on the road with them. When they were away from New York, they really had a hard time, because they didn't really play that well. In New York, when they were on and had their clique around them, there was nothing like seeing the Dolls at the Mercer Arts Center. It was exploding. But as soon as they got out into the Midwest where people wanted to hear lead guitar, they weren't as strong. We'd do three-act bills. It was the Dolls, us and Mott the Hoople or something. And the Dolls would pull shit like, "We're not going on until we get a case of champagne." They would make the show run late. Plus they had a blossoming drug problem which made it hard for them on the road. If they couldn't get enough stash for more than three days, that was it; they couldn't do a tour.

TYLER: Arthur Kane! [*The Dolls' bassist*]

PERRY: Arthur Kane's the first guy I ever saw where I said, "Hey, he's an alcoholic."

TYLER: He was way into his addiction in '74. Way ahead of us.

PERRY: I'd wake up in the morning and look out the window, and I'd have a hangover, too. But he'd be out staggering around in the clothes he had on the night before, with his fucking leopard platform boots down to here and his leotards all ripped up. He'd be staggering around the pool at 10 in the morning in the bright sun. And he'd say [*in a croaking voice*], "When's the liquor store open?" And he'd go over and wait for it to open. I couldn't get over that. I was years away from being that bad. And they would tell me how they would have to carry him, and the only way they could get him going was with a quart of vodka right before the show.

But the Dolls were a gas. We learned a lot watching them. That second album of theirs, *Too Much Too Soon* [Mercury, 1974], was so appropriate for them, you know?

GW: Did you feel something in common there?

PERRY: Well, there was a similarity. The whole line-up and all that. Johnny [*Thunders, the Dolls' lead guitarist*] and I were pretty good friends. I bought some guitars from him and sold him some. [*Dolls singer*] David Johansen—I got to hang out with him for a while. Our paths crossed a few times, too. [*laughs*]

GW: Back then, did you consider Aerosmith a glam band?

PERRY: No, not a glam band. We were trying to be like Peter Green's Fleetwood Mac. Be fuckin' real. Our roots are definitely Fleetwood Mac and the Yardbirds, and of course the Beatles. But that's not to say we didn't wear a little bit of stretch latex ourselves.

TYLER: Purple pants.

GET YOUR WINGS (Columbia, 1974)

For many years Aerosmith regularly included one cover song on their albums. Their debut featured their version of r&b singer Rufus Thomas' "Walkin' the Dog" which had previously been popularized by the Rolling Stones. Get Your Wings *contained a cover of the Yardbirds' adaptation of the rockabilly song "Train Kept a Rollin'," which became a substantial hit for Tyler and company. Aerosmith would go on to cover several other Yardbirds songs.*

GW: Tell us about "Train Kept a Rollin' " and Aerosmith's affinity for the Yardbirds in general.

PERRY: It was the only song we had in common when we first got together. Steven's band had played "Train" and Tom and I played it in our band. Steven's band was really tight and played Beatles songs and things like that. The band Tom and I had was just the opposite—loud, noisy, a lot of feedback and out of tune sometimes. But the common ground we all had was playing "Train Kept a Rollin'."

TYLER: That song was an extraordinary place to start from. Because it's everything that an ordinary I-IV-V rock song isn't. That type of E chord thing.

GW: It's in E, but with a G and A chord.

PERRY: Proto-metal for sure. It's a blues song, if you follow its roots all the way back. To me, it's as important as "I'm a Man" [*the Yardbirds' guitar* tour de force *based on Muddy Waters' "Mannish Boy"*]—as far as the rhythm goes. The push pull. I always thought if I could just play one song, it would be that one because of what it does to me.

TYLER: God, the Yardbirds were so fucking far away from anyone else. [*He starts singing the Gregorian chant melody to another Yardbirds song, "Still I'm Sad."*]

PERRY: The Yardbirds were definitely taking that blues thing—as a lot of those English guys did—and putting larger guitars on it. They had a melodic sense, you know, with Jeff Beck in the band. They were a pop band trying to incorporate some of that blues edge and still get played on the radio. The fact that Eric Clapton quit the Yardbirds because he was a purist and only wanted to play the blues—you have to scratch your head over that one. Because you look at his career three years later and what's he playing?

TYLER: Two singles that I wore the fuckin' plastic out on were "For Your Love" [*the Yardbirds' harpsichord-driven first American hit*] and "House of the Rising Sun" [*the Animals' hit version of the New Orleans folk song*]. The way those chords work. Perfect!

GW: What was the origin of the unique, start/stop rhythmic feel in Aerosmith's recording of "Train Kept a Rollin' "?

JOEY KRAMER: Probably just jamming on it at soundcheck and experimenting with putting a James Brown kind of beat behind it. I played with a lot of r&b-type groups before joining Aerosmith.

PERRY: We used to put James Brown songs in our set.

TOYS IN THE ATTIC (Columbia, 1975)

Indisputably one of classic rock's all-time masterpieces, Toys *contains two of Aerosmith's best known and most loved songs: "Walk This Way"* and "Sweet Emotion." The latter song marked Tom Hamilton's emergence as a significant contributor to Aerosmith's songwriting.

GW: The band hit a new plateau with *Toys in the Attic*. To what factors do you attribute that, looking back on it?

HAMILTON: That was the one where it really clicked. It was our third album. We'd learned how to do it by then. We were starting to have a solid relationship with [*producer*] Jack Douglas and a solid idea of how to make a record as a band. Jack was into refereeing and making sure any ideas that came up got tried out. That's how we ended up having a song like "Sweet Emotion" on there.

KRAMER: We had to try all those ideas. We only had something like six songs!

GW: Did that bass riff for "Sweet Emotion" come first?

HAMILTON: Yeah. I wrote that line on bass, and realized I should think of some guitar parts for it if I was ever going to get a chance to present it to the band. I didn't think I ever would. But it was at the end of the recording and Jack said, "Tomorrow's jam day, if anybody's got a stray riff hanging around." I said, "Yeah, I do." So I spent the day showing everybody everything and we took it from there, refining it into what it is. Steven had the idea of taking that intro riff, which became the chorus bass line under the "sweet emotion" part, and transposing it into the key of E, and making it a really heavy Zepplinesque thing.

WHITFORD: We kind of bastardized that lick from [*Jeff Beck's*] "Rice Pudding," didn't we? [*i.e., the transitional guitar riff that comes between verses and leads into choruses—GW Ed.*]

HAMILTON: That part came from all the times that we listened to [*Beck's album*] *Rough and Ready* [*Epic, 1971*].

GW: Who played the talk box part?

PERRY: I did.

HAMILTON: That's another Beck legacy thing.

GW: Do you recall what kind of guitars you played?

WHITFORD: I believe I had a '57 gold top Les Paul and a 100-watt Marshall.

TYLER: [*to Perry*] Remember, we didn't know how to end it? We got into a big fight. Blow [*cocaine*] all over the place. It was late and we were at the end of our rope. Finally I said, "Just fuckin' play a drum fill and we'll go into…[*sings outro riff*]." And we did it. It was such a magic moment.

PERRY: We knew it would be killer live—a show stopper. So then the fuckin' record company gets it and they say, "What can we maul to get this on the radio?" You listen to the single version of "Sweet Emotion" and it's pretty chopped up. They edited it down to just the melodic element. But that's how it was done back then.

GW: Who came up with the riff for "Walk This Way"?

TYLER: The guitar lick? Joe did.

PERRY: It was at a soundcheck in Hawaii. I was into the Meters at that point and I was trying to play something funky. So we started it down there and finished it on 44th Street at the Record Plant.

ROCKS (Columbia, 1976)

Another all-time classic Aerosmith album, Rocks' radio hits included "Back in the Saddle" and "Sick as a Dog." The latter song was another Hamilton/Tyler composition.

GW: After "Sweet Emotion" became such a hit, was there pressure to duplicate that success with "Sick as a Dog?"

HAMILTON: It wasn't pressure. All of a sudden I had some kind of credibility as a songwriter. That was just one of my three-chord wonders.

I think I came up with the verse part first. And then I did the parts for the intro, the B to E part, and came up with this little, jangling arpeggio thing. That's still one of my favorite things—hearing big, distorted chords with an arpeggiated piece on top. I'm such a Byrds fan; it comes from that. I don't know how many people reading this are familiar with "Mr. Tambourine Man" [*the Byrds' 1965 hit recording of Bob Dylan's song*], but that song has a really cool arpeggiated, jangling guitar thing going over a chord statement.

TYLER: I get down and bow to [*Byrds leader*] Roger McGuinn daily. I am not worthy!

PERRY: Tom played rhythm guitar on "Sick as a Dog." I played bass for the first half of the song. Then I put the bass down and played guitar in the end, and Steven picked up the bass and played it for the rest of the song—all live in the studio! One take.

GW: So Joe, how did you end up playing six-string bass on "Back in the Saddle?"

PERRY: One of my favorite guitar players—Peter Green—used to play one. I don't think he ever did a solo with one on record. But he would, live. In the middle of a song, they'd just do this little segue with him playing six-string bass.

GW: With Fleetwood Mac, you mean.

PERRY: Yeah. So in the back of my mind I always thought that was a cool thing. So I found a six-string bass and started playing it. I liked the way it sounded.

GW: Was that a Fender Bass VI?

PERRY: It was. One with four switches. But it was stolen about four years ago—the original one I had played on every tour. I found a replacement for it, another old Bass VI, but it's not a four-switch model; It's got three. I've also got one of those 1960 or '61 thinline, EB-6 355-shaped Gibson six-string basses, which are very rare. There are only 60 of those around. And I've also got an SG shaped EB-6, like a Jack Bruce.

GW: What do you remember about writing the music for "Back in the Saddle?"

PERRY: I was very high on heroin when I wrote "Back in the Saddle." That riff just floated right through me. Drugs can be a shortcut to creativity. All throughout history, medicine men and priests in all those primitive cultures used drugs to get to that spirit place. Ask any writer. You get to that place where your fingers are flying on the keyboard; you know the stuff is just flowing through you. But for a lot of writers, getting to that uninhibited place is difficult. So it's a shortcut just to have a beer. And it works for a while. But then you reach a point where it takes two beers to get there, then three. And after a while it's not working for you any more, and your liver's going, and the doctor is saying, "If you drink any more, your nose is going to turn into a cauliflower." That's just us excessive bastards, you know. But with all drugs, you burn out on them, for different reasons. With heroin, your body just caves in. After a while all you care about is getting that buzz. Then you don't care about picking up a guitar. So it ends up blocking your creativity rather than helping it.

DRAW THE LINE (Columbia, 1977)

Draw the Line went Platinum faster than any previous Aerosmith album. But trouble was brewing within the band.

GW: Looking back at your music, when do you first hear the drugs taking their toll?

PERRY: Definitely on *Draw the Line*. That was a very un-together album.

TYLER: What I specifically remember was not being present in the studio because I was so stoned. In the past, I always had to be there and hear every note that was going down—who was playing what and were they in tune. But for that album, I was so stoned on tuinals. Heroin doesn't come close to what tuinals do to you. You take two—whether you eat them or shove them up your ass—and you're fucking gone. Sorry. You're over the line immediately. And that line is Fuck-All Land. I just didn't care anymore. To be honest with you, it was really only when I didn't have my drug of choice, which was cocaine, and I started messing around with [barbiturates] like chloral hydrates and what everybody in America takes today: Xanax. I tried to take as much of that as I possibly could. *Draw the Line* is when it got to be a habit of being so stoned that I had to be doing the mondo salute.

GW: What's the "mondo salute"?

TYLER: I'd just get so out there that my eyes would cross. Instead of passing out, I'd be cross-eyed. See, I grew up in the Sixties. There was no such thing as stopping. If you couldn't do all the drugs on the table and still walk out the door, you weren't cool.

PERRY: So show him what the mondo salute is.

TYLER: Because I was seeing double, I'd just hold my hand over one eye.

PERRY: With your hand over one eye, you don't see double anymore.

TYLER: Then I could leave the room without bumping into tables and chairs.

PERRY: No big deal.

TYLER: How else are you supposed to drive when the line down the middle of the road is two? How do you know which side to stay on?

NIGHT IN THE RUTS (Columbia, 1979)

The album title is a (presumably stoned) anagram of the phrase "Right in the Nuts." Joe Perry quit Aerosmith during recording sessions for this album.

HAMILTON: With *Night in the Ruts*, we were on our way back from *Draw the Line*, to my mind. But unfortunately, the band broke up.

PERRY: We were still fucked up, but the record sounds more cohesive than *Draw the Line*. *Night in the Ruts* was a rockin' record. Most of those tracks were live in the studio, and a lot of the solos were live in the studio, as I remember.

TYLER: I think we wrote better songs on *Night in the Ruts*. Like "No Surprise." Joe came up with this fucking great guitar line, which is how we wrote for years. He came up with a line and I wrote lyrics. But this time, I went crazy trying to figure out what to do with that guitar line. For a year. Or maybe it was three months. I was so stoned I don't know, but it seems like a lifetime. I just couldn't figure out where to hang my hat. Do I do a vocal melody in unison with the riff? A contrary motion thing? And then one day, it just suddenly came into focus, and I heard it: I'll answer him! [*He illustrates by singing the call-and-response between the guitar riff and the first line of the vocal.*] I just went, "Yes!" and it was the fuckin' best song on the record. Except for "Chiquita."

GW: It's interesting to hear you two talk about writing together on *Night in the Ruts*. Because, by all reports, you weren't on speaking terms.

PERRY: Well, we always had the common bond of the music. All the other shit that went on was just "all the other shit," you know? My wife hated Steven's wife, and "why was I giving him drugs?" and all that. But when it came to making music, we still made music. We still had that vision.

HAMILTON: But in the end, the personal stuff got out of hand. The management we had then would allot three months for us to write and record an album, and then they'd book tour dates. Making a record was just a break in the touring. We got to the end of the period set aside for *Night in the Ruts* and there was no more time. We had to go on the road. We were flying back and forth and finishing the album on breaks. It was too much stress for the band. We freaked out.

PERMANENT VACATION (Geffen, 1987)

Brad Whitford followed Perry's lead and left Aerosmith in 1981. The following year, the three remaining original band members cut Rock in a Hard Place *(Columbia, 1982) with guitarists Jimmy Crespo and Rick Dufay.*

In 1984, Perry and Whitford made peace with their former bandmates—on Valentine's Day, fittingly enough—backstage at Boston's Orpheum theater. The original Aerosmith line-up got back in the saddle and recorded their first album under a brand new contract with Geffen Records: Done with Mirrors *(Geffen, 1985). It is perhaps best seen as a transitional record, between the classic Seventies Aerosmith and the newly rejuvenated, turbo-charged and sober Aerosmith that was just around the bend.*

Universally hailed as the band's comeback album, Permanent Vacation *reflects the healthy new Aerosmith of the late Eighties. They'd undergone treatment for their drug and alcohol addictions and hooked up with producer Bruce Fairbairn at his studio, Little Mountain, in Vancouver, Canada. Perry and Tyler also began collaborating with outside professional songwriters, notably Desmond Child and Jim Vallance. Hits such as "Dude (Looks Like a Lady)" and "Angel" brought Aerosmith to a new generation of listeners, via MTV and radio.*

GW: What was the first song you wrote completely straight—once you'd gone through rehab and gotten sober?
PERRY: [*to Tyler*] "Hangman Jury," wasn't it?
TYLER: Wasn't it "Dude"?
PERRY: I'm not sure. I remember working on "Hangman Jury" with the other guys, though, when you were still in the can.
GW: How soon after completing "Dude (Looks Like a Lady)" did you

realize that you'd written something that will be a staple of drag revues well into the next century?
TYLER: Well see, originally it was [*singing*] "cruisn' for a lady." As long as I had that kind of chorus line, I knew I was okay. Or even just the last part [*sings the final three notes of the chorus line*]: "ladaay." Or it could've been "crazaay," or "baybayy." Same difference; I had it. And it was just a matter of time before it became "dude looks like a lady." We had just bought a sampler. Joe was farting in it. Burping in it. And we were catching soundbites. That sound you hear in the intro was actually a soundbite of the very first time we plugged it in and Joe played something. I said, "Save that, and we'll put it in one of the songs."

We'd written that song and I was having trouble with the lyrics. So that was the first one Desmond helped out with. But we already had the "Dude looks like a lady" part. And we had the bridge: [*sings*] "What a funky lady. She like it like it like it like that." That's the best fucking bridge I ever wrote. For me, the whole song is me on a clavinet patch on a keyboard and Joe on the guitar. The keyboard got buried in the mix, but you can hear it on the bridge.
WHITFORD: [*Engineer*] Bob Rock was a big element in what was going on soundwise, on *Permanent Vacation*. Bruce [Fairbairn] was sitting back doing what he does best—evaluating and guiding the music. It was very cool having Bob there. He's famous for guitar sounds, and rightly so. But unfortunately, Bruce and Bob parted ways right in the middle of the project. They had a disagreement over money. But our second engineer was Mike Fraser, who is also extremely talented behind the board. He took over when Bob left.

Joe didn't have much guitar equipment then. A lot of it had disappeared during the crazy years. I was turning him on to a lot of older equipment. He kept liking what he heard. Then he went out and started his collection which, today, is unbelievable.
HAMILTON: It takes up the whole studio. It's like a rain forest!
WHITFORD: Vox amps, Marshalls, Silvertones… He's got some amps I've never seen before.
GW: People always talk about how "Angel" launched the whole "pow-

er ballad" phenomenon. But when I listen to it, I mainly hear r&b.
TYLER: Yeah, it's got the r&b element, but the chorus is so in-your-face. See, I love that song. It brings tears to my eyes; it's so emotional. But with the radio playing it so much, and the way the chorus is set up...
PERRY: It's definitely got that big, wet production. You can probably name dozens of power ballads from that era that typify what that was. Whitesnake had one, Bon Jovi had one...
TYLER: That record, I'm scared of it today. We wrote the chorus. But others took that chorus and put it on a silver platter. There are other ways to do it. Like the bands today. There's a great chorus to "Smells Like Teen Spirit." But why shove it down someone's throat? Or at least shove it down someone's throat without the silver spoon.

PUMP (Geffen, 1989)

Many hold this to be the best Aerosmith album ever. Or certainly, at least, on a par with Seventies classics like Toys in the Attic *and* Rocks.

Another Bruce Fairbairn production, the album finds Tyler branching out into social commentary with "Janie's Got a Gun." Mostly though, this is Aerosmith doing the raunchy rockin' stuff they know best.

GW: Was "Love in an Elevator" really based on a real-life experience? Or is that just something you tell journalists?
TYLER: Uh...it was real life.
GW: You don't want to elaborate?
TYLER: Well, you ever give a girl head in an elevator? Did you ever get a blowjob in an elevator? Were you ever jerking off and your mom called? Do you like to make love in a dark corner when you know people are looking and you may get caught? Knowing you may get caught puts a whole other slant on having sex. I don't know if that stems from my rowdiness, but I've experienced that. It's just one of those things. The first time I went [*sings*] "love in an elevator," it just slipped out. I didn't sit down and think, "What do I want to do with this song?" Although I'll tell you what I did think. Know how when people get in an elevator they always avoid eye contact? They're all looking up at the floor numbers. Oh yeah, 1,2,3,4,5... really gotta study that real hard. They're lookin' up there because

they're embarrassed. So, "Love in an Elevator," what a great theme! To maybe get people to think about that when they're actually in an elevator would be so cool.

By the way, that song got panned at first. "It sounds like a bunch of blues riffs," someone from the record company told us. That's quote, unquote.

PERRY: More of that sexist stuff again.

GW: On the other hand, "Janie's Got a Gun," staked some new territory for Aerosmith: concerned, politically correct, social commentary.

TYLER: It took me nine months to write the lyrics to "Janie." I came up with the first line and then I got stuck. Why did Janie have a gun? I didn't know. I was sitting there racking my brains forever. Then I picked up an issue of *Newsweek* magazine, and it had an article on all the people who'd died of gunshot wounds that particular week, with pictures of each one of them. I thought about that for a week, and I put it together with the abuse issues in America. Drug addiction isn't the only thing that's swept under the carpet. There's child molestation and fathers going ape on their daughters. I would go so far as to say that six or seven out of 10 fathers do something sexual with their daughters. That's just how it is. You don't hear about it that much because the daughter is embarrassed and scared. Doesn't want to say anything about "Daddy." So I just went with the child abuse theme. And as soon as I did, it wasn't hard to complete the lyric.

GET A GRIP (Geffen, 1993)

The last segment of Aerosmith's "Vancouver trilogy," this disc took the band into the Nineties and set the stage for Nine Lives.

PERRY: We did 8,000 overdubs on that album. Way over the top. I just remember it was hard to mix.

TYLER: We had two people in Vancouver who couldn't mix it, although they'd worked with us previously and done great jobs. One person actually said it wasn't on the tracks. 5K was added to everything.

PERRY: We'd been up in Vancouver three months. Our families had left. We figured, "Fuck, a week and a half to mix and we'll be outta here." Then Fraser brought the tracks up and said, "I can't get it." And Bruce was pulling his hair out. Then we sent the tapes to Brendan O'Brien, who did a great job of mixing them. Never having heard the material before, he just stripped it down to the basic elements.

TYLER: We asked him, "How did you do that?" He said, "Well, you guys did it. It was on the tape there."

GW: With *Get a Grip*, you began working with a lot of different co-writers, not just the usual core team of Desmond Child and Jim Vallance.

TYLER: So sue me. As someone once said, "If this was easy, everybody would be doing it." I have times when I write lyrics on my own. I mean I'm perfectly capable of that. But sometimes it's more fun to share the craziness of coming up with ideas with other people. Like Richie Supa [*co-writer of "Amazing"*] or Mark Hudson [*co-writer of "Livin' on the Edge" and "Gotta Love It"*]. We sit in a room and laugh so much, it's like, "What, are we working?" But at the end of the day, you come up with a song.

PERRY: That's the thing about bringing other people in. You constantly keep the pot stirred, and you're constantly getting new ideas. Steven and I have been writing together for 25 years now. It's not that we can't write anymore. It just makes it better to have other people in there sometimes. They put their slant on what they think an Aerosmith album should sound like. And it's great. They hear different stuff than we do.

TYLER: Some people are really interested in who wrote the words, others are really interested in the melodic structure. Others could give a shit and are just interested in dancing to it. So what are you gonna do?

Bob Marley

Guitar World, December 1996

Rastaman Vibration

Bob Marley was reggae's greatest poet, philosopher and prophet. Here is the story of the man and the music he introduced to a grateful world.

By Alan di Perna

THOSE WHO WITNESSED Bob Marley in concert say he could put the audience into a state of mass hypnosis. Dreadlocks flying, his wiry body buoyed by bass vibrations, Bob would dance to the edge of the stage, then suddenly freeze like a statue. He'd stretch his arm straight out in front of his face, his hand cupped as if holding a mirror or crystal ball, channeling pure, spiritual energy from the "third eye" region of his forehead. Behind him, on a massive red, gold and green backdrop, the image of His Imperial Majesty, the Emperor Haile Selassie I of Ethiopia, Ras Tafari, the Conquering Lion of Judah—the man Bob Marley called God—would be towering over the musicians and singers on stage. Moved in body, mind and soul, the crowd would surge forward like a single organism.

Many who experienced Marley in concert on one of those resplendent nights have never forgotten it. For a brief while, time seemed to hang suspended in the ganja-perfumed air.

"One good thing about music," Bob sang in "Trenchtown Rock," "when it hit, yuh feel no pain."

Robert Nesta Marley has been the single greatest force in introducing reggae to America and Europe. During the Seventies, Marley brought this vibrant music of Jamaica's poor black ghettos to worldwide prominence, where it was eagerly embraced by rock icons like the Rolling Stones, Eric Clapton, the Clash and the Police, who subsequently introduced reggae to the world. The roots of rap and hip hop also go back to reggae. Marley's own music just seems to keep growing in popularity. *Legend* (Tuff Gong), the most recent compilation of his greatest songs, has gone eight times Platinum and has spent over a year at the Number One spot on *Billboard*'s Top Pop Catalog Albums chart, beating out the Beatles, Led Zeppelin, Fleetwood Mac, Pink Floyd, U2 and Jimi Hendrix. Today, there are people discovering the music of Bob Marley who hadn't yet been born when Bob left this life, on May 11, 1981.

For a musician, exploring reggae can be like plunging down a deep vortex, *Alice in Wonderland*-style. Rock and rollers who want to play it generally find they have to reorient themselves rhythmically, learning to feel 4/4 time a whole new way.

Reggae doesn't come from Wonderland, but from Jamaica, a tiny Caribbean island a few hundred miles south of Florida, just below Cuba. It's a former English colony, and the island's predominantly black population is descended from Africans who were brought there as slaves by the English. This accounts for the "strange language" of reggae. It's what's called a patois—a dialect of a European language (English, in this case) spoken by people colonized or enslaved by speakers of that language. When drunken frat boys try to imitate Jamaican patois, they always seem to end up sounding more like mentally impaired Scotsmen than genuine Rastamen. There's more to it than saying "mon" at the end of every sentence. The pronunciation, vocabulary and grammar of the dialect all differ from that of standard English, but it is every bit as expressive and functional—for every purpose from conducting business to making love to waging revolution. "We nah give up" is more concise and more forceful than standard English's "We are not going to give up." The lilting cadences of Jamaican patois are also very well suited to poetry, proverbs and, of course, song lyrics.

Reggae music reflects the natural beauty of Jamaica's lush greenery, mountains, beaches and sparkling ocean, as well as the harsh realities of oppression and the extreme poverty suffered by the island's poor black people—or *sufferahs*, in patois. The system of beliefs behind reggae is called Rastafarianism. It finds a promise of freedom and a return to the African homeland in ideas derived from the same Bible read by the slavemasters while they were transporting their human cargo across the Atlantic ocean.

"Reggae music is the *heart* music from the people in Jamaica," Marley told interviewer Chris Boyle in 1979. "Reggae music natural. Don't fantasize at all. Natural as it can get."

SKA—THE ROOTS OF REGGAE

The first thing anyone notices about reggae is its rhythm—irresistible, joyous. Where does it come from? From Africa, originally. But its more recent lineage traces back to the late Fifties/early Sixties and a style of music called ska.

In those days, the first cheap, mass-produced transistor radios infested the island like a solid-state virus. For the first time, Jamaicans were able to pick up r&b radio stations from New Orleans and Miami—faint, tinny, nocturnal transmissions from the big country to the North, across the Gulf of Mexico. Strange, yet familiar. The New Orleans sound of artists like Fats Domino, Huey "Piano" Smith and Professor Longhair is itself the product of a rich Creole culture (African slaves plus European masters). It makes perfect sense, then, that the music would have a special resonance for Jamaican musicians, who began playing their own version of it. The result, ska, is characterized by chords played on upbeats against a walking bass line. The chords were typically voiced on piano, guitar, by a horn section, or by some combination thereof. One very unique feature of early ska is that the bass drum plays along with the snare drum, on the two and four, rather than alternating with the snare on the one and three beats. This helps give the music its characteristically jaunty lurch. Bob Marley made his debut during the ska era with the 1963 single, "Judge Not."

THE RISE OF BOB MARLEY

Born February 6, 1945, the son of a black woman and a white English naval captain, Bob sought one of the few routes out of the ghetto available to an impoverished Kingston youth—a career in music. Although "Judge Not" was his very first recording, the bouncy ska tune was Bob's own composition, inspired by a biblical theme, significantly enough. After releasing one more single as a solo vocal artist, Marley joined the Wailers, who made a strong debut with "Simmer Down," one of the all-time classics of the ska era. Although Americans tend to think of the Wailers as the instrumental group that backed Marley from the Seventies onward, they were originally a vocal harmony group, consisting of Peter Tosh (McIntosh), Bunny Wailer (Neville Livingston) and Marley. On the earliest Wailers sides, they were joined by several other singers, including Beverley Kelso, Junior Braithwaite and Bob's bride-to-be, Rita Anderson, but the line-up eventually consolidated around the magical triumvirate of Bunny, Bob and Peter. Initially, their look (matching shiny suits) and sound (smooth harmonies) were very much patterned after American r&b and Motown vocal groups like the Drifters, Platters, Miracles and Temptations.

"The Wailers were a group of singers from the beginning," Bunny Wailer told me in 1986. "So the establishment of the Wailers' history starts with singing."

Singers—both individual artists and harmony groups—were the main focus of the Jamaican music industry during the ska era, a tradition that survived into the reggae era. The Wailers were part of a teeming island music scene that also included artists like the Maytals (led by the soulful Toots Hibbert), the Pioneers, Justin Hinds and the Dominoes, Alton Ellis, Stranger Cole and Delroy Wilson.

THE STUDIO SYSTEM

Much like Nashville or Motown, Jamaican music was created via a studio system driven by producers like Duke Reid, Prince Buster, Leslie Kong and Clement "Sir Coxsone" Dodd. Most of these rough-and-tumble entrepreneurs had begun as "sound system men" who traveled from place to place in beat-up but colorfully painted trucks laden with speakers, amplifiers and turntables, which they'd set up and use to play r&b records that couldn't be heard on Jamaica's official radio stations. By the early Sixties, the top sound system bosses had graduated to producing their own records. Each of them owned his own recording studio, record label and often even the shop where the records were sold.

Each producer wanted to staff his establishment with a killer house band, which would back every vocal artist that came through the studio. The musicians were notoriously fast workers. Many of the records released during these years were first and second takes. It was also common practice to take a backing track—or *riddim*—created for one artist, overdub a new vocal by a different artist onto it, and release it as a brand new record. Needless to say, the talent was generally underpaid and overworked. A studio band could crank out 10 or 20 sides a day. Of necessity, the players had to be fast learners and skillful arrangers.

"We have a saying in Jamaica," reggae bass ace Robbie Shakespeare told me in 1987. "The first cut is the deepest. So we usually like the first take best. You run a song down once or twice, and then I think you should put it on tape as soon as you are ready. Otherwise you start getting too many arrangement ideas and you mess it up."

The most legendary of the early Sixties studio bands was Coxsone's aggregation, the Skatalites, who backed the Wailers on their early sides. The Skatalites, led by trombonist Don Drummond, had a string of Jamaican instrumental hits and are still performing today. Guitarist Ernest Ranglin, who recorded both with the Skatalites and as solo artist, pioneered a seminal ska guitar style that utilized crisp, muted, staccato passages and a vocabulary of riffs reminiscent of the James Bond theme and surf instrumentals.

RUDE BOY

The Wailers' "Simmer Down" was one of many "rude boy" records released during the ska years of the early Sixties. Rude boys were rough, often criminal youths from the Trenchtown ghetto of Kingston, Jamaica, where life has always been extremely violent. A parallel can be drawn between Trenchtown "rudies" and gang culture in American ghettos today. Gunplay was (and is) rampant in poor, urban Jamaica. One ska-era producer kept a pistol handy in his studio's control room. When the music started sounding good, he'd get excited and fire into the ceiling—his own quirky way of racking up the "hits." While many rude boy records, including "Simmer Down," encouraged youths to keep a cool head and avoid violence, they were still frowned upon by the more respectable members of Jamaican society. But the "rougher than rough," ratchet-toting *bwais inna yard* delighted at being glorified on phonograph records.

Ska made a dent in America in the form of "My Boy, Lollipop," a cute, catchy little single by 15-year-old Jamaican singer Millie Small. Charting worldwide in 1963, it was the first success for entrepreneur Chris Blackwell and his Island Records label, which would go on to be a major global force in reggae.

The late Fifties and early Sixties saw a massive wave of Jamaican immigration to England, people in search of a better life. The immigrants brought ska with them, and it was eagerly adopted by the English mod youth culture, which was born during the early Sixties. Along with the Who, the Kinks and Tamla/Motown records, ska became the soundtrack for the fashion-obsessed mods, as they shopped for narrow-lapeled suits and pork pie hats and rode their motoscooters to glory.

The sound of ska might have been unknown in today's world had it not been taken up by the mods. The post-punk early Eighties saw a major mod revival. Ska became a big part of the neo-mod movement popularized by Two Tone Records artists like the Specials, Madness and the Selecter. Once it was established as part of post-punk "alternative" culture, ska was subsequently crossbred with mid Eighties hardcore music. Today, ska can be heard in the various hardcore and neo-punk hybrids, played by the Mighty Mighty Bosstones, Rancid, No Doubt, the Dance Hall Crashers and a legion of college radio acts.

ROCK STEADY, REGGAE AND RASTAFARI

Meanwhile, back in Jamaica during the late Sixties, the music began to change. Sometime around 1966, the tempo started to slow down. The truism is that the slower rock steady beat originated so that Jamaicans could dance and party all night long, rather than burning out early on jumpy ska records. In rock steady, guitar and/or organ chords still fall on the upbeats, but there's a slinky, sensuous slur between chords, often reinforced by the drummer's hi-hat. The walking bass lines of ska were phased out during the rock steady era and replaced with sparer bass figures, typically built around triads and often doubled by muted guitar.

Rock steady only lasted a few years. By the end of the Sixties, another change—a profound one—had taken place in the sound, mood and content of Jamaican popular music. These changes can be summed up in a single word: reggae. Its arrival was exuberantly announced by the Maytals' 1968 single "Do the Reggay." Nobody's quite sure where the word came from, although there are many theories, some as imaginative as the music itself.

As rock steady gave way to reggae, the tempo once again slowed, becoming a deep, hypnotic pulse. Rhythm guitar accentuations became muted and tight, as in the classic reggae "chop." The rhythmic emphasis of the music changed, giving birth to the "one drop." This archetypal reggae feel leaves a space at the first beat of each measure—a sort of psychoacoustic manhole down which the listener's psyche can plummet, drawing him deeper and deeper into the groove. Bass assumed a more prominent role, as well, to the point where it was often said that bass is the lead instrument in reggae. But a reggae bassist doesn't "solo" like a lead guitarist. Instead, he plays a regular repeating pattern, typically two bars long, again with a silent beat or "hole" somewhere in the riff. Much like a tape loop, the bass contributes greatly to reggae's trance-inducing effect. Meanwhile, as reggae developed in the Seventies, it proved an excellent vehicle for rock-style lead guitar soloing.

The lyrics changed as dramatically as the music. Singers sang less about romantic love and good times, turning instead to more serious political and spiritual concerns. The force behind all these changes was the rise of Rastafarianism, which became a dominant religious force in Jamaica.

Rastafarianism began in the first half of the 20th century, arising from a prophecy made by Jamaican black separatist leader Marcus Garvey that a black king would be crowned in Africa. In 1930, prince Ras Tafari Makonnen was crowned the 111th emperor of Ethiopia, taking the name Haile Selassie I, King of Kings, Lord of Lords, the Conquering Lion of the Tribe of Judah. (So the image of a lion, often crowned and carrying a monarch's staff or sword—seen everywhere at reggae events—is a symbol of Ras Tafari.)

The founders of the Rastafarian religion proclaimed that the king crowned in Ethiopia was the true and living God—or Jah (from the same linguistic root as "Jahweh" or "Jehovah"). As Selassie traced his lineage directly to King Solomon and the Queen of Sheba, and thus to the house of the Biblical King David, his divinity seemed all the more assured to the Rasta founders.

"Jesus tell us that he would come again," Bob Marley told Chris Boyle in 1979. "Haile Selassie is the Christ who them speak of."

Rastas regard themselves as the Biblical Lost Tribe of Israel, and see the coming of Selassie as a harbinger of the final judgment, when Babylon shall be thrown down and all black people will repatriate to Africa. Babylon is modern Western technological society, with its systems of oppression and destruction. ("Babylon shit-stem," as the pun-loving Rastas say.) It is the present day manifestation of the debauched Biblical kingdom of Babylon, where the ancient Israelites were held in captivity.

As they await the time of repatriation, Rastas try to live a peaceful, *ital* (natural) life based, in large part, on the Bible. For example, the Rasta's abundant dreadlocks aren't a fashion statement, but an adherence to Biblical injunctions like the one in Leviticus 21:5 not to "make baldness upon [the] head" nor to "shave off the corner of [the] beard." When "walking inna Babylon," Rastas would often cover their dreadlocks with woven hats called tams—typically in the traditional Rasta liberation colors of red, gold and green—to avoid harassment.

(Tams are also worn by female Rastas in accordance with the Old Testament rule that women must cover their heads.) Although, of course, as reggae became a worldwide pop phenomenon in the Seventies, many decided to sport the look without accepting the beliefs.

True Rastas are vegetarians, again in obedience to Biblical commands like those in Exodus (22:31 and 11:13) not to eat any "flesh that is torn of beasts in the field" or any "creeping thing." And, as part of their natural, herbal lifestyle, Rastas make liberal use of ganja—marijuana, that is: *cannabis sativa*, collie, the iscience tree, "the healing of the nations" (Revelations 22:2)—again in accordance with Biblical references to the goodness of "the herb." The intent is not to "party" or get "fucked up," but to attain a spiritually conscious state. True Rastas do not drink alcohol or use heroin, cocaine, crack, Ecstasy or any other chemical substance. As reggae singer Pato Banton put it in a well-known song of his, "I do not sniff the coke/I only smoke the sinsemilla."

Rastafarianism was part of the Jamaican music scene from its early days. Some of the Skatalites were Rastas. A few ska songs had Rastafarian themes, like Laurel Aitkens' "Lion of Judah." But the Rasta lifestyle and beliefs gained tremendous momentum during the late Sixties with the rise of the black power movement and growing awareness of African heritage. Bob Marley and the Wailers were at the vanguard of this new chapter in Jamaican musical history. The cover of the Wailers' 1973 album *Catch a Fire* (Tuff Gong) shows Marley, his locks just starting to dread up, drawing on a huge spliff. It was thus—as a Rasta freedom fighter—that the world would come to know him in the Seventies.

One direct Rasta influence on the rhythm of reggae came through *Nyabinghi*—a style of drumming used to accompany chants of praise at rasta *grounations* (spiritual gatherings). The style involves three drums: First, there's a large bass drum, struck with a wooden hand mallet, that generally establishes the tempo in deep, resounding whole notes. (If you listen carefully, you will a hear a Nyabinghi bass drum in the Bob Marley song "Natural Mystic.") Over that goes a drum called the *fundae*, which plays a regular, recurring pattern. Thirdly, there's the repeater (or *repetah*), which plays energetic, improvised figures, usually in a call-and-response relationship with the vocal chant. "The repetah is the highest pitched one," Bunny Wailer told me in 1986. "The fundae is like the middle; it holds what you'd call the riff pattern. And the bass is the bottom. So there are all three sections in the drums as in all music."

The Nyabinghi beat can be heard on "Rastaman Chant," from the Wailers' 1973 *Burnin'* album (also on Tough Gong). The prime exponents of earthy, primal Nyabinghi-driven reggae are Ras Michael and Yabby You. Ras Michael is a particularly enrapturing performer. A robed patriarch, he sits at the edge of the stage, beating out a kind of spiritual Morse Code on a hand-crafted repeatah.

"You see, the music of the Rastaman is Nyabinghi," Ras Michael told *The Beat* in 1985. "You get all the other variations and aspects of reggae music, which is one drop, which Bob Marley talk about, 'cause him know of that."

DUB AND DJ STYLEE

While Jamaican music was making the transition from rock steady to reggae, something else was brewing. For years, sound system DJs had been in the habit of chatting or "toasting" over the instrumental B sides of Jamaican singles. The A side of a vinyl 7-inch would have the full vocal arrangement of a song. The B side was the dub or version side, containing the instrumental track without the vocal. Around the turn of the Seventies, live dee-jaying was taken to visionary new heights by a man called U Roy (Ewart Beckford). Where earlier DJs simply urged crowds to dance and have fun, perhaps recommending the track on the turntable as a real "scorcher," U Roy would launch into totally free-associating, ganja-inspired rants, combining rasta reasoning, folk wisdom, jokes, boasts and just plain weirdness—all punctuated by multi-octave yelps lifted from American soul music but taken into another dimension: "Good *GAWWD*, Y'all!"

What U Roy did was so entertaining someone decided to capture him permanently on record rather then letting his work die in the air above the sound system each night. Before long, there were records by other DJs, including I Roy, Big Youth, Dillinger and Prince Jazzbo. A healthy rivalry grew between the DJs, who started dismissing their rivals as mere copycats on their records. If all this sounds familiar, it should. Jamaican "toasting" was one inspiration for what happened in the Bronx during the mid Seventies, when MCs at street parties would rock the mic over a backing created by "scratching" instrumental breaks from phonograph records. All of this means, of course, that reggae was there at the birth of rap. Over time, the two cultures have grown together, with rap artists and reggae DJs often making guest appearances on one another's records.

Originally, the version side of Jamaican singles contained the exact same instrumental track as the A side, with the vocals removed. But in time, engineers began to mess with the version side tracks in wildly experimental ways. This gave birth to the art form known as "dub." An engineer called King Tubby is the great originator of dub, a pioneer in the concept of "playing" the mixing console like an instrument. Using the console's mute switches and a primitive analog delay unit, he'd "catch" a rhythm guitar scratch, or one word of a vocal, and send it into orbit, repeating it over and over again as the delay decayed into grainy oblivion. Tubby established much of the basic dub vocabulary, including radical mutes that drop the floor out from under the listener, flanging out the drum kit, or plunging it into an ocean of reverb.

Another powerful dub magician is Lee "Scratch" Perry, one of Jamaica's greatest—and strangest—talents: a producer, songwriter, singer and all-around metaphysical prankster. "I am a madman," he sang on a 1986 recording. That was no bluff. Perry is a high tech shaman, notorious for enacting bizarre rituals in the studio. On one of his most infamous singles, "Judgment Inna Babylon (Chris Blackwell is a Vampire)," Scratch claims to have seen the Island Records chief "drink de blood of a chicken out of a rum glass."

But then, there *is* a bit of a rivalry there. Perry was Bob Marley and the Wailers' producer from '68 through '72, in the years just before they gained international fame with Blackwell on Island. It was Perry who helped the Wailers make the transition from the rock steady era to reggae, recording the original versions of such well-known Marley songs as "Small Axe," "Trenchtown Rock," "Duppy Conqueror," "Sun is Shining," "Concrete Jungle" and "400 Years." Some reggae aficionados prefer the rougher, rawer quality of these recordings to the better-known Island versions.

Meanwhile, Perry's exalted position in the dub pantheon is assured. Other latter-day dub masters include Adrian Sherwood and the Mad Professor (who also lives up to his name). Recently, dub sounds have come to the forefront of hipness, in the form of electronic dance music styles like ambient dub, trip hop, jungle and drum & bass.

REGGAE IN AMERICA

Around the turn of the Seventies, mainstream America got a few small whiffs of *what a g'wan* down in Jamaica. Desmond Dekker had a surprise hit in '68 with his reggae song "Israelites." Paul Simon's early Seventies hit "Mother and Child Reunion" sported a lightweight reggae beat that garnered media attention for Simon, and for reggae. The all-Jamaican film *The Harder They Come* made its debut in 1972, starring reggae singer Jimmy Cliff as a Trenchtown youth who rises to musical stardom, gets cheated by the record biz and turns to a life of crime. The film's New York premiere was attended by John Lennon and a host of other luminaries. Word went out on the rock scene that an exotic new kind of music had arrived from Jamaica.

An event even more momentous for reggae came in 1972: Bob Marley and the Wailers made their American debut with *Catch a Fire*. The significance of the album's original cigarette-lighter-shaped jacket (now a collector's item) was hardly lost on early-Seventies, "party down" Americans. *Catch a Fire* sold reasonably well, and the Wailers became an international touring act. But fame took its toll on the original Wailers trio. Bunny Wailer was the first to leave. By all accounts, Babylon living just didn't agree with Bunny, who couldn't tolerate the cold of North America and northern Europe, and did *not* like flying in airplanes. Peter Tosh was next to go, the result of long-standing tensions over Marley's ascent to the leadership of the Wailers. But the Wailers' loss was the world's gain, as both Bunny and Peter went on to become prominent reggae solo artists in their own right.

With the departure of his longtime partners, Bob Marley increasingly became the central icon not only of the Wailers, but of reggae music itself. By this time, he'd assembled an incredible backing band, the classic Wailers instrumental line-up. This included one of the greatest rhythm sections of all time, the brothers Aston "Family Man" Barrett on bass and Carlton Barrett on drums. On guitar was Earl "Chinna" Smith, a seminal roots axeman who has appeared on thousands of reggae albums. In 1974, American guitarist Al Anderson was added to the line-up, bringing a scorching, Hendrix-influenced rock guitar feel to Marley's music. Keyboard duties were handled at various points by Earl "Wire" Lindo and Tyrone Downie. Percussionist Alvin "Seeco" Patterson had been with Marley ever since his earliest days in Trenchtown. Providing sweet vocal harmonies were the I-Threes: Rita Marley, Judy Mowatt and Marcia Griffiths, each of whom launched fine solo careers as well.

Bob himself played rhythm guitar, usually on an old Les Paul that can be seen in innumerable concert photos. But his main focus was on singing and writing. Marley blossomed as a songwriter in the Seventies. His songs transcended reggae's specifically Jamaican musical conventions and became universal in their expressiveness. Lyrically, Marley had an uncanny ability to capture the everyday feelings of all people, regardless of race, gender or socioeconomic standing. He wrote some mighty big guitar riffs too, for songs like "Them Belly Full," "Get Up Stand Up," "Exodus" and "I Shot the Sheriff."

Eric Clapton was quick to notice that. Marley's American and European careers received a major boost in 1974 when Eric Clapton recorded Marley's song, "I Shot the Sheriff." The hit cover version introduced Marley and reggae to Clapton's white, middle class Seventies-rock audience, millions of whom might otherwise never have heard reggae. This may explain why American AOR radio jumped on Marley's 1976 *Rastaman Vibration* like drunken sailors on a dance hostess. You could hear it blasting from every college dorm room in the late Seventies: "Rasta-mon vibration, yeeaah...pos-i-tive." Legions of brand new fans got their first taste of reggae while acting on the album's printed advice: "This album jacket is great for cleaning herb."

But the mainstream rock consumers weren't the only ones who felt the vibe. The punk revolution of the late Seventies adopted reggae as the only other honest form of music out there. Johnny Rotten praised it in interviews. Patti Smith was often seen in her Lion of Judah T-shirt. The Clash made heavy use of reggae in their own compositions and covered Jamaican classics like Toots and the Maytals' "Pressure Drop" and Junior Murvin's "Police and Thieves." Stiff Little Fingers did Bunny's "Roots Radics Rockers Reggae," while Blondie covered the Paragons' "The Tide Is High." The Ruts forged their own reggae-influenced style. Elvis Costello and the Police adapted the one drop to their own purposes. Bob Marley graciously returned the compliment by recording "Punky Reggae Party" in '77.

Marley's breakthrough opened the door for other great Jamaican artists, including vocal harmony groups like Burning Spear, the Gladiators, Culture, the Mighty Diamonds, the Ethiopians, the Itals and the Meditations, smooth "lovers rock" crooners like Dennis Brown and Gregory Issacs and a new breed of singer/deejays whose ranks included Eek-a-Mouse and Yellowman.

Back in Jamaica, Marley had attained the status of a great statesman, if not saint. He paid a frightening price for this distinction in 1976, when he became the target of a politically motivated assassination attempt. A gang of gunmen burst into Marley's Kingston home on a late November evening and opened fire. The singer and his band had been rehearsing, but were on a break. Musicians cowered in the bathroom and behind equipment cases as bullets shattered windows and tore through the woodwork, the ceiling and the Hammond organ in the rehearsal room. Marley was in the kitchen eating a grapefruit when an assailant armed with a rifle entered the room. Put it down to poor marksmanship or the mercy of Jah, but no one was killed in the raid. Marley sustained gunshot wounds to his arm and ribcage. A bullet grazed Rita Marley's head as she fled from the house. Band manager Don Taylor took several bullets in his legs.

Just days later, Marley and the Wailers played the Smile Jamaica concert in Kingston with his arm in a sling. The video footage of the event is riveting. His wounds still fresh, knowing that his assailants could very well still be at large and out in the audience, Marley got up on a public stage at a large outdoor event. While his fear was evident in his every movement and facial expression, also clear was the supreme courage he called on to conquer that fear.

By this time, Marley had become so important politically that he was able to persuade the leaders of Jamaica's two rival political parties, Prime Minister Michael Manley and his opponent Edward Seaga, to come up on stage and shake hands at one of his 1978 concerts. After that evening, Bob Marley became a saint for many Jamaicans and other lovers of reggae music.

Some of Marley's peers weren't so lucky. Peter Tosh was murdered during a burglary attempt in his home on September 11, 1987. Wailers drummer Carlton Barrett was shot dead not long after that. Numerous other reggae musicians have died violent deaths. But while bullets couldn't kill Bob Marley, lung cancer and a brain tumor took his life in 1981. He was greatly mourned and given a patriarch's burial in Jamaica. To this day, his life and passing are commemorated at annual Bob Marley festivals around the world.

REGGAE AFTER MARLEY
It was a rock-crit cliché in the early Eighties to wonder how reggae could ever go on without Bob Marley. But as Bob's son Ziggy told me in 1989, "Reggae nah need one 'hope' fi mek it be. Reggae bigger than any one man. Remember in the beginning, even when Island Records start off, it's not just Wailers they have. They also have Toots and the Maytals and many more. Y'unnerstan'? We wan' the cup a fill. We have 'nuff talent in Jamaica."

True enough, there's been no shortage of great reggae music in the past 15 years. In the early Eighties, Black Uhuru, Third World and Steel Pulse achieved mainstream recognition. Veterans like Bunny Wailer and Burning Spear have continued to do first-rate work. England has come forward with some great talent, including UB40, Pato Banton and Tippa Irie. Dub poetry has established itself as a genre with Linton Qwesi Johnson and Mutabaruka. Out of Africa have come the reggae sounds of Alpha Blondie and Lucky Dube. Ziggy Marley and the Melody Makers have come to occupy a central position on the post-Marley reggae scene. With albums by two more Marley offspring—Damian and Julian—currently in the works, it looks like the dynasty is secure.

The late Eighties saw the rise of a whole new style of reggae-based music called dance hall, characterized by brisk, all-electronic rhythms, a gruff, rapid-fire style of dee-jaying (or "sing-jaying") and sex-obsessed lyrics. Much like gangsta rap, from which it took much of its cue, dance hall draws a line of battle between generations. Many longtime reggae fans derided dance hall for its morally "slack" lyrics and the toneless style of the artists, who were often defiantly off key. A great schism sprang up between dance hall and the more traditional roots or "conscious" reggae. But Ziggy Marley takes a broader view:

"Dance hall still reggae music," he said in '89. "Me nah know why they want to change it or separate it. It's the same music from Jamaica, with only one little difference: now dem play no live instrument. But it still mek you dance. The main thing about dance hall music are the bass and the drum. That alone mek you dance. That is the basis of reggae."

The current scene would seem to reflect Ziggy's vision of unity. Today you'll find roots artists like Beres Hammond, Yami Bolo, Inner Circle and Maxi Priest sharing the same stages and studios with dance hall dynamos like Shaggy, Shinehead and Cocoa-T. Think of it this way: Reggae is like a tree. Its great strength lies in its roots. But its branches stretch across the entire musical horizon.

Guitar School, July 1993

Gimme Three Chords

Guitarist Gary Rossington explains the origins of some of Lynyrd Skynyrd's—and rock's—finest moments.
By Alan Paul

"WE USED A lot of D-C-G progressions," Lynyrd Skynyrd guitarist Gary Rossington says with a shrug and a laugh about his band's songwriting process. "There's only seven chords, so you gotta use the same ones over. It's all in what you do with them. I could write a dozen different songs with the same three or four chords, but they'd all be entirely different."

Rossington and company certainly have always had a knack for doing a lot with a little. For while Skynyrd is renowned for its aggressive, three-guitar attack and the seemingly endless soloing such a line-up produces, timeless songs are what made the band a staple of classic rock radio. Skynyrd produced a series of instantly memorable four-minute rockers, including "Sweet Home Alabama," "Gimme Three Steps" and "What's Your Name," as well as extended ballads such as "Simple Man," "Tuesday's Gone," and, of course, "Free Bird." Remarkably, "Free Bird," one of rock's most-played, best-loved songs, was one of the first songs Lynyrd Skynyrd ever wrote—penned when singer Ronnie Van Zant and guitarists Allen Collins and Gary Rossington were still in their teens.

Like virtually all of their material, "Free Bird" was written as a collaboration between Van Zant and one of the group's guitarists.

Gary Rossington of Lynyrd Skynyrd

This loose but consistent formula served Skynyrd extremely well, producing classic songs which quickly made them one of the nation's most popular bands. By 1975, however, when third guitarist Ed King, suffering from burnout, left the group, Skynyrd had fallen into a bit of a creative rut, as reflected by the album *Gimme Back My Bullets*, an unusually flaccid affair. Before anybody could write the band's epitaph, they added guitarist Steve Gaines, whose songwriting and phenomenal playing infused them with a new energy. The rejuvenated band shines on 1976's live *One More for the Road* and the following year's *Street Survivors*. The latter is one of the best-arranged and -played guitar albums in rock history.

Tragically, before the group could reap the fruits of this rebirth, their chartered plane crashed into a Mississippi swamp on October 20, 1977, killing three members—including Gaines and Van Zant—seriously injuring everyone else and seemingly forever putting an end to the group.

A decade later, the surviving members of the group got together for a "Tribute" tour with Van Zant's brother, Johnnie, taking over as vocalist. Enthusiastic audience response led to a full-time reunion, which has produced four albums, most recently *Twenty* (CMC International), so named to honor the twentieth anniversary of the crash. Rossington recalled the origins of some of the band's best-loved tunes.

"Free Bird" *pronounced leh-nerd skin-nerd* **(MCA, 1973)**
"We were just beginning to write—that was actually one of the first songs we ever completed—and Ronnie kept saying that there were too many chords to find a melody. He thought he had to change with every chord change. We kept asking him to write something to these chords and he kept telling us to forget about it!

"Then one day we were at rehearsal and Allen started playing those chords, and Ronnie said, 'Those are pretty. Play them again.' Allen played them, and Ronnie said, "Okay, I got it." He wrote the lyrics in three or four minutes—the whole damned thing! He came up with a lot of stuff that way, but he never wrote anything down. His motto was, 'If you can't remember it, it's not worth remembering.'

"We started playing it in clubs, but just the slow part. Then Ronnie said, 'Why don't you do something at the end, so I can take a break for a few minutes?' So I came up with those three chords at the end, Allen played over them, I soloed and then he soloed—it all evolved out of a jam. We started playing it that way, but Ronnie kept saying, 'It's not long enough. Make it longer.' We were playing three or four sets a night, and he was looking to fill them up.

"Everybody told us that we were crazy to put 'Free Bird' on our first album. They said it was too long. Even our record company begged us not to include it. When it first came out, radio stations did all kinds of awful edits until it got big enough where it didn't matter any more. It humbles us to think that it's played so much. But it's not magic—it's still just a song to us."

"Gimme Three Steps" *pronounced leh-nerd skin-nerd* **(MCA, 1973)**
"This is a true story. Ronnie went into a bar to look for someone, but Allen and I were too young to get in, so were waiting for him outside. We were waiting and waiting, then he came running out with a big ol' guy chasing him, yelling.

"He was dancing with this chick when this guy came in and said he was going to beat him up. Ronnie said, 'Just give me three steps and I'm gone.' The guy was a redneck, he had a gun and was drunk—a nasty combination of things. Ronnie said, 'If you're going to shoot me, it's going to be in the ass or in the elbow,' and took off like a bat out of hell.

"We all got in the car and split, and after Ronnie told us what happened, we laughed and wrote the song right there. We drove over to Allen's house, got his guitar and finished it.

"We've always considered ourselves a working-man's band, so we thought every song should tell a story that people can relate to. When we finish a song, you know what it's about, whereas some groups have songs you may dig, but not understand. I think that's why our songs have lasted as long as they have."

"Sweet Home Alabama" *Second Helping* (MCA, 1974)

"I came up with the banjo/steel guitar part—it's just a fingerpicked D, C, G progression—and the little opening riff, which I played over and over again. Ronnie started writing lyrics at rehearsal one day, saying, 'Play that again. Play that again.' After about an hour he had all the words. Ed took it home and put in all the little fills and licks and arranged it.

" 'Sweet Home Alabama' was basically a joke song. We traveled through Alabama a lot, and marveled at how pretty it was and how nice the people were. Neil Young was, and still is, one our favorite artists, so when he came out with 'Southern Man' and 'Alabama,' criticizing the South, we said, 'Well, what does he know? He's from *Canada.*' So we threw that line about him in there. We were told by some people to take out the parts about Neil and [*former Alabama governor*] George Wallace, but we said, 'Hey, it's just a song. And we're going to record it the way we wrote it.'

"Most of our songs happen real quick or don't happen at all. Actually, Ronnie wrote most of his lyrics driving around Jacksonville checking out different neighborhoods—especially poor ones, black and white—or in the shower. You know how people sing in the shower? Well, Ronnie did that, but he made up songs—melody, verse, chorus, bridge and all. Many times when we were on the road, he'd end up running into my room with a towel around his waist, dripping wet, saying, 'Check this out. Write some music to that real quick.' I'd try to write a few chords to get a rough idea of where the song was going, then either Allen or Ed or I would go back and finish the song."

"Call Me The Breeze" *Second Helping* (MCA, 1974)

"We always liked J.J. Cale. We heard 'Breeze' one night sitting around the house, and Ronnie said, 'Let's do that!' But it didn't work the way he did it—a real straight shuffle—so I wrote the arrangement, which was completely different. If we had changed the lyrics, it would have been a completely different song. We did the same thing to Merle Haggard's 'Honky Tonk Night Man.' "

"Crossroads" *One More for the Road* (MCA, 1976)

"We did that as a tribute to Cream, one of our all-time favorite bands. We saw them on their farewell tour and they completely blew our minds, so we made this a regular part of our set. In fact, it was our encore for years, until 'Free Bird' became so big that we basically had to do that last. By the time we recorded the live album, it had been such a part of our set for so long that we felt we had to include it. Also, our producer, Tom Dowd, engineered the Cream version and he told us the story about how it came together, and that really inspired us to want to re-record it."

"I Know A Little" and "You Got That Right"
Street Survivors (MCA, 1977)

"I think these two songs sum up what Steve Gaines meant to the band. He wrote both of them and sang 'You Got That Right' as a duet with Ronnie. He was a great songwriter and singer—and an incredible guitarist. I've never heard anybody, including any of us, play the picking he did on "I Know a Little" quite right. Steve had a lot to do with the writing and arrangements throughout this album, and his playing was so good it really inspired us. When he joined, we were kind of in a lull. We were still doing well—selling a lot of tickets and records—but the music was getting a little boring. We needed a little spark of inspiration, and Steve provided it. We started getting together and jamming at night. It put us back in the frame of mind we had had when we first started.

"Steve was so good, he was a freak of nature. He used to piss us off because he could do so many things that me and Allen couldn't. Every time I ever went to his house or his hotel room, he had his black Les Paul on. He'd order room service and eat with his guitar on. He'd sit around and talk and not play it for an hour, but it would be strapped on. He'd watch TV with it on, play it during commercials, then stop. It was his third arm."

"What's Your Name" *Street Survivors* (MCA, 1977)

"That's another of the first songs we wrote. Me and Ronnie were sitting in a hotel room one night playing around with some chords I wrote that day, and he started singing. The original lyrics were, 'It's eight o'clock and boy is it time to go.' Ronnie had just gotten an itinerary from his brother Donnie, who was in .38 Special and their first stop was Boise, Idaho. So Ronnie changed the first line to, 'It's eight o'clock in Boise, Idaho,' which immediately made it a real on-the-road song.

"It's all a true story. One of our road crew got in a fight at a bar with a hotel guest, so they kicked us out. We said we'd leave if they'd send a bottle of champagne to our room. The song's just about being young and free—21 and unmarried. We'd go to a town, meet a chick, then forget her name. And when you'd come back to town, you'd say, 'What was your name, honey?'"

Richard Williams of Kansas

Guitar School, October 1995

Songs for America

Kansas used to be one of the biggest groups of the Seventies—but is the band just dust in the wind today? In this overview of Kansas' 20-year career, Richard Williams lets it all hang out.

By Joe Lalaina

VERSATILE, HARD ROCKING and original, Kansas is pure classic rock—with a progressive edge. Their mega-hits "Carry on Wayward Son" and "Dust in the Wind"—to this day, two of the most played songs on FM radio—established the band as one of the most popular of the Seventies, a time when progressive rock was the style of choice for many artists. While contemporaries like Yes, Genesis and Pink Floyd kept their music consistently spacey, Kansas' unprecedented blend of hard-hitting guitar and lyrical violin instantly set the band apart.

"A lot of music, especially today, sounds too homogeneous," says Kansas guitarist Richard Williams, who lost his right eye one Fourth of July in his early teens when a homemade bomb blew up in his face. "When we first came on the scene, there was far more variety in the influences coming over the radio. I have a hard time distinguishing one alternative band from the next, and they're all influenced by one another. Some of the guitarists in those bands sound good on album—I like their stripped-down feel—but whenever I see them perform on the late-night TV shows, I'm immediately convinced that a lot of those guys can barely play. It makes you wonder if they're the ones playing on their albums."

Williams has played lead guitar on all 14 Kansas albums, the first 10 of which saw him sharing the playing with the band's chief songwriter, Kerry Livgren. More recently, Williams played alongside veteran guitar virtuoso Steve Morse on two Kansas releases. Now, he has the spotlight all to himself. (The band's new violinist, David Ragsdale, is an accomplished guitarist as well, and occasionally plays some guitar for the band.) Kansas' new album, *Freaks of Nature*, features Williams and fellow original members Steve Walsh on vocals and Phil Ehart on drums.

Guitar School recently spoke with Williams prior to Kansas' concert in Norfolk, Virginia, and he was more than happy to take us through Kansas' 20-year career, album by album.

KANSAS (Kirshner/CBS, 1974)

"We were just a bunch of hicks from Kansas recording at a major studio—the Record Plant in New York. It was the first time we'd ever been in a recording studio, so we didn't have a clue what to do. The only previous recording experience we had was on a four-track! We wanted to record the album through Marshalls, but the producer, Wally Gold, told us, 'Nobody records through those big amps,' and made us play through these little Fender amps. But the last album Wally had produced was a Barbra Streisand album! He's a great guy, and was instrumental in discovering us, so he got his foot in the door and got credit as producer. I never listen to that album now—it's too painful to listen to my playing. I just couldn't get any tone out of that little Fender amp. It was just, 'Okay, one, two, three, four—that's good enough.' The entire album was cut and mixed in about two weeks.

" 'Can I Tell You' was the song that got us our record deal. I wrote the opening riff in my parents' basement, and then Robby [Steinhardt] put a cool violin part over it. Of the three tunes we submitted to Don Kirshner's people, it was the only one that caught their ear. That song was my claim to fame. Had I not written it, I'd be selling shoes somewhere."

SONG FOR AMERICA (Kirshner/CBS, 1975)

"We were working in Los Angeles with a real producer, Jeff Glixman, and the record company wasn't breathing down our backs. There was no pressure to come up with hits. That's a good environment to be in—leave us alone and we'll do fine. If a band starts getting record-company pressure, it can really mess up their chemistry.

"The song that stands out most is the title track—we still play it on tour and it very much captures our style. Once the melody kicks in, I still get goose bumps. Every time I play that song in concert, I'll look over at my wife and she's totally into it, with tears rolling down her face. She was a big fan of ours back in that era, which was when we first met."

MASQUE (Kirshner/CBS, 1975)

"It was recorded in Bogalusa, Louisiana, at Studio in the Country. The studio was so isolated—and a far cry from working in L.A. or New York—that the only thing we had to do was get on with the business of recording. Unfortunately, the record company was pressuring us for a hit single and it affected our writing. The album turned out far too heavy and dark-sounding for them, and no one was sure what to do with it. A good album, but we were still learning to get the sounds we wanted. *Masque* sounded great in the studio, but the end product lost a lot of balls. 'Icarus—Borne on Wings of Steel' and 'Mysteries and Mayhem' are two real popular Kansas songs. I'd love to re-record a lot of our early stuff with the violin taking the place of the second guitar."

LEFTOVERTURE (Kirshner/CBS, 1976)

"The most important Kansas album—the one that put us on the map. Kerry has always been a great songwriter, and on this album he was really coming into his own. Writing has always been too painful for me—I've never aspired to be a songwriter; I'm much better at playing guitar and arranging—but songs seem to just flow out of Kerry. On the last day of rehearsals for the album, Kerry comes in with yet another song, and Steve [Walsh] goes, 'Oh, no! Not another one!' It was 'Carry on Wayward Son,' and we didn't even rehearse it—it was put together in the studio. It took four albums, but we finally had a big hit. By the time *Leftoverture* went Platinum, we'd paid back the recording costs of every album up until that point."

POINT OF KNOW RETURN (Kirshner/CBS, 1977)

" 'Dust in the Wind' put that album over the top. It was just a fingerpicking exercise that Kerry had come up with, and he wrote a song around it. Kerry is not a singer, and I remember him mumbling the melody to Steve. Everyone in the band knew it was going to be a hit. We just knew it! 'Dust' was an even bigger hit than 'Wayward Son,' and the only single we've ever had that went Gold. The title track of the album was released as the first single, and that turned out to be a Top Twenty hit. The keyboard technology was really progressing around this time, and Kerry was beginning to take more of a keyboard role in the band. Meanwhile, I was playing guitar on everything. *Point of Know Return* is a great album, but I prefer *Leftoverture* in retrospect."

TWO FOR THE SHOW (Kirshner/CBS, 1978)

"We were just coming off two multi-Platinum albums, so we thought we were infallible. But the big mistake with that live double album was that the record company dumped two million copies of it in the stores, and it didn't sell two million. So all of a sudden we started getting returns back, which the band has to pay out of its royalties. Fortunately, most of the returns have been bought over the years. The thing I didn't like about that album was that it was dry and not very live-sounding. There was not enough crowd miking done."

MONOLITH (Kirshner/CBS, 1979)

"We were still bulletproof, riding high on the success of the previous two studio albums. *Monolith* wound up selling more than a million copies, but for some reason it was considered a failure. It didn't make any sense, especially now in retrospect. I'd cut off one of my balls just to sell a million albums again! [*laughs*]

"Things were starting to change within the band, both musically and philosophically. Dave [*Hope, bassist*] and Kerry became born-again Christians, and band members were getting married, moving to different cities, and shifting their focus away from the band. And Kerry could afford not to work and tour so much because he'd made a lot of money with songwriting. Although some of the songs on *Monolith* were really good, like 'People of the South Wind,' it was depressing to see the downward slope of the band coming."

AUDIO-VISIONS (Kirshner/CBS, 1980)

"The last Kansas album with the original line-up. On *Leftoverture* and *Point of Know Return* we were like a big pirate ship—we were a team. Once we got to *Monolith* and *Audio-visions*, we weren't a team anymore. Everyone had their own self-interests. We thought no matter what we did, people would like it. I don't know if it was cockiness on our part, but we just couldn't see the end of our career. And once Kerry found himself spiritually, he lost touch. Anyone can identify with the searching soul of 'Carry on Wayward Son,' but no one wants to be preached to by Jim Baker."

VINYL CONFESSIONS (Kirshner/CBS Associated, 1982)

"The band was really falling apart by now, and a lot of Robby's violin parts were getting phased out by the latest keyboard technology. Steve had quit the band, and I was just two steps behind him. But I rode out the storm because I had too much invested in the band, and I'm stubborn. Quitting really doesn't solve anything. Steve tried a solo career—his band Streets was really good—but things didn't work out and he wound up sinking a lot of his own money on the project. The sum of all of us playing together was far greater than each of us individually.

"Steve quit on the last day of rehearsals, but we already had studio time booked and a producer bought and paid for. We headed out to L.A. to start recording; meanwhile, we were interviewing vocalists—what a nightmare! We interviewed so many good singers, but chose John Elefante; he was the safest guy to go with because he had a voice similar to Steve's."

DRASTIC MEASURES (CBS Associated, 1983)
"That was Kerry and Dave's last Kansas recording. I like the album, and 'Fight Fire with Fire' is a great song. We were having problems with Elefante—he was an L.A. punk who thought we were just a bunch of old fossils. He thought his little garage band was better than anything that Kansas had ever done. And he was a little mama's boy. He'd come into rehearsals and say, 'I played our demo for mom, and she thought it wasn't happening.' That's the kind of crap that Phil and I have had to juggle for all these years to keep Kansas alive."

POWER (MCA, 1986)
"Steve Walsh rejoined the band, and it was our first of two albums with Steve Morse. Man, that guy can play—the most amazing guitarist I've ever worked with. I remember, when rehearsing for the album, being completely knocked out by his playing. *Power* turned out to be an album with many great songs—'Taking in the View,' 'Three Pretenders,' 'Tomb 19' and the title track. Just last year, me and our bassist Billy [Greer] were walking around in Germany and heard this incredible song coming from a jukebox, but it took awhile before we realized what it was. It was 'Three Pretenders.' It's the greatest feeling to hear something you've played that you haven't heard in a long time, and you like it. Overall, *Power* is a great album, but didn't sell very well. We thought we were off to a new career, a transitional period with Morse in the band, but there wasn't any violin and many of our fans had difficulty accepting that."

IN THE SPIRIT OF THINGS (MCA, 1988)
"A technical fandango, produced by Bob Ezrin. The head of MCA happened to be a friend of Ezrin's. During a casual conversation, the record company head told Ezrin that Kansas was getting ready to do an album. Ezrin told him he'd love to work with us, so off we

went into the studio for two months of huge recording costs—and when we finished, the record company wanted more material. The total cost of making that album was $400,000! So much time was wasted getting computers to work, and there were so many keyboard patches from hell. That album taught us that even the best technology cannot make a great album. Fortunately, there's one great song, 'Bells of Saint James,' in the tradition of our older material. It could've been a big hit, but right after the album was released, MCA fired most of its staff. *In the Spirit of Things* was barely released, so it's difficult to find."

LIVE AT THE WHISKY (Intersound, 1992)
"The initial idea was to record a video—the CD was just an afterthought. Eventually, the CD paid for the whole project. The stage [*at the famed Sunset Strip club in Los Angeles*] was so small, with microphones crammed all around us. The end product sounded great, and that instantly changed our philosophy on recording. I mean, who cares if some of the guitar bleeds into the drum mics? We wanted a raw feel—I did not touch up a single note—and something where you can hear the personalities of the players. Not some technical marvel that no one will care about."

FREAKS OF NATURE (Intersound, 1995)
"We were originally going to record the album in Atlanta, but wound up doing it at Caribbean Sound Basin in Trinidad, an incredible facility and one of the nicest studios I've ever worked in. We were totally away from the nonsense of daily life and concentrated solely on recording.

"*Freaks of Nature* brought us back to how we used to do things—a group effort, with heavy violin parts and straightforward rock and roll. We took the rawness of *Live at the Whisky* and brought it to a studio setting. There's more of an ensemble feel, as opposed to the slick technology of *In the Spirit of Things*. Through all the years of turmoil, I stuck it out because I wanted to see where Kansas would go—and I like where it went."

Alex Lifeson of Rush

Guitar World, November 1996

Time and Motion

Alex Lifeson dissects several key songs from Rush's past.
By Chris Gill

"**Anthem**" *Fly by Night* (Mercury, 1975)

"We were trying to be quite individual with *Fly by Night*, which was the first record that Neil [*Peart, drums*], Geddy [*Lee, bass*] and I did together. That song was the signature for that album. Coincidentally, the name of our record company, which is Anthem records in Canada, came from that song. Neil was in an Ayn Rand [*author of* The Fountainhead] period, so he wrote the song about being very individual. We thought we were doing something that was different from everybody else.

"I was using a Gibson ES-335 then, and I had a Fender Twin and a Marshall 50-watt with a single 4 x 12 cabinet. An Echoplex was my only effect."

"**2112**" *2112* (Mercury, 1976)

"We started writing that song on the road. We wrote on the road quite often in those days. 'The Fountain of Lamneth,' on *Caress of Steel*, was really our first full concept song and *2112* was an extension of that. That was a tough period for Rush because *Caress of Steel* didn't do that well commercially, even though we were really happy with it. We wanted to develop that style. Because there was so much negative feeling from the record company and our management was worried, we came back full force with *2112*. There was a lot of passion and anger on that record. It was about one person standing up against everybody else.

"I used the ES-335 again, and a Strat which I borrowed for the session. I couldn't afford one at the time. I used a Marshall 50-watt and the Fender Twin as well. I may have had a Hiwatt in the studio at that time, too, but I think it came a little later. My effects were a Maestro phase shifter and a good old Echoplex. There were a limited number of effects available back then. The Echoplex and wah-wah were staples in those days."

"La Villa Strangiato" *Hemispheres* (Polygram, 1978)

"That was all recorded in one take. Because we were writing on the road, we used our soundchecks to run through songs that we were going to record. We would come off the road, have a few days off and start recording. It was all recorded at the same time with all of us in the same room. We had baffles up around the guitar, bass and drums, and we would look at each other for the cues. My solo in the middle section was overdubbed after we recorded the basic tracks. I played a solo while we did the first take and re-recorded it later. If you listen very carefully, you can hear the other solo ghosted in the background. That was a fun exercise in developing a lot of different sections in an instrumental. It gave everyone the chance to stretch out.

"By that time I had my ES-355, and my acoustics were a Gibson Dove, J-55 and a B-45 12-string. I had my Marshall in the studio. I had the Twin and two Hiwatts, which I was also using live, but the Marshall was my real workhorse. The Boss Chorus unit had just come out at that time, but I think I used a Roland JC-120 for the chorus sound here. That was the first of many 'chorus' albums."

"The Spirit of Radio" *Permanent Waves* (Mercury, 1979)

"There was a radio station here in Toronto—it's an alternative station now—and 'the spirit of radio' was that station's catch phrase. That song was about the freedom of music and how commercialized radio was becoming. FM radio in the late Sixties and early Seventies was a bastion of free music where you got to hear a lot of things that you wouldn't have heard otherwise. It was much like MTV was in the beginning, before it became another big network that feeds a large but very specific segment of the viewing audience. Radio has become a lot more commercialized since then. The station that we wrote that song about won't play our music.

"By then I was using mainly a Strat that I had modified by putting humbuckers in the bridge position. I also used the 355, which I used in the studio for the next couple of records. My amps were Hiwatts, the Marshall and the Twin. I also had a Sixties Bassman head and cabinet. The flanger on that song was an Electro-Harmonix Electric Mistress which I still have. I used the Boss Chorus Ensemble, and I had graduated to the Roland Space Echo, which replaced my Echoplex."

"Limelight" *Moving Pictures* (Mercury, 1980)

" 'Limelight' is about being under the microscopic scrutiny of the public, the need for privacy—trying to separate the two and not always being successful at it. Because we've never been a high-profile band, we've managed to retain a lot of our privacy. But we've had to work at it. Neil's very militant about his privacy.

"My guitar was a different modified Strat with a heavier and denser body. We set up a couple of amps outside of the studio as well as inside, so we got a nice long repeat with the echoing in the mountains. The approach on that solo was to try to make it as fluid as possible. There was a lot of bending with lots of long delay repeats and reverb so notes falling off would overlap with notes coming up. I spent a fair amount of time on that to get the character, but once we locked in on the sound, it came easily."

"New World Man" *Signals* (Mercury, 1982)

"Most of *Signals* was completed, but we wanted to add one more song. Neil had been fooling around with the lyrics, so we wrote and recorded 'New World Man' in the studio, all within one day. It has a very direct feel. Doing that in one day was a lot of fun. The pressure was on but off at the same time.

"It was almost compulsory to do solos at that time, but I didn't want to feel that every song had to have that kind of structure. I wanted to get away from that, and to this day I feel that way. I enjoy playing solos and I feel that my soloing is quite unique to my style, but I'm bored with that structure.

"I used a Tele for the whole song through the Hiwatts with a little bit of reverb and chorus."

"The Big Money" *Power Windows* (Mercury, 1985)

"That was a tough one that took a long time to complete. It was recorded in Montserrat. The guitar was tuned up a whole step with the E string at F#, and I played a lot of open chords. I did a lot of drop-ins where I hit a chord and let it ring, then dropped in the next chord and let it ring and so on. When we started recording the song, it sounded too ordinary, so we tried dropping in those chords during the verses as an experiment.

"I remember doing the solo in this studio in England, SARM East, which is in the East End of London. We set aside a week for solos, last-minute vocals and mixing. The control room was tiny. There was barely enough room for me to turn my body around when I was playing. But I got a really great sound with the repeats and lots of reverb. I loved to be soaked in that kind of effect at the time.

"I used a white modified Fender Strat that I called the 'Hentor Sportscaster.' The name came from Peter Henderson, who co-produced *Grace Under Pressure*. The amp setup was a couple of Dean Markley 2 x 12 combos, two Marshall 2 x 12 combos, two Marshall 100-watt JCM 800 heads and two 4 x 12 cabinets. I also ran a direct signal. By that time I had a pretty comprehensive rack with two t.c. electronic 2290s and a 1210 that I used for phasing, and I had a Roland DEP-5."

"Time Stand Still" *Hold Your Fire* (Mercury, 1987)

"We were in a bit of a reflective period at that time. Everything seemed to be moving by very quickly. Aimee Mann came up and did vocals in the chorus of that song. It was a lot of fun to work with her. She was very nervous. I don't think she had done that sort of thing very often, especially with a band like us. We weren't necessarily playing the kind of music that she was into or listening to, but she liked the band. We made her feel relaxed very quickly, turning the whole session into a fun thing.

"That was the year that I got the Signature guitars with single-coil active pickups. It's very apparent on that song. The guitar has a clear, metallic sound to it that really sings. I got into that bright tone, and my sound was still very chorusy. I had gotten rid of all my Hiwatts and the Dean Markleys and was using primarily Marshalls again. I used 2 x 12 combos as well as the JCM 800."

"Show Don't Tell" *Presto* (Atlantic, 1989)

"By then we were working with Rupert Hine as our producer. Oddly enough, I had been working on the basic ideas of that song at home and brought it to the studio when we started writing the record. We developed it from there. It was much heavier in the early version. The tempo had come up a little bit. Rupert's approach to the guitar sound was a little lighter than I wanted. That was partly my fault, because I was still using the Signature a lot, which didn't lend itself to a very thick sound. That amp line-up stayed the same as before, and effects would come and go. I was fiddling around with whatever was new at the time, as I've always done.

"We'd taken a seven-month break, which at that time had been our longest hiatus. We needed to clear the cobwebs and get away. We came into *Presto* feeling a lot more enthusiastic about working. The change to Atlantic Records was good because we felt like we needed a change all around. We were going into the Nineties, and it made everything fresher."

"Stick It Out" *Counterparts* (Atlantic, 1993)

"I used a Peavey 5150 and a 100-watt Marshall JCM 800. I had a JC-120 as well that I used for some clean things, but primarily everything was done on the Peavey and the Marshall. The guitar was a '72 Les Paul Standard that I had used on certain songs in the past. I used a dropped-D tuning and ran the guitar straight into the amp with no effects.

"We had gone back to working with Peter Collins, who produced *Hold Your Fire*. We used a much more direct approach to recording, moving back towards the essence of what Rush was about as a three-piece. In retrospect, *Counterparts* didn't work as well as we'd hoped, but it led us in the right direction. We're much more satisfied with *Test for Echo*, which we view as a progression from *Presto*."

"Test for Echo" *Test for Echo* (Atlantic, 1996)

"There's a lot of different stuff on there. I tuned the entire guitar down a whole step to a D standard tuning. I got a new Les Paul Custom with beautiful sustain, a heavy tone and a compact, but not too small, sound. In the choruses I used a Godin Acousti-Caster, which has a really interesting sound that is at the same time almost acoustic but definitely electric. I used primarily Marshalls: 50-watt and 100-watt JCM 800 heads and two 30th Anniversary models, with four cabinets—two vintage 4 x 12s and two new 1950 cabinets with Celestion 25-watt speakers. I used a DigiTech 2101 to knit everything together. The important thing with that is to use it through a good speaker simulator, like the Palmer. The compensated outputs on the 2101 don't quite do it for me, but through the Palmer it has nice body and width.

"I feel like we've arrived with this record. There's a particular feel that I don't think we've had before, a nice groove and a lot of really good Rush songs. I feel like we were all really together on this album. Although we strive for that all the time, it's not always achievable. The mood was so good in the studio, and we were so unified in direction."

Guitar World, November 1996

El Loco

ZZ Top's Billy Gibbons recalls three decades of Texas excess.
By Alan Paul

CLOSE YOUR EYES, crank up ZZ Top's new blues-rockin' *tour de force Rhythmeen* (RCA), and you'll swear that you've traveled back 20 years in time, to an era when muscle cars, tanktops and tight, tight jeans ruled supreme. But for all the band's skill at evoking that wonderful if tasteless time, there are some aspects of the Me Decade that even the mighty ZZ Top and their heralded juju power simply cannot summon back.

"Being a rock star in the Seventies was wall-to-wall craziness without any threat of penalty," Top guitarist/vocalist Billy Gibbons snickers. "It was all great fun. I remember walking into New York's Gramercy Park Hotel and seeing a guy in crushed velvet hot pants, lace-up knee boots and a feather boa, with multi-colored streaks and tips in his hair, and thinking, 'Why are *we* the ones being tagged weirdoes?'"

Bearded Billy and company took the era's excessive ethos to a new level with 1976's Worldwide Texas Tour, which featured a huge, Texas-shaped stage, 75 tons of equipment and a bevy of live animals, including buffalo, steer and snakes.

"That tour was definitely an all-time great," says Gibbons. "Something of which we can always be proud. I'm not sure who orig-

Billy Gibbons of ZZ Top

inally thought that concept up, but like most of the ZZ Top think-tank sessions, it didn't require too much to convince us to put the plan into action. The challenge for us always is pulling things back in—making it somewhat reasonable so that they can actually be accomplished. We still enjoy thinking about that tour, even though the animals often got better treatment than the band."

We interrupted Billy's fond ruminations about his barnyard past to ask if he would care to share some of the sonic secrets behind four of ZZ Top's most fiery slabs of Seventies vinyl. Amiable as always, Billy and his beard nodded their assent.

"La Grange" *Tres Hombres* (Warner Bros., 1973)

"That is straight guitar into amp, a 1955 Strat with a stop-tailpiece through a 1969 Marshall Super Lead 100. That fuzz sound in the lead and in the front and back end of the composition is just pure tube distortion. Pickup-setting differentials account for the different tones. The opening part was played on what we used to call 'the mystery setting' in the dark days before the existence of the five-way toggle switch, when finding that perfect 'tweener required dedication.

"That Marshall amp—which was a trusted friend through the first six records—was an import, brought over by Jeff Beck's at-the-time tech. I had four of those babies and they were my main road amps for years. I ran them through cabinets with those so-called 'greenback' speakers. They still retain a distinctive, rich, enjoyable tone and are well worth owning. I must, however, advise anyone fortunate enough to find one to beware of the variable power plugs. The 220 setting doesn't work very well outside of the 220 countries, as I can tell you from experience; we had more than a few paper clip nights over the years."

"Tush" *Fandango* (Warner Bros., 1973)

"The first three albums were recorded exclusively at the R.H. Studios outside of Dallas and the special sound that always seemed to be accessible there was due in part to the fact that the equipment was nailed to the floor and nothing ever moved so you could always count on a sound. Quite a good sound, I must say.

" 'Tush' was Pearly Gates, my beloved Les Paul, played through the same Marshall Super Lead, and we sure enough did stop and enjoy the G tuning for the composition's slide element. This song was largely straight guitar to amp, but I also utilized a real odd, esoteric device called the Cooper Time Cube, which was a simplistic application of the complex world of physics. In a small rack-mounted can sits a small speaker right up next to maybe 50 feet of one-inch rubber tubing, which is coiled, spring-like. The soundwaves actually take longer to travel, having to make these corners, creating a type of delay which is quite unlike the familiar sound of a digital delay. That was a real left-field piece of gear which they had—and still have, I might add—in that studio. Some of the guitar sounds that appear to be doubled on the early albums are actually the byproduct of that oddball Cooper Time Cube."

"I'm Bad, I'm Nationwide" *Degeullo* (Warner Bros., 1979)
"We wrote this about the great Texas bluesman Joey Long, a Gulf Coast lead guitar picker who appeared on a great number of wonderful records by the likes of Slim Harpo and Barbara Lynn. He played on Lynn's great hit record 'We Got a Good Thing Going,' which was covered by the Stones, and which was really one of the important recordings that shaped my understanding of where it was I wanted to go with my life. It was good. And so was he.

"Joey loaned me a multi-stringed mandolin-like instrument from Parral, Mexico, and I put it to good use on 'Nationwide.' If you listen closely, you can hear close-miked mandolin-sounding rhythm accompaniment. The lead track was played on a custom-made, half-sized, real short-scaled guitar tuned to G. It was actually standard tuning cranked up a minor third, which remained quite playable thanks to the guitar's short scale.

"The song's tail end alternates between three distinct effects created by two pedals: an Echoplex doubler and a Maestro octave box alternating every third bar between having the octave up and the octave down. The song also contains some Hohner clavinet, which was owned by one of our famous Memphis pals, Carlos De Marlos. It's such an interesting sound that it ignited Dusty's [*Hill, bassist*] interest in learning some keyboard skills and it was he who subsequently handled all the tickling of the ivories."

"Cheap Sunglasses" *Degeullo* (Warner Bros., 1979)
"This song was actually written during a trip from the Gulf Coast up to Austin, Texas. A bright spot of creativity flared as we were passing the hamlet of La Grange and I recited all three verses of 'Cheap Sunglasses' within the scope of 20 miles. And that's the way they stayed. Though that may sound simplistic, the lyrics speak for themselves. 'Simplistic' is indeed a word which may come to the mind of some.

"The lead track was performed on a fake Fender guitar which I used for the wiggle stick—there is a little dive bomb in the solo section. I played it through a Marshall Major, a short-lived 200-watt beast, which had one blown tube. Hence the rather bulbous, rotund sound. There's also a little bit of digital delay for that Bo Diddley impersonation at the tail out, and a Maestro ring modulator, which produces the strange tag to each verse. It appears three times, and it's a pretty funny sound. That is one insane effect put to good use."

Guitar World Presents CLASSIC ROCK

Neil Zlozower

Edward Van Halen

Guitar World, April 1995

Good Times, Bad Times
The Greatest Guitar Stories Ever Told

DID YOU HEAR about the time Chuck Berry gave Keith Richards a shiner and then set him on fire? How about when Ozzy Osbourne mistook Randy Rhoads for a girl? And what of the childhood events that drove Angus Young to wear those velvet shorts?

The world of guitar is filled with a million twisted stories, and in the following pages we have compiled some of our favorites. Some are funny, some poignant, others sick, but all are unforgettable. Black eyes, broken limbs, unusual encounters—it's the stuff that myths and legends are made of. And it's all in a day's work for the likes of Edward Van Halen, Jimi Hendrix, Howlin' Wolf, Kurt Cobain, Pete Townshend and James Hetfield.

Without further ado, *Guitar World* presents an incredible compendium of the most bizarre—and often pivotal—events in the annals of guitar.

HAMMER-ONS OF THE GODS
Van Halen Discovers Tapping

"As far as the tapping thing is concerned, I never really saw anybody do it, okay?" says Edward Van Halen. "I'm not saying, 'Hey, I'm bitchin',

I came up with it,' but I never really saw anybody do it before me."

Van Halen will admit, however, that the initial inspiration for his legendary two-handed technique came from a surprising source—namely, Led Zeppelin's Jimmy Page. "I got the idea a long time ago while attending a 1971 Zep concert," Edward explains. "Page was playing his classic solo in the middle of 'Heartbreaker,' and all of a sudden a light bulb went off in my head. I thought, 'Wait a minute, he's pulling off to an open string—that's simple. Now, what if I use the finger on my right hand to pull off to a finger on my fretting hand? I could move things around and do a lot more.'

"That was the beginning. I just kind of took the technique and ran with it."

But how did Ed keep tapping a secret in the years before Van Halen recorded their debut? "I remember when we first started playing original sets at the Whisky in Los Angeles, I'd turn around and keep my back to the audience when I tapped. No one could see what I was doing! My brother, Al, would always say, 'Ed, be cool, man. Don't let those *mothers* rip you off.' "

—*Brad Tolinski*

SHATTERED
Pete Townshend Smashes His First Guitar

By 1965, Pete Townshend had already acquired a reputation around London as the most violently aggressive guitarist on the scene. His convulsive windmilling, the way he'd bang his Rickenbacker around, scrape the mic stand across the strings and elicite feedback squeals from his amp shocked and delighted audiences in an era when rock bands still wore suits on stage. His creatively abusive way with the instrument reached its ultimate and inevitable climax one evening in '65, at a gig in London's Railway Tavern—a venue with a particularly high stage and low ceiling. There are many versions of the story, but the best is the one Pete himself told to his friend and biographer Richard Barnes in the latter's book, *The Who: Maximum R&B*:

"I started to knock the guitar around a lot, hitting it on the amps to get banging noises and things like that, and it started to crack. It banged against the ceiling and smashed a hole in the plaster; the guitar head actually poked through the ceiling plaster. When I brought it out, the top of the neck was left behind. I couldn't believe what had happened. There were a couple of people from art school I knew at the front of the stage and they were laughing at me. One of them was literally rolling about on the floor, and his girlfriend was kind of looking at me, smirking. So I just got really angry and got what was left of the guitar and smashed it to smithereens. About a month earlier, I'd scraped together enough [money] for a 12-string Rickenbacker, which I only used on two or three numbers. It was lying at the side of the stage, so I just picked it up, plugged it in, gave them a sort of look and carried on playing, as if I meant to do it. The next week I went back [to the club] and there was a whole crowd waiting to see this lunatic break his guitar."

—*Alan di Perna*

PAUL-VERIZED
Gary Rossington Almost Loses His Baby

Lynyrd Skynyrd's Gary Rossington and his 1959 Sunburst Les Paul are like father and son; he says he finds it virtually impossible to perform without his "baby." He has, in fact, used the guitar on every one of Skynyrd's albums and at all their concerts. In 1977, however, he came close to losing his beloved guitar:

"When we were recording *Street Survivors* in Miami, I got lazy and left the guitar on a stand for the night," recalls Rossington. "The next morning, I went to play it, and the whole headstock just fell right off—it was held on only by the strings. I started cryin' like a baby. The whole band freaked out, we canceled the day's sessions and I took off walking. I got about a mile down the road when two friends came by and picked me up. They said, 'What happened back there? Your whole band is acting like they're in mourning—they're all cryin' and mopin' around.'

"So I went back, and the studio's maintenance man said, 'I got some glue—I can fix that guitar.' And I was like, 'Glue? Man, this is a precision instrument, and it's ruined. You can have it.' And I gave it to him. When I came back the next morning, I went to grab another guitar to play, and he handed me my Les Paul—fixed perfectly."

The headstock is still held in place by the maintenance man's glue, and Rossington still uses the guitar. "I was offered 30 grand for it and I just laughed," he says. "The thing is not an investment—it's part of my arm."

—*Alan Paul*

OH BOY!
Buddy Holly Unplugged

Buddy Holly looked like your grandmother's idea of a nice boy. Hair—short and neatly combed. Clothes—always clean, never flashy; he actually wore a bow tie on the *Ed Sullivan Show*. Even Holly's Stratocaster looked wholesome. But the "nicest" thing about Holly were his songs. Unlike contemporaries like Elvis Presley and Gene Vincent, whose sexuality oozed out of every pore, Holly sang about eternally innocent sweet love in such classics as "Oh Boy," "Maybe Baby" and "That'll Be the Day." But there was another side to nice-boy Buddy Holly.

At least, that is, according to Little Richard. In *The Life and Times of Little Richard*, Richard remembers a Holly very different from your grandmother's ideal: "He was a wild boy for the women."

One time, Richard recalls, when the two rock and rollers were on the same bill, he and his girlfriend, Lee Angel, were in his dressing room, going at it hammer and tongs. Suddenly, Holly entered and, without even pausing to clean his glasses, dropped his pants and joined in.

"He was having sex with Angel...when they introduced his name on stage," says Richard. "He was trying to rush so he could run on stage. He made it, too. He finished and went to the stage, still fastening himself up. I'll never forget that. He came and he went!"

—*E.F. Glumm*

HELL TO PLAY
Robert Johnson Sells His Soul

Robert Johnson was "King of the Delta Blues Singers," the artist who got under the skin and into the soul of Eric Clapton and countless other rabid devotees. Part of his appeal is romantic: according to an enduring legend, Johnson sold his soul to the devil in exchange for the spectacular guitar playing, singing and writing abilities that ultimately made him the most influential and obsessed-over bluesman of all time.

Call it a myth, but the facts of Johnson's career and life suggest that he did, in fact, have a thing for the Evil One. There is the song "Me and the Devil Blues," not to mention the terrifying "Hellhound on My Trail." One of the bluesman's acquaintances even remembered that Robert died "crawling along the ground on all fours, barking and snapping like a mad beast."

But the most convincing evidence of Johnson's alleged pact with Satan was the supernatural speed with which he improved his guitar playing skills. Delta bluesman Son House recalled that he and another bluesman, Willie Brown, often mocked Johnson, who at the age of 20, in 1931, was a terrible guitarist who made "such a racket you never heard." One day Johnson disappeared, and when he returned a year later he had a surprise in store for the two older bluesmen. House remembered:

"All of a sudden somebody came in through the door. Who but him! He had a guitar swinging on his back... I said, 'Well, boy, you still got a guitar, huh? What do you do with that thing? You can't do nothing with it.' He said, 'Well, I'll tell you what... Let me have your seat a minute.' So I said, 'All right, you better do something with it, too,' and I winked my eye at Willie [Brown]. So Robert sat down there and finally got started. And man! He was so good! When he finished, all our mouths were standing open."

—E.F.G.

FINGERS, BLOODY FINGERS
Black Sabbath's Tony Iommi's Darkest Hour

It should have been one of the greatest days in young Tony Iommi's life. His band had just landed a tour of Germany, which meant that he could finally kiss his odious factory job goodbye. Then, out of the blue, disaster struck. On his last day at work, the guitarist caught his hand in a machine press, snipping off the tips of two of his fingers in the process.

"I couldn't believe it," the Black Sabbath guitarist recalls. "I was furious, because I wasn't even going to go to work that day! My mom *made* me go. She said it was the 'responsible' thing to do.

"After the accident I thought my playing days were over, because I went to several specialists and they all said, 'Forget it.' Then a friend of mine bought me a record by [jazz guitarist] Django Reinhardt and told me to have a listen. I said, 'He's unbelievable.' Then he told me that Django was only able to use two fingers on his fretting hand. It started me thinking, "Well, if he was able to play that well with two fingers, I'm gonna have a go at it."

And go at it he did. Iommi ruthlessly attacked his problem like a man possessed. First he created two thimbles made of plastic and leather to extend the length of his truncated fingers. Next he detuned his guitar one half-step to Eb, to make bending easier. Finally, he began using extremely light strings to maximize playing comfort. Ironically, the combination of these three things gave Iommi a revolutionary new sound, deep, dark and ominous. It was the guitar sound that would give birth to Black Sabbath and, ultimately, sow the seeds for death metal, thrash and grunge.

—B.T.

BOOIN' IN THE WIND
Bob Dylan Goes Electric

Today, folk rock is such a well-established genre that it's hard to appreciate the magnitude of the ruckus Bob Dylan caused 30 years ago when he appeared on stage at the Newport Folk Festival in a black leather jacket with an electric guitar slung from his shoulder. To the mid-Sixties folk purist, the electric guitar was the embodiment of evil—rock and roll. In other words, banal, commercialized, socially irresponsible, witless teen Pablum. On his first four albums, Dylan had seemed the antithesis of all that: an eloquent, committed protest singer; a forthright, homespun performer in the tradition of Woody

Guthrie and Pete Seeger, armed with just an acoustic guitar, a wheezy harmonica and his ragged, edgy voice. But Dylan's musical perspective has always been just a little larger than his audience's. He always dug rock and roll.

In 1963 and '64, Bob Dylan had been the toast of the Newport Folk Festival. He got a very different reception in '65. It was actually no huge surprise when Dylan came onto the Newport stage on the afternoon of July 25, 1965, flaunting an electric guitar and backed by the Paul Butterfield Blues Band. March had seen the recorded debut of Dylan's new, electrified rock and roll sound on *Bringing It All Back Home.* By June, he already had—horror of horrors—a hit single with "Like a Rolling Stone." Many of his original fans felt deeply betrayed.

Dylan and his backing band got through three numbers before the crowd began to heckle him openly. "Get rid of that guitar!" someone yelled. "Go back to the Ed Sullivan Show," jeered another voice (referring to the television variety show where British Invasion acts like the Beatles and Rolling Stones had made their American debuts). As the derisive laughter swelled, Dylan left the stage. Peter Yarrow (of the popular folk trio Peter, Paul and Mary) pleaded with the crowd to bring him back with a round of applause. When Dylan finally did return to the platform, he had tears in his eyes and his old acoustic guitar in his hands. He faced the hostile audience and sang "It's All Over Now, Baby Blue."

But a whole new thing had just begun.

—*A. d P.*

SUIT TO KILL
Angus Adopts The Schoolboy Look

Shorts and blazer. Necktie and cap. Angus Young's schoolboy outfit is as much a part of his stylistic signature as his Gibson SG and roaring lead guitar work for AC/DC. The perfect complement to Young's diminutive frame and a hilarious sendup of macho metal guitar posturing, the school suit is recognized even by people who couldn't identify a single one of AC/DC's songs.

"It was my older sister's idea, really," says Angus of his distinctive stage get-up. "When we were growing up, I'd come home from school every day and pick up my guitar, without bothering to change out of my school uniform. My sister always remembered that. She'd come to call me to dinner and I'd still be in my school suit, playing away. She thought it was cute. So she was the one who said to Malcolm and me, 'You know, it would be a great thing if Angus would get up on stage with that school suit. 'Cause nobody's ever done anything like that.'

"The school suit helped people remember who we were when we were first starting out. It gave a visual side to the band. But it's not a con. When I get up there, I become that schoolboy."

—A. d P.

FIRING LINE
Metallica Fires Dave Mustaine

Metallica always knew how to party, but they also knew when to stop. Except, that is, for lead guitarist Dave Mustaine, who partied himself out of a job. On April 11, 1983, the band decided that it was time to fire Mustaine. The decision was made partly because of his increasing problem with alcohol, and partly because Metallica had become interested in a guitarist named Kirk Hammett, who was playing with their thrash rivals, Exodus.

Drummer Lars Ulrich clearly remembers the split: "We were having a wonderful time touring the United States in our U-Haul when we ran into some problems around Iowa and Illinois involving a drug called 'Alcohol & Dave.' Dave got really drunk. He'd probably had 15 or 20 beers and was driving the truck while we were crashed-out in the back. He almost killed us 10 or 15 times! We stopped to get something to eat, and Dave and our tour manager, Mark Whittaker, got into a heavy argument. It was obvious that Dave was in no shape to drive, so Mark made Dave crawl in the back of the van where he immediately went to sleep.

"The four of us started talking about how Dave wasn't stable enough to be happening on the road. He was a great guy, a great friend, but he just couldn't handle his liquor. So that night, just out of Chicago, we shook hands and decided this was the end, and that we'd get Kirk."

The band members cringed at the thought of firing Mustaine, but they felt it was inevitable. But first, they had to figure some way to get him off the tour and back to their home base in San Francisco. Lars, who couldn't afford a plane ticket for Dave, bought him a Greyhound bus ticket, instead. The bus was scheduled to depart at 10 a.m., making it necessary for the band to dismiss the guitarist at the crack of dawn.

"Everybody was bummed out," recalls the drummer. "It was such a weird scene. We tapped him on the shoulder at 8 a.m., woke him up, and said, 'We've decided you're not in the band anymore.' Dave looked around the room and said, 'Oh, no!' He probably thought he was dreaming. After 10 or 15 minutes of our telling him why we wanted him out, he realized he wasn't gonna get us to change our minds. And then he made the statement of the year: 'Okay, when does my plane leave?' "

—B.T.

BLITZKRIEG BOPPERS
The Birth of the Ramones

On January 23, 1974, an unemployed, 22-year-old construction worker named John Cummings and his buddy Doug Colvin took the subway in from Queens, New York, and walked into Manny's Guitar Center on West 48th Street, just off Times Square in Manhattan. There they purchased their first guitars, with John buying a blue Mosrite for $50 and Douglas going for a $50 Danelectro bass. John, who'd just been laid off, thought it might be fun to start a band with some of his friends while collecting unemployment.

Most loud rock guitarists in those days played with their arms, but Cummings quickly developed a personal guitar style that relied on what he called a "limp wrist action"—all downstrokes and barre chords. No one was around to teach him leads, and he didn't feel as if the revved-up, three-chord rock his band was writing needed solos anyway.

A few months later, on August 16 and 17, 1974—with their friend Jeffrey Hyman on vocals and Tommy Erdelyi, who owned their rehearsal space, on drums—the group played its first gigs at a dingy bar called CBGB, on New York's skid row. Only now, they were using their new stage names—Johnny, Dee Dee, Joey and Tommy Ramone.

Club owner Hilly Kristal recalls: "They did their famous 17-minute set: 20 songs in 17 minutes, performed very loud with loads of energy, from one to another to another. Nobody had ever done that before. It was like hitting people over the head, but by the time you were screaming, 'I can't take it any more!' they were finished."

—B.T.

D.I.Y.
The Origin of Brian May's Red Special

Queen exploded onto the rock scene in 1973 with a distinctive look, a brilliant singer and Brian May, who produced an instantly identifiable sound with his extremely unusual guitar. While his contemporaries all favored factory-built Gibsons or Fenders, May's instrument of choice was his homemade Red Special.

"By the time I was 17," May recalls, "I had already figured out how to wind a pickup for myself. I stuck it on this acoustic guitar that I had, and I was off. When it came time to build my guitar, I knew what I wanted—a guitar that would sing and have a lot of warmth to it, but also a nice articulating edge. When my dad and me designed the guitar, we had that in mind. We tried to design a solid-body guitar that had all the advantages of a hollow-body—the ability to feed back in just the right way."

The Red Special is a living, breathing monument to May and his father's inventive domestic craftsmanship. The spring in the vibrato tailpiece was scavenged from a motorcycle kickstand, the fret buttons were fashioned from old pearl buttons and the oak body responsible for May's smoldering tone on such Queen classics as "Bohemian Rhapsody" and "We Are the Champions" came from a 500-year-old fireplace mantel.

—*Tom Beaujour*

GYPSY KING
Django Reinhardt Beats the Odds

Just mention Belgian-born Gypsy guitarist Django Reinhardt to a jazz fan and the superlatives begin to fly: the *most beautiful* tone, the *best* improviser, the *fastest*. Reinhardt, who many believe was the *greatest* jazz guitarist of all time, is best known for his 1930s recordings with the acoustic string ensemble, The Quintet of the Hot Club of France, which also featured violinist Stephane Grappelli.

But Django's career, stellar as it was, almost came to an end before it really began. In 1928, when he was 18, the guitarist was at his home outside Paris when he dropped a lit candle on some celluloid flowers that his wife had made. The resulting fire burned both of his hands and his body, particularly damaging his left hand, which the doctors considered amputating. Fortunately for Django, and the world of guitar, this notion was soon dropped. He headed for a clinic, where he began an intensive therapy regimen that included playing the guitar.

After 18 months of determined physical and mental effort, Reinhardt was deemed recovered. The ring finger and pinkie of his left hand were permanently withered, so he was left with only his index and middle fingers to fret the guitar with. Merely learning—relearning—to play in such circumstances would have been something to write home about. But Django Reinhardt overcame this monumental handicap to become the *greatest ever*.

Every time he played one of his spectacular single-string runs, he mocked the word "can't."

—E.F.G.

BURN BABY BURN
Jimi Hendrix Plays Monterey

On leaving the stage at 1967's First International Pop Festival in Monterey, Jimi Hendrix reportedly collapsed into the arms of the Rolling Stones' Brian Jones, was tongue-kissed by Nico (the late German actress/chanteuse/model) and congratulated by African jazz great Hugh Masekela. Reporting for the *Los Angeles Times*, Pete Johnson wrote, "When Jimi left the stage, he graduated from rumor to legend."

The popular media has canonized Woodstock as the big hippie rock festival. But *the* crystallizing event of the psychedelic era was actually the Monterey Pop Festival, which took place two years earlier, on June 16–18, 1967, in a picturesque town on the Northern California coast. The line-up was as stellar as it was diverse. The Who, the Grateful Dead, Janis Joplin, Otis Redding, Ravi Shankar, the Paul Butterfield Blues Band, Mike Bloomfield's Electric Flag, Buffalo Springfield (Steve Stills and Neil Young's band) and Canned Heat were among those who performed. But perhaps no act was as highly anticipated as the Jimi Hendrix Experience. Following an old blues and jazz tradition, Jimi Hendrix was a black American artist who had moved to Europe to achieve widespread fame and respect. With his British rhythm section, consisting of Noel Redding on bass and Mitch Mitchell on drums, Hendrix had become the sensation of Swinging London. He traveled back to America specifically to play Monterey. The festival was to prove a triumphant homecoming.

It was Paul McCartney who recommended both Hendrix and the Who to the festival's promoters. In so doing, he inadvertently touched off a backstage contretemps between Jimi and Pete Townshend over who would go on first. Ordinarily, bands vie for the "headline" prestige of going on last. But since both groups smashed their instruments as a finale—something that Hendrix had, in all fairness, appropriated from Townshend—whoever played second ran the risk of seeming a major anti-climax. To settle the dispute, festival organizer John Phillips tossed a coin. Hendrix lost. He would have to play after the Who. "If we're going to follow you," he reportedly told Townshend, "I'm going to pull out all the stops."

Brian Jones introduced Hendrix to the audience, hailing him as "the most exciting performer I've ever heard." Dressed in a frilly shirt, second-skin red pants and a feather boa, Jimi didn't make a liar out of his friend from the Stones. The assembled love children had never, um, experienced anything like his otherworldly guitar tones or unabashedly sexual stage moves. Jimi was visibly nervous, yet cosmically loose, playing the guitar with his teeth, behind his neck and between his legs, humping his Marshall stacks and offering up tripped-out, stream-of-consciousness raps between songs. The set was a mixture of Hendrix's own compositions—including "Foxy Lady" (already a hit single in Britain) and "The Wind Cries Mary"—and such well-chosen Sixties covers as Billy Roberts' "Hey Joe," Bob Dylan's "Like a Rolling Stone" and the Troggs' hit, "Wild Thing."

The last-named song closed the set. Flinging his colorfully hand-painted Stratocaster down on the stage, Hendrix straddled the instrument and, holding a can of cigarette lighter fuel at crotch level, proceeded to eject flammable fluid all over the body and neck. Once he'd set fire to the guitar, he smashed it against his amp and threw bits of charred wood out into the crowd.

The stunned hipsters lucky enough to be in that audience were the first Americans to realize what would soon be overwhelmingly apparent to the whole wide world: rock and roll had acquired a bold new talent who would change the music forever.

—A. d P.

THE BEST MEDICINE
Duane Allman Learns How to Play Slide

Before Duane Allman, electric slide playing was mostly a matter of rehashing the chord-based triplet made famous by bluesman Elmore James in his signature tune, "Dust My Broom." Duane left "Broom" in the dust with his huge tone, horn-like phrasing and extended improvisations. Incredibly, he only learned how to play slide guitar in 1967—just two years before the release of The Allman Brothers Band's self-titled debut.

Duane's great bottleneck awakening happened when he and his brother, Gregg, were living in West Hollywood, California, with their band, the Hourglass. One day, Gregg decided to go horseback riding. Duane, nursing a bad cold, didn't want to go, but Gregg convinced him to come along. Duane was thrown from his horse and sprained his wrist. The guitarist, Gregg later recalled, went home with a sore arm—and nursing a mighty grudge against his younger brother.

The Allmans did not speak for several days, and then Gregg, in an attempt to mend fences, bought Duane some Coricidin, a cold medicine, and a new album by the Rising Sons, a band featuring Taj Mahal and Ry Cooder. Duane loved the album, especially "Statesboro Blues," a blues standard that featured Cooder's slide work.

"I heard Ry Cooder playing slide and I said, 'Man, that's for me!' " Duane said in a 1971 interview. Using the empty Coricidin bottle as a slide, Duane began playing along with the record. But, he recalled, he didn't immediately master the technique: "I went around the house for about three weeks saying, 'Hey, man. This is a gas!' But everyone would look at me, thinking, 'Oh no! He's getting ready to do it again,' and just lower their heads, as if to say, 'Get it over with, quick!' Then I got a little better at it. Now everybody's blowing my slide playing out of proportion. It's just fine for me as a relief from the other kind of playing. But it's just guitar playing."

—A.P.

MANIC IMPRESSION
Jimi Hendrix Meets Howlin' Wolf

The legendary Chicago blues singer Howlin' Wolf (1910-1978) and his guitarist Hubert Sumlin exerted an enormous influence on a wide variety of rock greats, including Eric Clapton, who recorded Wolf's version of "Spoonful" and "Sitting on Top of the World" with Cream, the Rolling Stones ("Little Red Rooster") and the Doors ("Back Door Man"). Sumlin, master of the perfectly placed bent note and one of the first exponents of distortion, was a particular favorite of Jimi Hendrix, whose version of Wolf's "Killin' Floor" appears on both *Live at Winterland* and *Stages*. Sumlin recalls the first time he and his imposing, six-foot-six, 300-pound boss met the young Jimi:

"He was just a little ol' dude living in England. It was before his band, the Experience, hit it big. We played in Liverpool, the Beatles' home, and in walked this little ol' hip guy wearing earrings and a bandanna. Wolf said, 'What the fuck is this guy? I ain't saying nothing to that motherfucker.'

"He came right up to Wolf and asked if he could play his guitar. Wolf just nodded and Hendrix picked it up, turned it over and played it with his teeth. Wolf looked at him big-eyed, and said, 'You hired, man, you hired!' Jimi said, 'No thank you, Mr. Wolf. But I admire you and the blues. You guys are 100 percent. Beautiful, man.' "

—A.P.

FLYING HIGH AGAIN
Ozzy Auditions Randy Rhoads

When Ozzy Osbourne was fired from Black Sabbath in 1979, he was suddenly forced to put together his own band. "It was a shock because Sabbath had always been there," Ozzy recalled later. "I had never auditioned anyone before, so I was petrified.

"The auditioning process was so embarrassing. Back then, everyone was trying to clone Jimi Hendrix; I heard nothing but 'Purple Haze' and 'Foxy Lady' riffs. One guy even hooked up several tape recorders and echo units so he could simultaneously play both the lead and rhythms to Hendrix tunes—it was a nightmare!

"I had almost given up when somebody told me about this great guitar player in town named Randy Rhoads. Shortly afterwards, Randy came over to my Los Angeles apartment. He was so frail, tiny and effeminate that I thought he was a girl. But out of politeness, I invited him to play the next day.

"Unfortunately, when he turned up, I was stoned out of my mind—I mean, I was on another planet! Some guy woke me up and said, 'He's here.' I looked up and Randy started playing from this tiny amp. Even in my semi-consciousness, he blew my mind. I told him to come by the next day, and that he had the gig.

"The next day I told someone I dreamed that I'd hired a guitar player. They told me I didn't dream it, and that he was coming that day. I thought, 'Oh God, what have I done? I hope he can play.'

"Randy turned out to be very instrumental in bringing me out of me. My first two albums with him are by far the greatest things I've ever done. He was too good to last."

—B.T.

HOT LICKS
Why B.B. King Calls All of His Guitars "Lucille"

The year was 1949, and B.B. King, then a 24-year-old budding blues guitar star, was performing at a bar in Twist, Arkansas. Suddenly, two drunken patrons began arguing, and soon came to blows. Their flailing knocked over a kerosene lamp which quickly set the building ablaze. The bar's terrified patrons poured out onto the street.

King, who in his flight from the flames left his guitar behind him, realized that he could not spare the $30 to purchase a new instrument, so he raced into the bar to retrieve his well-worn axe. Although he did rescue the guitar, the young bluesman almost lost his life in the process; the building collapsed, killing two men, moments after he escaped.

When King learned that the brawl had been over a woman named Lucille, he decided to name his guitar, and every guitar he would ever own, after the incendiary woman, in order "to remind myself never to be foolish like that again as long as I lived."

—T.B.

PRESENTS

Guitar World Presents is an ongoing series of books filled with extraordinary interviews, feature pieces and instructional material that have made *Guitar World* magazine the world's most popular musicians' magazine. For years, *Guitar World* has brought you the most timely, the most accurate and the most hard-hitting news and views about your favorite players. Now you can have it all in one convenient package: *Guitar World Presents.*

Guitar World Presents Classic Rock
00330370 (304 pages, 6" x 9") $17.95

Guitar World Presents Alternative Rock
00330369 (352 pages, 6" x 9") $17.95

Guitar World Presents Nirvana and the Grunge Revolution
00330368 (240 pages, 6" x 9") $16.95

Guitar World Presents Kiss
00330291 (144 pages, 6" x 9") $14.95

Guitar World Presents Van Halen
00330294 (208 pages, 6" x 9") $14.95

Guitar World Presents Metallica
00330292 (144 pages, 6" x 9") $14.95

Guitar World Presents Stevie Ray Vaughan
00330293 (144 pages, 6" x 9") $14.95

FOR MORE INFORMATION, SEE YOUR LOCAL MUSIC DEALER, OR WRITE TO:

7777 W. BLUEMOUND RD. P.O. BOX 13819 MILWAUKEE, WI 53213

Prices and availability subject to change without notice.
Some products may not be available outside the U.S.A.

CPSIA information can be obtained at www.ICGtesting.com
Printed in the USA
BVOW03s2226151013

333865BV00013B/644/P